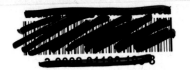

D1079921

ger

YOU can't MAKE ME!

How to get the BEST out of your teenager

PATRICK RYAN

Newleaf

Newleaf
an imprint of
Gill & Macmillan Ltd
Hume Avenue, Park West, Dublin 12
with associated companies throughout the world
www.gillmacmillan.ie

© Patrick Ryan 2010
978 07171 4674 1

Print origination by O'K Graphic Design, Dublin
Printed by ColourBooks Ltd, Dublin

This book is typeset in 11/15 pt Minion.

The paper used in this book comes from the wood pulp of managed forests.
For every tree felled, at least one tree is planted, thereby renewing natural
resources.

A CIP catalogue record for this book is available from the British Library.

5 4 3 2 1

This book is dedicated to Nellie Coughlan, otherwise known as Nanny, Granny, Nan-Nan, Mam, Mammy, Nel and Mrs Coughlan, aged 102 years, who has spent seventy-six years of her life as a parent, grandparent and great-grandparent, and has yet to be heard to utter the words 'adolescent' or 'teenager'.

For the inspiration that emerged out of never hearing those words being spoken by her, I am truly grateful.

Contents

Acknowledgments

This book would not have been written without the substantial support of important people in my life during the time I was writing it. In particular the following people encouraged my learning as I ventured into the world of words in a new way:

Sarah Liddy, my editor, for having the vision to see what I was trying to write about, the wisdom for guiding me in the right direction and the patience for just letting me get on with it.

A special thanks to the editorial and production team for taking such good care of this work and for sharing their expertise to bring it to fruition.

David Coleman for coffee, chat and fun experiences over the last couple of years.

Tom Geary for providing the best model of mentoring that I have been fortunate enough to experience.

Tracey Butler, Shirley Ryan and Mairead Condon for guidance on the mechanics of putting my ideas together and for numerous conversations about young people and what we do with them and to them!

James Ryan for reading earlier drafts and not being afraid to point out areas that needed development.

Catherine and Aislinn, who for three summers have had to listen to the tapping of the keyboard against the lapping waters of beautiful west Cork. Another adventure over, a new one beginning and a lot of learning in love in between. Thank you for being there and for the unending love, joy and inspiration that you bring to my life.

Introduction

You're the parent of a teenager – what now?

So, you've got a young person in your life who is going through a set of changes which have turned your life upside down. The pace of these has knocked you off your feet and you are questioning yet again why you ever became a parent.

You think that there were big changes when he was a toddler, but the current ones are being played out in every aspect of your life, and he is more than willing to play them out in public too. Rows, breaches of the peace, tears, shouting, untidiness, moodiness and bad manners are apparently about to take over your very existence.

You are very anxious about the growth spurt that is under way but you cannot put your finger on when and how this anxiety became like a constant ache in your life. You have listened to the horror stories about young people, seen the newspaper photos showing 'night of exam' scenes that scare you senseless and heard the statistics about underage sex and drug use. A slow realisation has become a fear that the family is about to hit a series of very sharp rocks and be broken to pieces. All because of one young person. Welcome to adolescence, twenty-first-century style!

First things first

Well, hold on one minute. Can it really be possible that all is doom and gloom when it comes to being a parent of a teenage son or daughter? This doesn't make sense if we are also to believe that being young is all about vitality, energy, talent and fulfilling potential. The doom and gloom versus the energy and excitement. How do we make sense of that?

In coming to understand how to be a better parent it is necessary to develop a profile of what it is you bring to the relationship with your teenager. This will allow you to balance the anxiety of being a parent with the excitement of seeing your child grow into their full potential. You need to ask yourself key questions about where you developed your ideas and identity as a parent. We will look at such questions in the following chapters.

Your answers to these will help to determine whether what you bring to the relationship with a teenager is useful or whether it could do with a make-over. In my experience, the vast majority of us could do with a substantial overhaul in the way we think about teenagers, and we need in particular to examine how we influence their thinking and behaviour.

What's this book about?

You Can't Make Me is a book based on the idea that society's current obsession with teenagers and 'all that is wrong with them' completely misses the point about how people develop. Simply viewing teenagers through the lens of what might go wrong takes away the opportunity to enjoy their lives with them.

This obsession offers us adults a scapegoat for many of the problems in society. It's an easy way out for explaining difficult issues that we fail to grasp and sort out. Drug and alcohol misuse, promiscuous sex and anti-social behaviour are often too easily explained by thinking that they are simply to do with teenagers.

We don't stop often enough to ask where these teenagers learned about drink, drugs and sex. We shy away from looking at the context that these problems have emerged from. Why?

Because many of the attitudes and beliefs that underlie such behaviours are substantially formed in the home. Not on the street, not in school and not from friends, but in the relationships that we build with teenagers under our own roofs. We are responsible for them.

And if their attitudes are not formed there, they are taken up from other soft sources, often without being questioned. This is easier than accepting that as parents, we have full responsibility for how attitudes, regardless of their source, are taught to children.

Too many values and morals coming from TV versions of reality are accepted as the norm and parents feel unsure whether they want to stand up to the empty promises that such TV values promote. We are not confident enough in our responsibility to protect young people from getting themselves into mischief and trouble. We're not fully sure of what we are doing.

Because who ever taught us how to be effective parents of teenagers?

Blame the parents?

No way. I have not written a book that seeks to blame parents and other significant adults for everything that is wrong in society. I have written a book that I hope gets to the heart of what shapes young people – their thinking, their emotions, their morals and ultimately their behaviour.

Central to this is the crucial role of parents and what it is that they bring to the relationship with the teenager. Teenagers offer a mirror into family values and attitudes. They cannot be seen to be separate from the people with whom they have shared their lives since birth.

I want to explore how adults influence a range of life experiences that either makes young people robust, energetic and positive contributors to the world around us or turns them into energy-sapping, destructive forces on whom we end up wasting vast amounts of time and energy trying to rein in and control.

Understand the parents?

Absolutely yes. In order to understand the world of the young person, the first step is to look at parents. Parents need to examine their own beliefs about adolescence. In particular, they need to understand more clearly what it is they do that keeps the healthy and unhealthy parts of the teenager going. In other words, they need to look away from the child and towards themselves for answers and for the context in which their child is growing up.

Doing this requires parents to ask themselves the very questions that they throw at teenagers in moments of frustration and desperation.

- Why did you do that?
- How will you explain that?
- Where did you get that opinion from?
- What makes you think you can treat me like that?

We use these questions to get answers from teenagers when we are seeking an explanation for something that has really hurt us or defies obvious, logical explanation. We need to turn those questions back on ourselves.

- Why did I do that to her?
- How will I explain that to her?
- Where did I get that opinion from?
- What makes me think I can treat her like that?

An approach like this makes for hard work. All relationships are hard work but they are more difficult if we can't stand back and look at ourselves in them. This approach also demands of us that we generate a clearer understanding of how we grew up. We need to look at our own journey through life, so that we come to realise the influence that this has on how we interact with young people today. Our teenagers have been created out of our DNA but also out of our beliefs, values, hopes and personalities.

Teenagers are of us. Teens are us.

Teenagers – big children or small adults?

I refer to adolescents as children and as teenagers. This is deliberate. I want to remind parents that for all the maturity of teenagers relative to when they were young children, they still require a strong sense of safety and of being nurtured that can only be provided by adults, and primarily by parents.

The use of the words 'child' or 'children' also serves as a reminder of the legal definition that determines when children are still children. These words inform us that the abandonment of parental responsibility of people under the age of eighteen is a form of short-sighted behaviour that can have very long-term negative repercussions.

Therefore, in my view, one of the key tasks for parents is to become aware of how flexible they are in their nurturing and relationship style. They need flexibility in order to take into account all of the changes that occur for the child during this phase of their life experience. Teenagers need parents!

Teenagers as problems or teenagers as people?

I have deliberately decided against writing specific chapters about various problem areas that might exist either for parents or for young people themselves. Teenagers are not defined by any problem they have or that their parents have with them. If only it were that easy.

Writing *only* about problems will not encourage a scrutiny of the more fundamental issues that can explain our relationships with teenagers. These issues often get hidden when the media headlights are turned on issues such as sex, drugs, suicide, gang activity, etc.

Such problems are obviously important and require all the attention they receive, and more. However, if we focus on them alone, important issues such as the parent–child relationship, morals, respect and authority are left to one side as if they were not important. This is a wasted opportunity. When these issues are left unattended, we often end up in the blind alley of blaming the teenager and setting up cycles of rows, tension and general bad feeling.

I have chosen instead to focus in this book on key areas that I have learned have significant influence on how we interact with teenagers. So instead of looking at underage sex, I set out to discuss relationships; instead of looking at problems in school, I discuss what school and exams mean to us and how this meaning can be changed.

Through all of this, I set out that it is what *parents* bring to all the important teenage issues that can help make them a positive or negative experience for child and parent alike.

Looking at only the problem areas would also strengthen the notion that parenting teenagers is all about a series of tasks that are aimed at keeping trouble at bay. It is much more interesting than that. It is about supporting the development of a person – a young person on the cusp of their potential, ready to add to the world their skills, talents, energy and enthusiasm.

Adolescent identity is all about human identity and is as much about goodness, strength, hope, energy, creativity, opportunity, growth and development as it is about the more popularly cultivated aspects of upheaval and ructions. Seeing teenagers through this lens offers us a different way of understanding problems when they come along as well as offering the best hope of keeping problems away in the first place.

Why does being a parent to teenagers seem difficult?

I believe that psychological growth occurs best in an environment where the individual is actively involved in creating opportunities that will stretch them and take them out of their comfort zone. Teenagers do this to families. They throw up scenarios that need new thinking. Parents need to adjust how they relate to their child. Teenagers require a new space in the family to grow up in and usually don't mind creating upset in order to get it.

How ready are parents for the learning opportunity that this offers? Oftentimes parents get caught out by the speed of change that naturally occurs with the teenage years. Not being ready means that instead of learning from the young person, parents fall back on a style of interacting that is about control and constraint rather than negotiation and nurturing.

Teenagers force us into questioning our reasons and behaviours. When this gets too much, we stress, react against them and try to control them so that they don't try it again. If we go along with the questioning, we are forced to pause, think and maybe come up with new ways of handling a situation.

This means that we need to see teenagers as partners in a relationship, not problems to be solved. For most of us, this is a big jump in how we normally see the parent–child relationship. Partners, not problems.

I will pose many questions throughout this book and I hope that they will generate conversation, debate, agreement and disagreement in order to trigger the opportunity to stand back from all the regular talk about teenagers.

Standing back can allow you to see the same issue differently. It gives you the chance to become more aware of exactly what type of parent you are and where you might make changes. The best learning will nearly always come after a chance to step back from 'the way you have been doing it all along'.

Teenagers offer us the chance to do a lot of stepping off and on as we travel with them on their journey to adulthood. We can choose to see this as either a gift or a nuisance. That is a choice for us – not them.

So where are the answers?

It is most certainly not an objective of mine to provide answers – I do not know you or your child, and I do not have access to any magic or mystery that will reward you with life in paradise.

If you find answers in the following chapters, it will be because you have done something with the information that gives you a new lease of (parenting) life. You will have created a different perspective, a chance for a sigh of relief or a determination to evaluate what your own life is about. You will have created the perfect opportunity for you to learn how to be a better parent to your teenager.

My answers for your situation would be mine alone, and you would find enough holes in them to offer much entertainment. My thinking might, though, stimulate yours. It might allow you to make clearer to yourself the manner in which you are choosing to live your life as a parent. It may help to influence your relationships and to understand the young people who have little choice but to share this life with you.

Answers ultimately come from the people directly caught up in a situation. Those answers may be helped with advice, opinion and direction from others, but the best answers to your questions about teenagers will come from you and your teenagers. This book may be the trigger for the conversations that launch the questions.

What is my thinking based on?

The ideas in this book stem from my work over the past fifteen years with people of all ages who have sought psychological help for a range of difficulties. Initially, I was interested in the gaps and problems in their lives. We would spend time looking at the lack of positive experiences in their lives and how it was that they hadn't learned to take care of themselves. We would piece this together and develop a more useful way forward that would increase the likelihood of a more healthy experience.

That interest in what's wrong in people's lives remains, but nowadays I find myself engaging with clients less about the problems, difficulties and trouble in their lives and far more about what is satisfactory with their lives. I want to know what's right – what is working well, what is fine and what is just good enough.

This is a move away from a 'difficulties' way of thinking about the world and the people in it. I did this because when I stood back from the stories of the hundreds of people I have met through my work, one of the most significant facts to stay with me is that despite all the troubles, most were still managing to live their lives with some degree of success.

For the most part, they were at school, or in work, living with family, and interacting with groups of friends. These things were not enough to keep problems away, but it made a great place from which to start building people up. There were some elements of a foundation in place. As a result I became interested in what it was that allowed them to have some level of both happiness and unhappiness in their lives at the same time.

My thinking is also based on years of reading up-to-date

research on what it is that helps people to grow and develop, on what it is that children and adolescents need in order to reach their potential. So there is also a science behind my thinking, and one of my challenges is how to link this science with what I experience in my direct work with people.

Throughout the book you will be brought into contact with up-to-date psychological research that can be used to improve your relationship with your child but may also cause you to evaluate your own thinking about yourself and that part of you that is a parent.

This will help to reinforce the notion that in order to understand your teenager you also need to develop awareness of the type of person you are. Doing so will open up new avenues for managing the natural ups and downs that go with being in any relationship. Of course, with a teenager there are brand new parts to the relationship, parts that offer opportunity for togetherness and falling out, pleasure and pain, highs and lows.

I hope that in reading what follows, you find some things that discomfit you and some that offer hope. I hope your thinking is stretched and your emotions fired up. With these reactions I hope that there will emerge energy to rethink who and what your teenagers really are to you and you to them.

Welcome to adolescence and being a parent – twenty-first-century style.

CHAPTER 1

Adolescence: What Is it?

What are we dealing with?

Adolescence is not something to cure, fix, control or get rid of. It is not a disease, disorder or set of terror traits that warrants treatment or therapy. It is simply a word used by humans to define a phase of development from the age of thirteen to nineteen. It has become, though, particularly in modern literature and ordinary day-to-day conversation, a time to be feared by parents and stumbled through by the young people themselves.

Barely a week goes by without some survey or other informing us of the disasters that supposedly come the way of teenagers. Misuse of alcohol, drug-taking, underage sex and behavioural difficulties at school are just some of the horror stories that are apparently taking place on a regular basis. These things do happen and need to be understood.

Such difficulties also need to be seen and explored in the *context* in which they happen – way beyond the individual teenager himself and most definitely in the context of the adults who make up (or in some cases, do not make up) his life.

It is easier to be uncomfortable at the idea of sixteen-year-olds engaging in sexual activity than to face the uncomfortable fact that sexual exploration is a normal and natural part of this phase of our life cycle. It is also critically important in helping us to develop our own sense of who we are. What is often lacking, of course, is that this fact is not addressed with young people in a manner that is free of critical, negative or controlling values that fail to take into account the perspective of the teenager.

Many of us do what was done to us – we warn of the dangers, warn of the consequences and harass about the dire straits that, for example, unwanted pregnancy might bring. In doing so we are completely ignoring the danger that this might simply shut down the chance that teenagers will listen to us.

None of us tends to listen when we are being lectured at.

There is much in the old saying that goes, 'tell me something and I will forget it . . . involve me in it and I will understand it'. We talk *at* teenagers so much of the time, and we hit them with so much negativity in these talks, that it is no wonder they shut down. And even if there is something important to be told, it gets lost in how we talk and by how we place so much emphasis on things that might go wrong.

We forget that many teenagers do not engage in the type of futuristic thinking where awful things *might* happen.

We need to remember that the teenage years are just another phase of development in the human life cycle, nothing more, nothing less. This is a challenge to parents and would-be parents of teenagers who believe that this phase is something out of the ordinary in terms of the human condition.

It is my contention that it is no more out of the ordinary than any other phase of human development. It is as easy and as difficult as we perceive it to be. The father of a teenage girl may be quite happy to engage in the constant negotiations and arguments that she triggers, but made to feel helpless by the crying of his infant child. There are others who would swap places in an instant.

Attitude is critical. It tells us what we will find stressful and what we will find challenging and exciting. The attitude that you bring to a relationship with a teenager could well determine how positive the experience is for you and him.

Contradiction – more than the name of a perfume

Parents often are bewildered by the fact that teenagers can be 'so unpredictable' – happy one minute and depressed the next; best friends with the world in the morning and in the middle of war by the afternoon.

Consider this scenario: young teens Deborah and Jane, inseparable on a Wednesday as they prepare for a youth disco on Friday to celebrate the end of the school year. Except by Friday there has been a huge row, they're not talking, they've split their group of friends down the middle and caused mayhem at home because of the unfairness of it all and the fact that of all places they'd expect to get a bit of understanding, it would be at home, but no such luck. And all because Deborah bought a pair of jeans that Jane said that *she* might buy.

The young people I meet offer an answer to this as they regularly teach me a lesson along the lines of 'When I live out the unhappy part of my life, I am sad, angry or difficult, but when I live out the happy part, I can be good company with valuable contributions to make.'

This is no different from any other age group, but with teenagers we oftentimes perceive it as a problem. The trouble with this type of thinking is that it fools us into believing that it is the teenager who is the problem. It blocks us from looking at our own role in why it is we fail to understand the needs of teenagers. This in turn stops us from coming up with useful ways of interacting with them.

When we think about teenagers I wonder which part grabs most of our attention, the happy part or the angry part. Probably the angry and difficult part. Psychology teaches us two things about why this happens.

1. We tend to be more sensitive to information that poses a threat to our happiness. So an irritated teenager is like a big

flashing light on our radar – we pay them close attention in case our happiness is threatened.

2. Once we have stored this threat information in our memory, we are more likely to look out for information similar to it in the future. This creates a cycle: if we look out for it more, we are more likely to see it, and this in turn makes us believe in it more. Just to make matters worse, if information comes along that is opposite to what we believe, we are likely to either dismiss it or not pay much attention to it.

So we are primed by nature to collect information that might upset us, we then hoard it as if it's going out of fashion, and finally we reject anything that might help to dislodge it. Hardly a recipe for peaceful, harmonious relationships with teenagers who enjoy a bit of energetic interaction with parents as a way of learning about the world.

Teenagers – a threat? Only if I think so

Teenagers can pose a 'threat' to parents because sometimes this is what parents expect. For example, if I believe that teenagers are grumpy, unpredictable troublemakers, the information I will see most in the world is exactly that which confirms this belief. So I hear my fourteen-year-old son fighting with his brother 'all the time' (meaning once or twice a week) and this reinforces my belief about his troublemaking skills.

And because I'm so busy trying to confirm my beliefs about him, I miss the information that might help give me a different opinion. So I don't pay as much attention when he is helping his brother fix his computer game. Or, worse still, I see it but don't know how to make sense of it, so I just discount his help as being irrelevant.

We are all familiar with how easy it is to list off the difficulties of living with a teenager. Common complaints might include the following:

1. He's as awkward as be damned.
2. She'd fight with her own shadow.
3. He's as lazy as sin.
4. She treats me like I'm her servant.
5. He thinks money grows on trees.

It is easy to do this because the difficulties threaten the nice, easy atmosphere that you aspire to have in the home. I wonder what it would be like to list off the information that we hold about teenagers that balances this up – the good stuff, the healthy stuff, the positive stuff. Use the following table to see what you have managed to spot that is healthy this week.

Helpful attitude you noted this week in your teenager	Helpful behaviour you noted this week in your teenager	How did you respond to these?
1.	1.	1.
2.	2.	2.
3.	3.	3.

It's a bit more difficult to catch the positive stuff because it means that we might have to adjust our thinking about teenagers. The list of good, positive points about them might lead us to accept that it is our *thinking* about them and not what we *see* in them that is the problem. Keeping a list of what is good about our teenagers is useful because:

1. it reminds us of what they have to offer
2. it helps us to maintain an accurate picture of who they are

3. it helps us to remind them of how good they are
4. it gives us a basis to work from when we hit the natural humps and bumps that take place in any relationship.

How can one person have so many people inside them?

Teenagers have taught me about the human ability to live out many different and sometimes contradictory aspects of our personality at the same time. I observe this in the sulky teenagers dropped off by tired and frustrated parents, who become energetic, thought-provoking clients when we work together. They go out afterwards to meet friends as if they had not a care in the world. Many different parts, but all within the one person.

It is my belief that part of the challenge in being a parent to any child is learning how to respond to the many different aspects that make up their character. Asking yourself the following questions will help you to make a better decision about how to respond.

1. Do I have all the information about why my daughter is the way she is right now?
2. What do I know about what she was doing today?
3. What are my assumptions about her when she is in a (happy, sad, grumpy, funny, angry) mood?
4. What happens when I normally match her mood with a similar one myself?
5. What is the most compassionate thing I could do for her right now?

Such questions set up a thinking habit that opens up an opportunity to decide how to relate to your teenager at any given moment. It helps to remove the automatic pilot response that often occurs between parents and children. This is much more productive than wasting energy on trying to make them into one type of person who is easier to control. But it is hard work, for which most of us are ill prepared.

Too often we forget that in relating to teenagers, we are not relating just with one part of them, the so-called troublesome part. There are lots of components and we get frustrated when we try to control only some of these. We throw our hands up in desperation because we have focused on only one part of who they are, and this is normally the part that we say is negative.

We forget (or ignore) the parts that are fine. We don't 'catch' them doing things that are positive, useful and healthy. We struggle to compliment them on these things. We forget about using the language of praise that so often got us out of tight situations with younger children and that we yearn to hear ourselves on a daily basis.

So teenagers grow up with the notion that communication with parents is about being harassed about 'stuff' that's wrong. Stuff that to them seems normal and a true part of who they are. Consider the following table of sins!

What you say	What they hear	What you mean
I've got belts longer than that skirt	My clothes are wrong.	That really doesn't suit you. Or, I wonder do you know how you really look in that.
You're all caked up in that rubbish.	My make-up is wrong.	I can't believe I've got a daughter old enough to wear make-up. Or, she's such a pretty young woman now, I hope she's not taken advantage of.
How the hell can it take one person so long to wash?	Bathroom time is wrong.	Excuse me, I'd like to use the bathroom. Or, if only I had that amount of free time to enjoy a shower.

Needless to say, their friends are wrong, their attitude is wrong, what they eat is wrong, where they go is wrong and how long they stay out is wrong. That's a lot of wrong in somebody who is probably fairly all right.

Teenagers' responses to this type of communication are similar to those an adult's would be if the same was done to them. We get frustrated when someone tries to control different parts of us. We feel low if all interactions around us are based on a negative running commentary that fails to see what we have to offer. We will try and avoid the relationships that are based on this sort of communication. If confronted with them we will 'bark, bite and bang on the tables' (or feel the need to do this). So will teenagers.

A key to overcoming this type of commentary is to note when teenagers are doing just fine in their lives or when you have been comfortable when with them. Then make this explicit. For example, say it's been a week since you had a row with your son. Don't let this slip by without a comment like, 'It's been good fun with you this week,' or 'I enjoyed what you did with me on Tuesday.' Don't use it as a chance to sabotage the good week with something like, 'You were such a pain last week but this week has been a bit better,' or 'I wish you could be like this all the time.' These last two statements will annoy him because they contain accusations that he wasn't good enough previously and his natural response will be to defend himself.

TOP TIPS

1. Use all information available before deciding why a teenager is annoying you.
2. Know how you relate to *all* the different parts of your child's personality.
3. Catch, Comment on and Commend teenagers when they do ordinary things well.

Teenagers have the answers – can we hear them?

Bearing in mind the above, the focus of my work with young people and their families is to try and remind them of the ordinary parts of the lives they share that are working fine. We set out to examine what makes this happen and then work towards trying to reproduce it in the areas that are not so healthy.

In other words, we work hard at using what is already working to sort out what is not working. For example, many teenagers have good relationships with grandparents or people who coach them in their hobbies while at the same time their parents struggle to get on with them. Teasing out what it is about Grandad or the sports coach that makes life bearable can bring to life some important ways forward for the parent–teenager relationship (e.g. regular praise, good listening skills, clarity in rules, negotiating a bit of freedom).

By focusing on what works, the reasons why the parts of the relationship that are not working well start to become less important in how everybody relates to each other.

Work to everybody's strengths and the weaknesses become less irritating because we end up paying less attention to them.

Get everyone to catch everyone doing something useful, healthy and helpful and give compliments on this. This is often brought to life at times of family crisis such as serious illness or bereavement. Suddenly, helping out is not seen as a chore and neither is complimenting the teenager for doing this. He helps, he is complimented, so he does it again.

Both the giver and receiver of the help and the praise will feel much better for it. In the process, both learn to ignore some of the irritating stuff about each other: the stuff that is rarely that important anyway and usually leads to rows that don't serve any useful purpose.

Only when the focus is placed on what is working in the

relationship with a teenager does it become useful to focus attention on the areas that are causing difficulty. Doing this highlights what is open to influence and change, such as how a parent and a teenager might choose to relate to each other. For example, take John, aged sixteen, who swears at his parents, doesn't listen to a word they say, comes and goes when he pleases and treats home like a classy B&B. He's also good at soccer, well liked by friends, and his relations think he's got a great sense of humour. His young sister adores him. So the questions for his parents are:

1. What do they do when he is not swearing or when he does listen?
2. What are the team skills he uses in soccer that could be negotiated into the home?
3. How do they enjoy his sense of humour with him?
4. What mistakes did they make when teaching him about his responsibilities around the home, and have they explained the mistakes to him?
5. What support will they withdraw if he continues to treat them with disrespect?

This has the benefit of decreasing the amount of energy and effort that is spent on issues where little influence is possible. So often, I have seen parents and teenagers have huge rows about a certain friend, or going to a disco, when in fact important issues like how and why certain rules are set remain unspoken about and are not negotiated between parents and their children.

Fight for what is worth fighting for and not for what is easy to fall out about.

Realistic goals with teenagers

The target that parents and I set together is to change the focus of the relationship with the teenager from 'What's the problem?' to 'What's the possible?' Once this is in place, we examine how, when, where and why so much of the parent–teenager relationship is lived through a cycle of almost never-ending judgments that are often rooted in criticism, sarcasm and one-upmanship.

Claire's parents brought her to see me because they were finding it increasingly difficult to deal with a range of discipline problems that would outdo the contents of any psychology textbook. One day Claire bumped into two pieces of furniture in my office within the space of an hour. A couple of questions later, we had established that 'being clumsy' was a regular experience for her. Two hours later, we had located a range of learning difficulties that required specific psychological assessment. Some of these were directly related to being clumsy. With the results, her parents found a new way to understand her and re-energised themselves to help her out. Suddenly the discipline problems were not the focus of who she was and the 'old' bonds between them all were re-forged.

Not all clinical work is so dramatic, but the example highlights how important it is to be able to get to know teenagers in totality in order to have any hope of understanding how best to interact with them.

So often, we get lost in conversation with teenagers because the only thing we can remember is that they out-manoeuvred us in the last argument and we ended up feeling like fools. To be able to stand back from this and not try to win the next argument is difficult, but it is a skill that can be practised and, like any skill, it becomes more automatic the more often we do it.

It's cool to be content

Within the parent–teenager relationship the target I find it useful to work towards is probably best captured in the word 'contentment'. For me this means a sense of ease and happiness that can be had in the ordinary things in life and the ordinary things that people do in life. This is not a new concept but one that in my view has fallen off the radar of what people want from life today – it is not on the materialistically oriented wish-list of people in today's world. This is usually a world of immediate gratification (I want it now) and entitlement (I have a right to it). We are less talented at holding out for a reward or persevering with a difficulty until we resolve it.

In our interactions with teenagers we want to stay ahead now rather than give a bit of ground and reap the rewards later.

We have set expectations for ourselves and our children very high and we have done this without thinking about the values by which we wish to live our lives. There are key questions to be asked about the values we carry around about being a parent of a teenager. The answers to these questions form the blueprint for parenting behaviour.

To understand why some parents are more successful than others we need to develop a profile of who we are as parents. In particular, we need an insight into the values that guide our behaviour as parents. Look at the questions across and note your responses. Better still, jot them down and see what changes you could make that would help you clarify what type of parent you would like to be.

Our expectations about our relationships with teenagers are formed by the answers to questions like these. Falling back on the argument that our parents didn't have these types of conversation with us, or that we are pretty all right in what we do is not a helpful strategy. It requires courage and a good dose of humility to engage with teenagers and tease out answers to these questions, but the rewards in the long term are substantial, real and fulfilling.

PROFILING MY VALUES AS A PARENT

1. How do I teach my teenager about the balance between their rights and their responsibilities?
2. Do I practise what I preach?
3. What message do I give out about money and how to be responsible with it?
4. What message do I give out about alcohol and how to be responsible with it?
5. What do I teach my child about the needs of a community over the needs of an individual?
6. How do I teach about the difference between wants and needs?
7. How do I transfer to teenagers my understanding about right and wrong?
8. What part does love play in my values and how do I bring this to life in my relationships with my children?

Staying ordinary generates contentment

If we are to make contentment a core target in parent–teenager relationships it is necessary to learn how to identify ordinary daily satisfactions. Friendly smiles, coffee with a friend, a walk, a wave from the postman are the stuff of satisfaction for us all, if only we would spare a moment to notice. Such small satisfactions are the fuel that can keep us going and keep us mentally fit. They ensure that we are protected from the type of thinking that runs along the lines of 'Nothing in my life is good, or brings me happiness.'

As a parent, being able to pinpoint ordinary daily satisfactions like seeing your teenage son meeting friends, watching him grow strong, etc. helps to remind you that most of the time, most things are just fine.

Pursuing the goal of contentment in psychological treatments has helped me to collaborate more efficiently and effectively with parents and teenagers. It helps me to encourage them to build an understanding of their distress out of the ordinary information that makes up their own life story. This stops the often fruitless search for answers from the latest fad or half-baked theory.

It also helps to fight against one of today's endemic myths – that there is a perfect way to live, a single roadmap to persistent psychological happiness, or one route to making all children being number one in the class (logically, not even possible on the best of good days).

TOP TIPS

1. Work to your own strengths and the strengths of your child.
2. Focus on what is possible in your relationship, not what is on your wish list.
3. Make contentment a target in the relationship with your teenager.

Perfection – a perfectly useless game plan

The idea of perfection flies in the face of 'good enough', an idea that has also taken a beating in modern culture with all sorts of books, gimmicks and notions about how to live the perfect life and raise the perfect child. Forget it! For me there are no seven steps to anything, ten ways to everything or six mistakes to nothing.

'Good enough' has to become just that, good enough – there is a time for saying 'This is as good as it gets, so let's all get on with it and enjoy it.' Fourteen-year-old Kate, who comes home from her friend's house on time three evenings out of five, is doing well. Not ideal, but good enough to warrant praise.

Without the idea of 'good enough', psychological satisfaction and contentment will be unobtainable. When that happens, depression, anxiety and a host of other psychological complaints will become the hallmark of our existence.

Striving for perfection in our children becomes a breeding ground for worry that we will not achieve it, which almost certainly guarantees that we will never achieve it. The result is what we are observing in society now. Hidden mental distress gets masked in drug misuse, alcohol problems, using sex to build self-esteem, and youth gangs replacing the family as the mechanism for growing up.

Teenagers need to learn that they are good enough. This is too tough a lesson to learn if we constantly surround them with feedback about how difficult they are or how we would never have done something like that in our day. We can help them learn by saying things like this.

- Thanks for the help with . . .
- You look well today.
- That's a good piece of work.
- I like what you're wearing.
- You're really good at . . .

It's also important to make teenagers feel special. They are not too old to be occasionally taken out for a treat, being surprised with extra money for something they would like, being asked if they would like to go somewhere with friends without having to fight for it.

25

Good enough means that praise for exam results is delivered clearly and is not contaminated with 'How could you do better?' That question can be asked at another time and probably in a better way – 'How can I help you to improve the grade?'

Seventeen-year-old John, who struggles to live within the rules of the house, needs to hear that you see his struggle, will try and help him and maybe that you struggled with rules when you were young. He also needs to hear that you love him, struggles and all. Thirteen-year-old Ali needs to hear that while it is okay to use fashion and make-up to feel good, it is actually who she is as a person that will ultimately determine if she feels good. She will not know this unless parents explicitly and deliberately give her the feedback that who she is is good enough.

Uncertainty – look for it, learn from it, live with it

Another key lesson that I have learned from young people is how they deal with uncertainty. In order to support their development so that they can increase the chances of reaching their potential and get the best from life, being able to live with uncertainty is crucial. This seems to be somewhat different from other age groups.

Most young children and adults are just not good with uncertainty. Young children need predictability to learn what the world is about. I'm not sure why adults need so much of it, as it seems to stifle a lot of freedom, creativity and energy in how they relate to others. Adults spend too much time trying to control things and people. Wasted time.

The ability to give up the idea that all situations and people can be controlled to the extent that certainty prevails is not that obvious in people today. This creates a trap because, with the advancement of technology and the fact that we live in a 'global village', we now get to hear of all sorts of disasters that befall people on a daily basis.

So on the one hand we are able to learn about child kidnappings as soon as they happen, earthquakes killing thousands, wars being inevitable and famine predictable. We feel unsure, uncertain.

On the other, we are being bombarded with glossy advertising that instructs us with various degrees of certainty how to find the right man, make the perfect dinner, wear the right dress, launch the perfect golf swing and write the perfect book. We are led to believe that we can have ultimate control.

I have observed that teenagers have a different way of approaching uncertainty. They wear the uncertainty of life on their sleeve as they work out the ways of the world. They are not afraid to meet head-on the reality that we live our lives surrounded by uncertainty. This is one of the triggers for throwing adults into a state of mild panic when we interact with them – they naturally bring uncertainty with them.

Teenagers are the mirror we don't want to look into

Teenagers tend to act as symbols of the things we would prefer not to have to think about – the stuff of life that cannot be made certain.

They want to talk about the fragility of relationships, the loss of love, the rejection of partners or the devastation felt when a young friend dies. They want to push the boundaries on safety and health by driving too fast, drinking too much and experimenting with drugs. They seem to deliberately set out to create uncertainty both for themselves and all those connected with them.

Teenagers don't get into too much of a panic about the uncertainty around them, preferring to stick with what is in front of them. This is useful because it may point to a mechanism that can also guide adults as to how to manage uncertainty. For many teenagers it is acceptable that while it is useful to try and control some elements in life, other things just happen and you may as well just try and get along with it.

Teenagers are naturally curious about the various rules and regulations that are used by parents, schools and society to put boundaries around aspects of their lives. Young people need to be allowed to examine, explore, seek out and experiment with all sorts of possibilities in their world so that they learn what we call 'worldly wisdom'. As a consequence of this natural part of who they are, they have to remain open to many things being uncertain, as otherwise their curiosity could not survive.

So the thirteen-year-old door slammer is pushing the boundaries of what is allowable at home – she needs feedback that clearly indicates what door slamming actually says about her:

All I know when you slam the door is that you are angry. I have no idea what it is that makes you angry unless you tell me. If you don't tell me then I'm left making up the reason and I'll probably be wrong, which will upset you more. When you slam the door, it's difficult for me to help you and I struggle to understand what's happening.

She needs to be asked why it is that door slamming was the only option for her at that particular time:

I wonder what would have happened if you had spotted that you were getting upset earlier and said that to me. Did you or I do or say something that made us miss an opportunity to calm things down earlier? I hate it when I get to boiling point – I wonder what we could have done differently?

She does not need to hear 'We don't do that in this house.' She knows that. She needs to be taught how to recognise and manage her emotions and develop another behaviour that gets rid of the physical build-up that she experienced inside her.

You can teach her about the signs she gives off that suggest when she is getting upset, such as:

- being irritated with small things
- using a different tone of voice
- being snappy with people
- the physical sensation of her stomach tightening or wanting to hit something.

Once she is aware of these signs, she can learn to identify when she's about to lose her temper and can then explore choices other than slamming the door.

Teenagers develop their worldly wisdom by not being too taken up with the need for certainty. More important, they are not that interested in the need for anything to be perfect. This would suffocate the spirit of adventure that is necessary to question and explore what is going around them.

So the natural state of uncertainty that is part of all our lives feeds teenagers' curiosity. Curiosity in turn protects against the negative aspects of perfectionism. Not a bad recipe for healthy living, then!

Of course, a balance needs to be struck between the usefulness of uncertainty and the need for stability. Parents need to guide and mentor teenagers so that they learn to do this. Exploring choices and teasing out their pros and cons allows space for uncertainty. Actually making the choices in a manner consistent with personal values, agreed family rules and expectations creates stability.

Down with perfection – and that sort of thing

When applied to the field of parenting, what the notion of perfection does is to delude parents into thinking that what they have attained is not good enough. It drives the belief that no matter what they do for their child it is not enough. It generates a comparison with other parents that can make them feel overwhelmed and helpless. It also undermines the right to assert that their best is usually enough. Parents will say things like, 'When I look at other families, all I see are happy relationships and obedient children. Why don't *they* fight over money, discos and friends?' Such comparisons are natural, but don't be fooled. All relationships require work to make them look easy. Focus on what you can do to learn more about your family relationships – that's good enough.

Instead of comparing your family to others, try to draw satisfaction from the aspects of your family life that do work well. Those times when we explain to children something that was causing them difficulty; or when we give them a new piece of information that opens up an exciting possibility for them.

Society has lost sight of a second meaning of the word 'perfect', which is that it represents something being 'complete'. The tendency to focus solely on the narrow definition of perfect – 'flawless' – undermines a sense of being able to derive reward and satisfaction from when we actually complete a daily function.

On a daily basis, parents *complete* a whole host of important functions and roles, very few of them *perfectly*, but without awful results. Yet many parents still feel inadequate and believe that they should be doing more. You need to understand clearly where this expectation about the need to do more is coming from and whether you have ways of protecting yourself from it when it gets too much. If you think about it, it is probably an old message that isn't really your own but you act as if it is.

TOP TIPS

1. Give up trying to be the perfect parent – there is no such thing.
2. Instil the value of being 'good enough' into your relationship with your teenager.
3. Talk about uncertainty and learn from your teenager.

Your history determines your geography

I am regularly drawn to the life experience of teenagers as a way of understanding the psychological needs of their parents. I have always been intrigued by parents' experience of their own teenage years. In particular, I ask parents how they managed their own changes from childhood to adulthood. I am curious as to how these transitions were influenced by those in charge of their care, education and social development.

Knowing your own story is important if you want to develop insights into how you interact with your teenagers. If your mother threw her hands up in frustration at you when you were a teenager, it is likely that you did not learn much about teenagers other than that they are unmanageable. If your father forbade you to have a boyfriend and issued threats accordingly, you could well hear yourself repeating the same threats.

Your history will give you very clear pointers as to the geography of the family map that you are creating with your teenager.

Psychological history does repeat itself unless we examine it, decide what's healthy and unhealthy and then take action to adjust our parenting style accordingly.

We usually learn that our history repeats itself when a crisis comes our way, and by then we have missed the opportunity to take preventative action. Take an example of Jessica, aged thirteen, whose mother learned that the sexual side of her personality was something to be ashamed of. Brought up in a family where sex was seen as 'dirty', and sent to a school where it was seen as sinful, she will struggle with talking openly to Jessica about sex and sexual health. A crisis will occur if Jessica becomes pregnant or develops a sexually transmitted disease. Jessica's mother will be enveloped in her own shame as well as the immediate needs of her daughter. The challenge for her will be how to prevent her own sense of shame being handed on to Jessica.

Most of us keep away from our history as if doing so helps us to be better people. This is simply not the case. To be better parents of teenagers we need to look our own history of being a teenager straight in the face. This is where we learned so many lessons about teenagers and as parents we need to know if these lessons were accurate and useful. We need to know if we can confidently pass on these lessons to our children.

But more usefully, these lessons can highlight ways to manage current difficulties that we might be having with teenagers. In other words, it is often the lessons that parents are carrying around that are maintaining the difficulties for their teenagers. These lessons need to be put out for a good airing and evaluation so that you have a good understanding of your own profile as a parent.

DEVELOPING YOUR PARENTING PROFILE

1. Where has your thinking about young people come from?
2. Why is there a need for anxiety about being the parent of a teenager?

---

3. What is the nature of your anxiety?
4. What benefit is it to you or your child?
5. Whose anxiety is it?
6. Do you really feel that anxiety or are you simply replaying messages that you hear in everyday talk?
7. Why do you believe that teenagers have to be difficult?
8. How might your own experience as a teenager be creating problems for the way you deal with your child now?
9. How are you replaying the messages about teenagers that were given to you by your parents?
10. How have you challenged these messages to make sure that you do not simply repeat them?

Clearing the fog

It is too easy to get caught up in the many well-publicised difficulties that supposedly accompany adolescents and to forget that young people are just ordinary people. We need to start challenging the belief that parents cannot be proactive contributors to the healthy development of their teenage children. Teenagers deserve to be identified in society as more than the reputation that some of their more unfortunate peers bring upon themselves.

It is also shirking responsibility to understand teenagers as just being difficult, as it focuses the responsibility for changing this on the individual adolescent. This response is pretty useless and inappropriate societally, given that young people are a product not only of their genetic material but also of their times. So, for example, focusing on the drug-taking habit of a fourteen-year-old, without paying heed to the circumstances of how that teenager came to learn that drug-taking is in some way a useful method of problem-solving, is head-in-the-sand material.

Equally, the answering-back, door-slamming fifteen-year-old is much more than the seconds it takes to come up with a smart answer or to swing the kitchen door off its hinges. There is a need to go beyond the obvious in order to open up understanding. The anger required to slam the door is anger *about* something. On page 50 there are some examples of statements and questions that can help you find out what that something is.

It is easy to focus only on the obvious and forget about the rich detail in what is not so easy to see. By holding on to the obvious we are creating the notion that young people deserve their reputation. However, when we look at *ourselves* we are more likely to go beyond our behaviour – we look for reasons. We need to look back into our own development as a way of attempting to bridge our life story with our current attitudes and behaviours when interacting with teenagers.

In other words, there is a need for adults to understand that their own upbringing directly influences how they bring up their teenage children. And this is not done in some silent, subtle manner. It is right at the heart of how a person becomes a parent. I examine this idea in more depth in Chapter 4.

TOP TIPS

1. Know your own story and how you play out the lessons that you learned in your relationship with your child.
2. Teenagers are more than their behaviour – see the bigger picture that includes their likes and dislikes, their beliefs and their opinions.
3. Teenagers are still developing – they are *not* adults. They need you to allow for mistakes and mischief.
4. Teenagers need parents!

Challenging our thinking

When we start to examine our thinking about any aspect of our lives, the first hurdle we have to overcome is the fear that we might find something we don't like. It is my opinion that if there is such a fear in the first place, there is probably potential to learn something.

For example, it is easy to bemoan the sight of drunken adolescents on a street at night, not knowing what they're doing, clothes half-stripped off them, stumbling from pathway to road. But do we think that our own teenager might be involved in this type of behaviour?

We have a reluctance to face the questions about why they are out on the street in the first place. Do we always know where our own child is?

We can ask who has given them money to buy alcohol, but what have we taught our own teenagers about the safe use of alcohol?

And whoever asks who will be there to work out with them the meaning of why they went on a drunken binge? How would you cope with this scenario if you were landed with it one Sunday morning?

The reluctance to address these questions exists because deep down we know we have some responsibility for the drunken teenager. If we start answering the questions, we will have to confront the issue that we, as adults in society, are responsible for the safety and well-being of the generation coming behind us. And while it is one thing to acknowledge responsibility it is a completely different ball game to turn that acknowledgment into actual behaviour. It is easier to assume, 'my teenager would never do that' than to go out to see if they are falling drunk around town at the weekend. And if they are, what can you do? Try these for starters.

1. Educate them about the dangers of alcohol for their developing bodies – that alcohol can get in the way of the proper development of their brains and bodies because they are still maturing.
2. Take them out some night and show them exactly what drunken teenagers look like when they fall around the place.
3. Model your own behaviour on your advice.
4. Reduce pocket money.
5. Explain the law to them.
6. Monitor their whereabouts.
7. Reduce time allowed with friends until their behaviour changes.
8. Have an open discussion policy about alcohol in the home.

Hard work and discomfort?

Adults need to allow for some discomfort as they begin to question the very nature of what they believe about teenagers. Sure, adolescence is a time of rapid change, but is not the first two years of life even more so? Or what about the last few years of life when the body slows down and we move towards our certain death? It seems that the teenage years have been isolated as the only time of drastic change in our lives that has a place in modern discussion and writing, and this is curious.

One possible reason is that the teenage years produce large amounts of stress for parents. My experience as a person, never mind as a psychologist, is that each move into a new phase of our lives introduces a need for the ability to manage the stress associated with that change. Surely the definition of change is based on something new or an unexpected happening, which in turn causes a stress to which we have to respond. Why is it that we maximise the sense of stress associated with the normal changes seen in adolescence?

We do not do the same thing with other equally momentous changes, such as the birth of children, getting married, moving house. Yes, we see these as being stressful, but we balance the stress with a focus on the pleasurable bits and by repeating these in stories afterwards that ward off the negative stress that we felt at the time.

We could learn a lesson from ourselves when we tell stories about our relationships with our teenagers. We need to look for what is good enough and offers contentment, and make these the basis for our memories. We need to work to be as truthful about what is good as what is bad.

Engage in tales of wonder, not tales of woe

None of the questions or comments above is easy to deal with, but I have learned that talking through them doesn't bring about the end of the world. Rather it engages people in a process of taking time out in order to get a better understanding of what makes a family work.

As a result, I generally set out to question how we interact with teenagers and, in particular, the beliefs and assumptions these interactions are based on. In doing so, I use family history, psychology and how society views adolescence in order to understand our preoccupation with teenagers.

Later I will examine the skill of communicating with adolescents in various ways, but not by looking at the young person as the centre of any problem that might exist in communication. Instead, I hope to challenge the reader to examine closely their own style and manner of communicating. Specifically, I will ask how changing this might have much greater influence over the behaviour of a teenager than trying to control the child herself.

TOP TIPS

1. Think about and monitor whether you maximise the negative things about teenagers.
2. Identify and challenge your own attitudes to teenagers.
3. Start to become comfortable with being uncomfortable.

So what can I do?

I try not to provide answers to the question, 'How will I deal with him or her?' My preference is to trigger questions about our assumptions and practices in engaging with teenagers. In doing so, a little creativity allows parents, with support, to generate perspectives that will allow them to change their own style of relating to and interacting with the adolescent. Change that comes from within yourself will always have a better chance of succeeding because you are directing it and because you have an investment in it.

It is my experience in clinical practice that answers or advice simply handed from professional to client rarely work over the long term. But a process like the following does work.

- *Working out how to relate with each other* – e.g. what annoys us, when do we talk best, when is it best to leave things alone, are we 'doers or talkers'?
- *Exploring the issues* – the who, what, where, when, how of each issue.
- *Taking each other's perspective* – summarising the other's viewpoint, imagining out loud what it must be like for them, pretending that you are the other person.
- *Generating possible solutions* – brainstorming, not picking holes in the other's answers, not judging any possible answer

until all possibilities have been suggested, not making fun of possible answers, not being the know-all.

- *Spotting possible obstacles* – what are the potential problems, what might stop a possible answer from working, what gets in the way of us relating?
- *Regular review of progress* – how have we been doing since the last time we chatted, what have I done to help us relate better, what have I done that hasn't helped, what have I noticed in you that lets you relate better?

Likewise, with teenagers, the process of relating, exploring and discussing needs to happen in an atmosphere that is based on acknowledging each others' strengths and values. Good communication founded on respect and dignity will help to develop the expectation that good enough relationships can be sustained with them.

We tolerate difficult behaviour with infants, we tolerate it with our romantic partners and we tolerate it with work colleagues. We need to live with the standard of 'good enough' with teenagers and learn to tolerate the differences between us. If we do that, then we will stop frustrating ourselves with trying to control them simply because we do not understand the perspective that they take on life.

And finally . . .

Hard work, patience, courage, humility, opportunity and uncertainty – these are all concepts that have surfaced in this chapter. All are required if the journey away from the idea of teenagers being troublesome is to be challenged. All are required if as a parent you decide to adjust the lens through which you see your child and focus on the myriad of possibilities that lie within you, your child and the relationship that you can create. Such possibilities really become visible when 'What's the problem?' becomes 'What's the possible?'

TOP TIPS

1. Understand your child as an offshoot of yourself as well as a person in his own right – look to yourself for potential ways forward in the relationship.
2. Don't waste time trying to create answers for the future – focus on what you can reasonably do in the here and now.
3. Enjoy the differences between you as much as is reasonable and see what you can learn from them.

CHAPTER 2

Common Myths and Uncomfortable Truths about the Teenage Years

In this chapter we will examine how common beliefs and myths about adolescence can influence our thinking and behaviours in relation to our own teenager.

So we know all about teenagers, then?

No, we do not. We are inundated with stories about them in media reports, we use information from our own experience of being a teenager and we trade stories with others who are happy to confirm how awful they are. That is not complete knowledge. That is where myth and fanciful thinking emerge from. Taking on board information about any topic requires us to be able to stand back and decide if the information that we are getting is actually of any use. One parent's joy at a shy teenage girl having a nice boyfriend is another parent's horror at the possibility of underage sex.

Therefore it is important to be able to evaluate the information that we have, ask where it has come from, decide how it has stood the test of trial and error and conclude whether it is useful to apply it to our own child. Simply following the logic of urban legend takes away our capacity to be confident in our parenting skills. Following the crowd makes us blind to the unique parts that make up our individual stories.

What are we not dealing with?

There is a range of myths that are endorsed in much discussion and debate about young people and their 'problems'. Drunk, rowdy, randy, depressed, hyperactive . . . the list goes on. These serve to get in the way of working out what is possible in a relationship with young people. We simply see the angry, grumpy teenager as a problem as opposed to a person who may have a genuine gripe. Or who at the very least deserves to be asked about the grumpiness before we jump to conclusions.

A walk through any bookshop will show you titles of books referring to the nightmare teens, the terrible teens, surviving the teens, and even asking if your teen reminds you of an alien! Compare that to the titles given to books about babies and infants and the lovely, appealing pictures that advertise them. Just as we know that not all babies are angelic pictures of happiness, we also know that not all teenagers are alien in any way to those with whom they share their lives, we are not dealing with aliens.

All of the one-sided thinking that teenagers are problems conjures up the notion of adolescence as some form of illness or disease that is out there ready to take us all in, chew us up and spit us out. In my experience, the vast majority of adolescents make their journey through this phase of their lives in a pretty ordinary way. There is as much stress as there is for the rest of us making the journey through our own changes and challenges that occur as a normal part of both growing up and growing older.

Most of the myths in common discussion seem to come back to the notion that teenagers have to be controlled, harassed and overpowered into submission like some invading army intent on destroying all around it. This is inaccurate, unfair and a cop-out because it fails to recognise that, in general, all behaviour is best understood in the context of the relationships that surround it.

Here are some common myths.

- Teenagers are moody.
- They are naturally unco-operative.
- They are difficult to deal with.
- They like to push boundaries and break rules to cause mayhem.
- It is normal for teenagers to fight with everyone in their family.
- They do this deliberately because they enjoy chaos and disorder.
- They are lazy.
- They have to be harassed into studying and helping with the household chores.

The list could go on. There is no doubt that there is a ring of truth to it, but it's a hollow ring. Most teenagers show only some signs of the list, and only on certain occasions. It's unfair to use such a list as a tick-box for all teenagers.

Why do we need myths?

Why do people accept such myths without question? To accept anything in our lives, it has to serve *some* purpose, otherwise we just wouldn't do it. Myths offer a comfort blanket, they let us off the hook and they let us shrug our shoulders and say, 'Well, all teenagers are like that, not just mine.'

Myths can allow us to abdicate our own responsibility for our contribution to the problem.

Fourteen-year-old Chloe, who screams and slams doors every time she is asked to help out at home, has learned that it is okay to treat people in this way. Somewhere in her development she has been shown that slamming doors is the way to manage frustration. She has never been shown that we sometimes have to do things that are not enjoyable, for the good of the family. Neither has she been taught that she can calm herself by:

- knowing when to leave a heated situation
- taking a deep breath to control rising frustration
- stopping talking for a while in order not to over-stimulate herself.

The screaming and door-slamming is not the problem; it becomes part of the myth. The lack of respect in how to deal with requests from others is one problem. The question for her parents is, 'What lessons about respect did we teach and practise for Chloe?'

If we want Chloe to change her attitude to such requests, we need to examine what it is that we did to bring these attitudes about in the first place. We need to ask these questions:

1. Did we teach her the link between rights and responsibilities?
2. Did we give her lots but request little back?
3. Does she treat home like a B&B because this is exactly what we have made it?

And as we have seen, another problem for Chloe is that she has not been taught how to soothe and calm her frustration without slamming doors. She fails to recognise the signs within herself that she is becoming increasingly frustrated (feeling anxious, getting irritated and snappy, etc.). Without this information, she is at the mercy of her emotions, becomes overwhelmed and gets rid of this feeling by slamming the door.

I think the answer to why we allow myths to develop about teenagers in our lives lies in a range of other questions that we need to put to ourselves. We need to further develop the profile of ourselves as parents by challenging specific behaviours we have or have not engaged in as preparation for relating to a teenager. We need to know what we bring to the relationship.

PROFILING YOUR PREPARATION FOR RELATING TO A TEENAGER

1. How did I prepare myself for my child's move from dependence to independence? (For example, by taking a course, reading a book, talking to other parents.)
2. Is most of my childcare practice based on the notion of controlling my child? How can I change from this in order to meet the changing needs of my teenage child?
3. Do I struggle with her independence because I struggle to influence it in a way that suits me?
4. Am I unable to cope with my teenager's new-found thinking ability that enables her to question rules that I have put in place?
5. Do her questions or answering back actually point a spotlight at the gaping holes in my logic?
6. Am I uncomfortable with the fact that I sometimes say one thing and do another?

For most of us the profile that emerges will make us uncomfortable because it highlights how little time we give to preparing ourselves to be parents. It strikes me that a common frustration experienced by parents emerges from a *perceived* lack of knowledge and skills about how to deal with adolescents. This can lead to a reaction of opting out of engaging fully with the process of trying to understand their perspective. It then becomes easier to simply describe them as being troublesome so that we can sit back and say, 'Well, I've done my best, it's all his/her fault.'

Where to from here?

Well, we need to identify the myths and then challenge them with what we really know about our relationships with teenagers. As mentioned earlier, one of the most common myths about adolescents is that their normal development is a rowdy, temper-filled and trying time. This is a one-sided view of teenage development. It is only partly supported by the findings from research; and neither does it hold up for all parents when they are asked if it's true.

Many young people are referred to professionals by parents, teachers and care workers because they believe the teenager has a problem. Interviewing the teenager often shows that she believes there is no difficulty whatsoever. This in itself, of course, can be part of a problem, but it nonetheless reminds us that the idea of 'storm and stress' is one that we sloppily wallpaper onto young people, not one that that they choose for themselves.

'Storm and stress' is a term traditionally used to describe and define what the teenage years are all about. It is what it says it is – disorder, chaos, intensity and anxiety. Unfortunately it has stuck in the mind of most of us when we think about teenagers. It is a faulty term because it does not allow for the many experiences with teenagers that involve neither storm nor stress.

A teenager who does not see a problem with their behaviour can also offer insight into a possible resolution to his parents' distress. Sixteen-year-old John, who is praised by his parents for being mature in helping out at home, will take that praise and apply it to staying out late, having girlfriends or drinking alcohol. He is being taught that he is mature: he is not being taught that maturity does not apply to everything; he is not being taught that there are things he still has to learn. He is also not being taught how to bridge maturity in one area to another area and that he still has some learning to do. He is not even being taught that sometimes maturity is a hindrance for young people.

How can parents challenge the myths?

1. Feedback

Parents need to make their feedback to teenagers very specific in order to reduce confused conversations that lead to rows. 'You annoy me so much' is pretty useless feedback. 'Walking out while I'm talking annoys me' is better because it links what you feel with a specific behaviour.

Such feedback is easier to understand and also reduces the potential for misunderstandings. Feedback that is unclear or not specific can trigger frustrations for young people because they are still learning the ways of the world. It can lead to making assumptions about people or situations that may not be accurate. How many times have you heard the logic of a teenager along the lines of 'you said I could stay out late, so I did', not realising that you meant it was in relation to one occasion and not an entire week of late nights?

2. Be aware that you might be the one looking for rows

Sometimes it is also worth recognising that we might be the ones who look for the rows. We might be the most difficult part of the relationship. If a parent has a need to control events in life and sixteen-year-old John has a need to test limits in order to learn about the world, my bet is that the parent needs the row in order to be able to put on the authority hat, issue a few orders and feel in control again.

Lecturing John about smoking and drinking is a waste of everyone's time. Asking him what it means to him to smoke and drink places the focus on his view of himself, his natural need for acceptance by his peers and a whole host of other worthwhile issues.

3. Challenge the idea that normal adolescent development is full of difficulties

There is a need to challenge the idea that normal adolescent development is full of argument and a phase in life that would be best gotten over by going to sleep for about six years.

Over eighty per cent of teenagers in surveys will talk about their frustrations in understanding families, in getting along with parents and teachers, but will not describe this in any way that borders on being hugely distressing.

4. Is the problem really a problem?

One key to undermining the notion of problems is to understand that oftentimes problems are only problems because we think they are. John, who spends his time out late with friends smoking and drinking, can be seen as a problem or as a young person trying to find the acceptance so necessary for him. If he is feeling unaccepted, this needs to be addressed – otherwise the smoking and drinking stay in place.

Sometimes we want teenagers to be troublesome so that we have something to complain about as a way of not having to address uncomfortable issues in our own lives.

Think about Chloe's parents. If they have tried to coerce her into certain behaviours and have not taken time to explain, or didn't have the patience to do this, it is easier to complain about her rather than admit weaknesses in their own ability. Placing Chloe at the heart of the problem is just a way of using her to soothe their own fear of weakness. Admitting their weakness to themselves, and to her, offers a different platform to work from. A different perspective often counteracts the power of a potential problem.

It is true that teenagers do not like limits being put on them and it is true that they do not like being told what to do, but is this any different from a two-year-old toddler who doesn't like limits being put on her, or being told what to do? Or indeed a forty-two-year-old adult who equally does not like being told what to do by people in his life? It's no different, but for some reason we have a reluctance to use the same rules to manage and influence relationships with teenagers.

5. Involve teenagers in the conversation: don't just lecture

For many parents of teenagers, Chloe and John are either acting within limits or they are not. If they are, everything's fine; if they are not they should be told clearly what the limits are. This is black and white thinking that is flawed because none of us likes being told what to do. We know it doesn't work with babies, school-agers or adults, so why would teenagers be any different? Telling them does not make it so. It pushes them away from us because it does not reflect the role that they can have in helping to create limits.

So if your language is peppered with statements like, 'I told you so', 'Don't make me tell you again' or 'How many times do I have to tell you?', it's likely that you are having a one-way conversation.

If, on the other hand, you involve your child as a partner in the conversation you increase the likelihood of a positive outcome. For example, if they are involved in creating limits and rules for their own behaviour they are more likely to have a sense of ownership of them and are therefore more likely to live within them.

If your language is full of statements and questions like 'I don't know what you think', 'How does that sound to you?' or 'What would it be like for you if . . .?' there are two people involved in the conversation, with a better chance of a happy outcome for both.

TOP TIPS

1. Be wary of falling into the trap of thinking that everyone else knows best – learn to trust yourself as a source of useful information about your teenager.

2. Ask yourself what preparation work you would like to have done before your child became a teenager and see whether some of that is still possible.

3. Link specific feedback to specific behaviour.

4. Give up on the idea that being a parent is about maintaining control.

5. If you are having lots of rows, ask what it is within yourself that is troubling you.

6. Ask a friend to advise you on whether you are a 'teller' or an 'involver' in conversation.

Teenagers – in or out of the family?

The vast majority of teenagers report healthy functioning relationships with mothers and fathers, brothers and sisters. They also report confusion at working out the changes in these relationships that come about as a result of their own physical and mental changes as they enter into their adolescent years. They report enjoying life with all its challenges and potential.

They enjoy the freedom found in new friendships and the liberation of being able to deepen friendships in a way not experienced up to now. They appreciate and thrive on feedback that highlights to them their importance in the family and to the family.

Teenagers like the observation that they do have more common sense than their younger brothers and sisters. They want to know that they can be trusted with things that were until now kept in the domain of adults or older children in the family. They enjoy immensely being asked their opinion on important family issues.

And believe it or not, they enjoy (and in my experience, quietly demand) the sense of connection with their family in a way that can be genuinely strengthening for the whole family unit. Family is profoundly important for teenagers – it can be the safest haven for them when life in the real world gets hectic. Teenagers definitely want to be in the family.

But there has to be a but!

However, teenagers also report that they get frustrated by the idea that in some way they are more trouble than any other children. If all that Chloe hears at home is that she is more trouble than her siblings, or she is compared directly with one of them, what has she to lose by acting out exactly what her parents expect her to do anyway? Moreover, if she acts differently, family members will probably not see this.

Parents tend to see only what fits with their view of their child. This causes a lot of problems if their view is faulty or incomplete, because what they end up commenting on is the very stuff that they need to ignore. For example, if you think your teenager is lazy you will only pay attention when he doesn't want to do something. You will see this as a sign of his laziness rather than the possibility that he doesn't know how, isn't feeling well or has grown tired of being asked to do this same task repeatedly without praise for the effort.

You would be better off ignoring your view of him as being lazy and spending more time establishing *with* him why he struggles when he asked to do certain tasks. If you don't, your teenager will get frustrated and this frustration will impact on his ability to engage with you and other family members.

Or, in the earlier example, Chloe will feel that she is being unfairly judged. Therefore, in true human fashion she will act out a self-fulfilling prophecy if the notion that she is trouble keeps getting hoisted on her. Her thinking becomes, 'If I hear it often enough I might as well act it out because everyone expects me to anyway.'

In my experience, adolescents hold in great respect those who stand up and fight their corner for them. When they see and hear this, they are more likely to own up to their own contributions to problems and even offer possible solutions. Parents need to develop this role by praising them when this happens rather than spending energy on telling all and sundry about how difficult their child is. Focusing on a difficulty only serves to make you feel helpless. Advocating for the perspective of teenagers makes you an ally and creates opportunities for strengthening the relationship with them.

Walking emotional time bombs?

Another myth is that the teenage years represent a time of constant yo-yoing of emotions: in other words, that teenagers are moody, with upswings and downswings that are neither predictable nor consistent. As a generalisation it is grossly unfair and misleading to both adolescents and their parents. Everybody's emotional state varies from hour to hour and day to day. If you are mindful enough to track your emotions very closely, you will find that your emotions constantly change in response to triggers both inside you (e.g. thoughts and physical feelings) and in the world around you (e.g. other people, the weather, work).

Teenagers are no different, but it is easy to see how parents can fall into the trap of seeing their child as over-emotional. Up to the teenage years, many children do not have the complex language skills to make those around them fully aware of exactly how they are feeling; let alone in a way that actually leaves you unsure as to how to act next, which is what parents often feel when teenagers express emotions.

Up to this time in a child's life, you can usually draw on some answer or controlling mechanism if the child attempts to outwit you. However, nature steps in, releases a wave of hormones in the teenager that suddenly skills them up, enabling them to spot the multitude of logical and emotional weaknesses that all adults carry around with them. In order to protect yourself, you will label this as hormonal or emotional and describe it as being negative. By doing this you miss the opportunity to fully engage with the teenager and learn what is actually going on for them when they are emotional about something.

If teenagers were actually that emotionally unstable, families would be going bust everywhere, schools would fall apart and there would be no such thing as ballet classes, football teams or school choirs because the consistency in personality that is required for daily functioning would be missing. Generally, adolescents, just like adults, have relatively stable personality characteristics, and that does include emotional spikes and troughs from time to time.

I sometimes offer parents the idea that when a teenager is in a sulky mood or practising for the world championship door-slamming competition, the adults' frustration is borne out of jealousy that they cannot (for some reason) do the same thing. Sometimes when we get irritated by something that someone is doing, it is because we would like to do it too. Think of John, the free-living smoker and drinker. Who wouldn't like to go out and meet friends, stay out late, have a few drinks, sneak a few cigarettes and come home when we feel like it?

Teenagers, because of physical changes in the early teenage years, have in their bodies a range of hormones and chemicals that have been released in order to spur their physical development and their mental development. This spike in growth, both physical and mental, can lead to some emotional outbursts that were not so obvious in the later years of their childhood.

However, it is important to recognise that these spikes in emotionality are just spikes. In fact, on a day-to-day basis, most adolescents, like the rest of us, actually have a pretty consistent and predictable personality right through the various aspects of their lives. It is useful to remember that having a teenager means being a part of a relationship and that by definition that means ups and downs, easy and tough, agreement and difference.

Understanding their mental world

I believe that for many parents in interaction with teenagers it is the lack of understanding of the mental world of the teenager that causes difficulties in interaction. This lack of understanding can often be traced back to their own upbringing, in which understanding was also lacking. It is hard work to empathise with something that you have not experienced or received yourself. If your parents were unable to understand your world as a teenager, you may not have the natural know-how to do this.

Parents often paralyse themselves with the myth that just being parents means that they have to know what to do at all times.

Particularly with teenagers, this happens because parents' own experience of being a teenager occurred in such a different time; and what their parents did then may not be enough to keep up with the teenagers of today.

If John was a teenager thirty years ago, then he would probably have been 'given a slap', taken to confession and confined to barracks with manual labour for weeks. Today, such action could lead to a phone call from social services! In such cases, it is often easier to give up trying to understand teenagers, but I believe this is because we try too much on our own and forget that we are in a learning relationship with them.

In other words, in teaching them we can in turn learn from them, particularly in the one area that they are expert in – their own lives.

TOP TIPS

1. Give feedback on the importance of the teenager to the family, for example, 'You're a great help looking after your younger brother'; 'Your opinion helped me work out a better way to sort out that family rule.'
2. Ask your child for their view of how the family is.
3. Ask yourself what you have learned from your child today.
4. Teenagers are experts on teenagers.

Are they high on emotion?

With regard to moods and emotions, adolescents do have 'high highs and low lows', but not all the time: it is useful to be able to keep that in mind before deciding on how moody your child is. In fact, it may be even more useful simply to go with whatever mood your child is in rather than trying to judge them on the basis of their moodiness. So don't harass someone who is having a bad day by repeatedly telling them that they are in a bad mood – they know that already. Acknowledge it and say that you'll link in with them later or tomorrow.

Teenagers seem to exhibit a broader range of experience of emotions than adults and can therefore seem more changeable. Maybe we are looking at this from the wrong perspective. What if we were to examine this from the view that adults control their own emotions too much? We know that adults laugh much less than children. We know that men struggle to express their emotions. Maybe the teenagers are right – we should all let go a bit more often!

And it is important to remember that in spite of the popular belief that adolescence is associated with high levels of conflict, this is just not supported in research findings. Being emotional does not have to mean that a row has to take place. Most young people, along with most of their parents, siblings, teachers, youth workers and team trainers, will find ways of handling their relationships in a way that is good enough most of the time. I do not think we can reasonably ask for much more than that.

It is a normal aspect of personality development that children and adolescents exhibit some increased emotionality. By that I mean that they exhibit a much broader range of emotional experiences than younger children or, indeed, some adults. With the onset of adolescence, the teenager has the ability to name a wide range of emotions while also being able to differentiate between changes in emotions from one event to another. Therefore teenagers do not necessarily act angrily in every situation, although it may appear this way. Sometimes they may be acting out of frustration or disappointment rather than anger.

Adults often misread situations and use general emotional labels to describe a teenager. Just as the word 'bold' is used to describe younger children when they do something we don't want them to do, we tend to use 'anger' as the catch-all word when it comes to teenagers. So for example, 'John smokes because he is angry at something'; 'Chloe slams doors because she is angry.' How about 'John smokes because it makes him belong'; 'Chloe slams doors because it's an effective way to get rid of unwanted tension'?

Being able to identify subtle differences in emotional responses is a key indicator of psychological maturity. It is also one that many adults struggle to achieve themselves, never mind hand on to their children. How good are you at noticing the difference between irritability, frustration, annoyance, anger, fury and rage? Can you tell when you move from one to another and do you know what is good for you to do as you experience each of these?

If the answer is yes, pass these skills on to the young people you meet; if it is no, provide yourself with the opportunity to learn with the many others who struggle with this. There are many communication, assertiveness skills and parenting courses that can help tackle issues associated with emotional communication. Sign up and feel the benefit.

The do-it-yourself method is to keep a diary of your own emotional responses and note the physical changes that occur for you when you feel different emotions. Then note how your thinking changes. Use this as a basis for discussion with your teenager to see if they experience something similar.

Many parents describe their teenager as being angry, while

the teenager herself might report rare experiences of anger but many experiences of disappointment or frustration. They might relate these to not being listened to or their point of view being disrespected or undermined in some way.

I believe that at a time in our lives when we have little time to attend to the smaller details of what happens in interactions, it is often easier for parents to use a simple label such as 'anger' than to work out the exact nature of the child's emotional response.

Of course normal adolescent interactions do contain some anger, but information from interviews with teenagers on the substance that drives this anger gives us a view into their world and their unfolding maturity process.

Normal adolescence gives the teenager the ability to begin to look around and see the bigger issues that impact on daily life. From middle childhood onwards they have been starting to understand that they are not in fact the centre of the universe.

As adolescence takes hold, they finally have the capacity to fully realise that the world is not all about them and that there are many issues and difficulties that people have to encounter and manage day to day. When they look around, teenagers, because of their age and their mental capacity, have the ability to see clashes between what adults say and what adults do.

All of this, layered on top of their emerging moralistic and idealistic thinking, creates a lively ingredient for a pot of ammunition ready to be launched at an unsuspecting world. In other words, making sense of the adult world is difficult work and yet teenagers are expected to live in it.

This process underlies the idealism that many adolescents go through with regard to what they see as important issues in the world. For example, they quickly see what the ideal scenario with regard to poverty should be but struggle to understand why adults can't sort it out. They don't have enough experience to understand the complexities that often prevent us reaching the ideal answer to a problem.

It is issues like inequality, unfairness and lack of justice that adolescents really get angry about because they go against many of the principles they have been brought up with. Many of them were also led to believe that such principles were non-negotiable and all-encompassing. Their anger is a reaction to the difference between what they were told and their now unfolding realisation that the world 'village' is a giant's leap from that innocent place of early childhood.

Teenage anger is often about some important principle being violated by someone who does not recognise its importance to that particular teenager at that particular time in their lives.

All that said, teenagers' ordinary day-to-day encounters with each other, with parents and with teachers are more often emotionally positive or neutral rather than being about anger at all. On the other hand, however, if an adolescent is angry with somebody and he expresses this through shouting and door-slamming, this is something that is very easy for adults to see and to label.

Therefore parents should realise that it is important to take note of the vast majority of the time when their child is *not* angry. It is at times like this that ordinary encounters with him should focus on developing, nurturing and sustaining the relationship rather than trying to control parts of it that if given too much attention will stand in the way of healthy relating.

Teach them how to have useful rows

It is also important to remember that healthy relationships include arguments and rows. Such arguments remind us of our individuality and also tell others of the limits that we are willing to be pushed towards but not beyond. Arguments help to clear the air, put life into dead point-scoring routines and refresh stale routines. They can be very, very healthy.

But wouldn't it be interesting if in an argument with someone we had the ability to draw from our memory all the happy times we spent with them and to throw this at them in the heat of the argument? Imagine the screaming match that went like this: 'I love your caring and kind side. You are so helpful with your little sister. It's great to be able to rely on you when you say you'll be in at a certain time!'

We don't normally do this, choosing instead to unleash a store of old incidents, which guarantees making matters worse. By doing so we lose the opportunity to generate some understanding of where the other person is coming from. So it is with teenagers, and even if we don't throw everything negative at them, we often hold an attitude that absolutely makes clear our disdain for their position.

Over ninety per cent of our communication is not verbal, so adolescents will know very clearly whether they are being respected or undermined when interacting with parents. They don't need to hear the words – they can judge it from *how* we behave towards them or look at them!

Teenage thinking – bridging the child and the adult

There is a notion that in some way adolescent thinking is generally child-like and that teenagers cannot therefore be trusted to know what is good for them. Choosing friends is one example that parents fret about in this regard. But many adolescents in fact have the same mental capacity as the adults that they live with. This is because many adults do not engage in full adult-like thinking!

Just think back on the times when you couldn't believe what was coming out of your mouth or when your emotions were as contained as those of a seven-year-old. We all have the capacity to go back to being childlike – a source of great entertainment (and ammunition) for our children.

Of course what teenagers don't have is life experience, or the street wisdom that goes with their newly developed adult-like way of thinking. Most adolescents will have developed:

1. the capacity to problem solve
2. the ability to look at problems from many different angles
3. the ability to take on board the perspective of others
4. the capacity to bring new information into their own thinking so that they can improve their own problem-solving skills.

These skills also help them to improve their arguing skills. They still require guidance and support, though, as they have to learn that their thinking is sometimes at odds with the reality of a situation, e.g. drinking alcohol is good for me because it helps me relax and make friends.

What is interesting to note is how often parents are not actually able to engage in thinking processes in the same clear way as their teenagers. This may be because of the busyness of their own lives or because of the emotional baggage that they have carried from earlier experiences in their own lives. In times of distress or a crisis, the parent often reverts to a thinking style that is much more childlike than the adolescent, who is able to stand back and see things through their idealistic lenses, without being hindered by years of the wear and tear of life.

Many adults, even though they have the capacity to think in a mature and complex way, do not engage with this skill day to day. Their ability to stand back and be clear leaves them, particularly if there is a bit of tension in the air. Therefore, imagine the clash that will occur if an adult is engaged in childlike thinking, an adolescent is engaged in adult thinking and they are trying to find common ground between them. Bulls and china shops don't even begin to describe the potential fallout.

Moral thinking

A related point here concerns the notion of moral thinking, in other words, arguments that arise out of behaviour that is at odds with certain moral standards within the family, school or neighbourhood. We know that a moral sense develops strongly during the teenage years. However, this does not mean that strong moral thinking automatically leads to strong moral behaviour. The two do not necessarily go hand in hand for either adults or teenagers.

Trying to convince a teenager that a particular behaviour is not 'mature' can be a bit pointless – they probably already know that. Consider this conversation:

Teen: Me and Jo had a huge row and she's such a bitch.
Parent: Why, what happened?
Teen: She's been telling everyone that I went out with her boyfriend and saying that I'm a two-faced cow.
Parent: That's awful – what actually happened?
Teen: Well, he said it was over and I went along with it.
Parent: You what? That was stupid. Why didn't you check first? You could have found out. You'd think at your age you'd have more sense . . .
Teen: Gimme a break: what'd you know anyway? Leave me alone and mind your own business.

The opportunity was lost to simply comfort and console and leave the judgment until later if it really was necessary. The teenager rejects the parent and the conversation because her distress wasn't heard.

What teenagers generally require help with is working out what happened that made them do something that they know was against some of their very own principles, e.g. going out with someone else's boyfriend. This is a source of confusion and therefore needs to be worked out with them. But how often have you as a parent chosen instead to launch into a rant about rights and wrongs in the mistaken belief that you are actually doing some good?

What is required is for you not to judge the situation too early but to listen to the story and guide the teenager's thinking towards some sort of useful answer. You don't need to take away all the pain and confusion in one go. Consider this conversation:

Teen: Me and Jo had a huge row and she's such a bitch.

Parent: Why, what happened?

Teen: She's been telling everyone that I went out with her boyfriend and saying that I'm a two-faced cow.

Parent: That's awful – what actually happened?

Teen: Well, he said it was over and I went along with it.

Parent: Oh dear, that sounds awful to get caught out like that.

Teen: Ya, and to make matters worse, he did the same with Debbie last week.

Parent: Sounds like you're hurting about being on a list for him.

Teen: Just feel crap that I've hurt Jo cos I was stupid enough to believe him.

Parent: Right, that's a tough spot. Wonder if there's anything you can do to sort it.

Teen: She's too mad right now anyway – oh, I feel such a bitch.

Parent: Sounds like you think it's best to leave it settle a while and then see . . .

Teen: Ya, maybe, we'll see. Ya, probably.

The opportunity was used to support the teenager in her distress and not to worry about the whys and wherefores of the situation. The end result is a consoled child with some pointers as to where to move to next to resolve the issue, and a parent in her good books.

TOP TIPS

1. Acknowledge your own emotions and express them so that your teenager learns how to regulate their own (e.g. 'I'm frustrated because I've asked you to . . .').
2. Realise that there are contradictions in your own life and learn how you live comfortably with these.
3. Everyone needs to revert back to being child-like every now and again. Just let it happen and don't store it as fuel for a future row.

Distance, disengagement and disowning the family

A myth that I hear being expressed by parents is that their teenager has disengaged from the family and as such is exhibiting signs that they have had enough of family life. Parents often interpret this as a sign of dislike or morbidity, or some sort of rebellion against parents.

Disengagement from family life as it was when they were young children is in fact a normal part of the teenage journey. It symbolises a move, a developmental shift towards more independent thinking and independent behaviour. It is not a comfortable place for you as a parent because the change seems to take off with such speed and haste that oftentimes you are not fully prepared for it. Of course, you also have the dubious honour of being able to spot the potential dangers that exist in the world of the teenager, and in your panic you double your efforts to try to re-engage with the child.

The response to this can often be that the teenager chooses to distance herself even more. Your endeavour for closeness may be somewhat at odds with how you were with the child in the previous years, when there may have been a bit more space given to her. The big difference is that when she was younger the amount of space and independence was controlled totally by you. With the onset of adolescence, this grip on control is challenged.

The rather bizarre result is that just as the teenager is able for some more space, you get anxious and try to reduce the amount of it. From my perspective, it is the *battle over control* that can unsettle parents when it comes to disengagement, not the actual disengagement itself.

From teenagers' perspective there is a normal urge to distance themselves from the family system in order to understand their own development. They also require space in order to understand the rules of the world around them and to develop the peer relationships that can sustain and nurture them. This can ultimately lead to a move away from the complete dependence on family that has been the hallmark of their existence up to now.

Space – a safe launch into it

In other words, they are creating a distance in order to get a perspective and it is important to support that space. It is also important to negotiate the balance between the space and the family's need to have all members contribute to the daily routine and functioning of the family.

The easiest way to do this is to make it clear that you recognise the need for time away for your teenager and that you give her that space if in return she agrees to be part of certain family events. For example, you might say that you would like her to be home for family meals, to avoid arranging to have friends call until other children have homework finished, or to help tidy up before visitors arrive. It's not that she ends up liking what she has to do that's important, but rather that she learns from you the give-and-take nature of getting needs met.

Space is healthy but sometimes when we distance ourselves from those close to us, we are not aware of this and need a gentle reminder or kind word to entice us back into the fold. This does not need to be a battle. Earlier we learned that being a valued part of family is hugely important for teenagers. So a respectful request to reconnect, put without fuss, is often enough. A statement like, 'I know you'd prefer not to, but I'd love it if you could come with me to your sister's game on Thursday' is much better than 'For God's sake, you're part of this bloody family too, you know!'

Ultimately, young people are preparing themselves for the separation of themselves from the family unit that will come with leaving school, gaining employment, going to college or heading off around the world. The process of moving away from the family in small steps is essential for a teenager to learn how the world works.

Interestingly, if this disengagement is supported by parents, it will actually help to strengthen the relationship between the teenager and other family members. This is because as the adolescent steps back from the centre of the family, she will inevitably make some mistakes that you can be there to offer support and guidance with, which will firm up the connection between you and her.

In many ways the distance is no more than the distance required for healthy functioning in any relationship. The most nurturing and sustaining of partnerships occur when both parties are able to exist both together as a unit and independently. This is where both people allow time and space for engagement together while at the same time giving freedom to promote individual growth, friendships and interests.

Distancing, increasing disengagement and separation are not the same as being completely cut off from family. Think of it like the hub and spoke of a wheel. The hub is the centre from which the spokes emanate and which gives them the strength to hold the outer wheel. The family unit is the hub, the spokes are the children and the wheel is the interaction with the outside world. The job of being a parent is to keep the hub solid and air in the wheels!

And of course it is important to remind ourselves that most adolescents and their parents continue to have a healthy sense of connection and this is crucial for the transition to adulthood that is not too far down the road.

Dancing with distancing – maintaining family rhythm

What needs to happen for all of this to work is some ongoing communication and discussion about the need for the teenager to disengage from the family while at the same time still being part of that family and still having something to offer. The relationship rhythm in families is constantly in movement. It is like one big dance and works well when everyone is dancing to the same music.

As referred to earlier, adolescents can engage in a type of thinking that is quite adult-like but without an adult's worldly experience. Parents therefore have an opportunity to access this particular thinking ability and invite the teenager to help with discussions. Topics can include the following.

1. The types of limits and boundaries that are set in the home.
2. Different types of choices that teenagers are free to make and those that require approval.
3. Setting time limits.
4. Different types of friends.
5. Use of alcohol.
6. Sharing household chores.

Because of the teenagers' increased ability to reason, negotiate and compromise, these are all up for grabs rather than simply issued as orders.

It is like setting up an experiment with teenagers. Involve them in the boundary making, reward them for this by having them put it into practice in the real world and then watch as they acquire experience of the world in an organised way.

For example, your teenager wants to stay out late with a group of friends who you know buy alcohol and drink it when the parents of one of them leave the house. You voice your concerns; your teenager dismisses them. You agree the time boundary, setting it later than you are comfortable with, but with the condition that as soon as alcohol is produced, your teenager will come home. Advise that you will monitor the evening. You would be surprised at the number of teenagers who will come home on time because they were part of the negotiation and have agreed to the condition. And the last thing they need is you turning up at the doorstep mortifying them!

It has been my experience of working with teenagers and their families that disengagement, far from being a sign of dislike, is actually a normal statement of an adolescent creating a thinking space out of which they attempt to understand the world.

They take time out to consider:

- how they are doing
- how they are getting on with friends
- what they would like to offer and receive from those around them.

They also:

- learn how they handle the complexities that life presents on a regular basis
- try to make sense of their mistakes, which helps their learning
- fantasise about being rock stars and models
- wish for different parents
- plan running away
- really plan giving up school
- wonder about falling in love and having sex and a whole host of other entertaining and necessary issues.

This is busy work! The distancing process needs to be appropriately nurtured by parents, but it can also be contained by setting boundaries around when it can happen, where it can happen and with whom it can happen. Equally, parents may need to reinterpret a sign of resistance not as open defiance of the rules and regulations they have set up, but more as an opportunity to engage with the adolescent to establish whether those rules and regulations are useful.

Many family attitudes and rules have been around for many years and have actually outlived their usefulness. These could do with a good review, a thrashing out and maybe a re-establishment of some different boundaries and limits. Most teenagers will react favourably to the news that you think your way of thinking might be old-fashioned and in need of a review and will happily contribute to your attempt to sort yourself out.

When to worry

It is only in the most severe instances that disengagement needs to be judged in some way as a sign of something morbid or fearful going on, a sign of a teenager being depressed or anxious. Generally, parents do tend to know when their child has cut herself off to such an extent that in fact there may be other more serious issues that need to be addressed in a more proactive way.

Parents get a hunch, an inkling that just won't go away, and it is best to follow up on this rather than choose to ignore it. I advise parents that such hunches are not just sudden inspirations that come out of nowhere. They are the result of years of observing and interpreting how the child is in the world and then reacting when something doesn't quite fit the pattern. The responsibility here is for parents, teachers and others in regular contact with the young person to act decisively in this instance and not to hope that whatever it is that is concerning them will go away.

Asking, explaining your concern and finding out that you are wrong is far healthier than wondering and worrying, only to find out later that there is something important and serious happening in the life of the adolescent. It also reminds the teenager that you are there watching out for them, and this is a powerful, positive message that will stay with them. Of course, you may not get to hear this for about twenty years.

TOP TIPS

1. Allow for distance in the relationship with your teenager, but try to make sense of why it makes you uncomfortable before you try and control it.
2. See engagement and disengagement as qualities rather than quantities.

> 3. Hunches need to be checked out. It is better to be proved wrong than to be left wondering.

And finally . . .

Adolescence is a time of exciting change for everyone concerned with the young person, but this change is just another part of a process of change that has been in play since conception. Parents and others are centre-stage players in all of this and therefore it is a fruitless preoccupation to try and hang all the woes of the family or the particular young person on the teenager. Any explanation of problems in the absence of the social, school, community and family context is flawed.

The majority of adolescents continue to live their lives in ordinary enough ways and have much to contribute to the relationships of which they are a part, by way of their increased capacity for thinking and communicating. Hanging on to urban legend and popular myth only serves to undermine young people and belies the many ordinary day-to-day interactions with them that form the basis of healthy, positive experiences for families and the wider community.

Myths also undermine the existing skills of parents that have been built up over more than a decade with their child. If parents can stand back from the fog that sometimes falls on parent–teenager relationships they can learn that they remain crucial for the healthy development of their child.

It is out of this crucial role that what is possible becomes much more exciting than whatever problem might exist.

CHAPTER 3

Forming a Person: What's Involved?

B y now I hope you can see that it is necessary to move away from the idea of the young person as someone who must have something done to him in order for him to be set on the right road in life. A lot of headlines ask questions such as what can be *done* about teenage drinking, what needs to be *done* about teenage sex, and how can teenage anti-social behaviour be *managed*. These are important questions, but they only examine surface issues, the problems that we see. Such questions fail to get at the complex reasons that underlie these very problems – the story behind the behaviour.

Focus on forming, forget about fixing

Practically every school counsellor, psychologist and doctor who meets an exasperated parent of a teenager will at some stage of the conversation have that parent plead with them for some expert advice on how to 'fix him', 'control her' or just plain simply 'do something with them'. This is somewhat perplexing in that it is generally not an approach we use when we encounter difficulties in relationships with others. When we fall out with our husband, we generally don't haul him down to the local doctor and ask for a fix.

With other significant people in our lives we are more likely to stand back and try to evaluate all the possible whys and wherefores of a situation in order to generate some

FORMING A PERSON: WHAT'S INVOLVED?

understanding of the 'what' that is causing us difficulty.

It seems that with teenagers, our first port of call is to ask what can be done with them. We don't bother trying to build up the context around a particular behaviour, we simply want it fixed. This approach is more likely to run parents into a cul-de-sac, which will leave them even more frustrated because they will then believe that they have tried everything and have failed.

When I work with teenagers and their families it is by acknowledging the full and active involvement in family life of every member, including the so-called troublesome child. This notion is based on the simple idea that all behaviour can only be fully understood if as many of the people affected by it can be used to sort it out. Some of the most important factors to understand are part and parcel of the personalities in the family set-up. Each of these personalities brings something different to each other in their various relationships.

Fourteen-year-old Tommy fights constantly with his younger sister and he is therefore seen as being difficult. Attention gets focused on Tommy alone because he is older. This one-sided approach to a problem fails to recognise that all relationships can only be fully understood by examining all participants in the relationship. Tommy gets the negative attention simply because of his age, something he has no control over. What about the personality of his sister?

Such a problem-solving approach would not be tolerated in trying to understand other groups in society. It is very restrictive to define any group of people by only one aspect of their personality. More so if that aspect is then used to explain *all* their behaviour.

So Tommy is fourteen, therefore he's a teenager, therefore he should know better, therefore he's to blame. Instead of trying to work out a better way of getting Tommy and his younger sister to relate *together*, parents plead with the older sibling to try get on better with his sister. This makes it look like Tommy is the one doing all the relating.

This seems unfair, but it is the experience that many teenagers will describe when I get into conversation with them. They detest being defined by the fact of their age. Indeed, by doing this, we make teenagers vulnerable to all sorts of misunderstanding because it makes us blind to everything they have to offer. It also robs you as a parent of the opportunity to explore deeply with teenagers the things that might be causing them distress.

Adolescence doesn't exist anyway!

A strategy that I often use to remind me how to treat teenagers with respect is to think there is really no such thing as adolescence. It is only a label that society uses to describe a group of people who are between the ages of twelve and eighteen. But it seems as though we have chosen to relate to the label and have forgotten that no one label can ever capture the diversity that is key to what being a person is about.

But as we can see, using age as a way of defining young people poses some problems. Consider the following questions.

1. Is a twelve-year-old in his teenage years?
2. How can an eighteen-year-old adult be described as an adolescent?
3. How do we label a ten-year-old girl who begins her monthly period?
4. Why are sixteen-year-old mothers described as teenagers but sixteen-year-old boys who play rugby described as young men?

This, I hope, is not just playing with words for the sake of it. It reminds me to relate to the young person I meet and not to whom I expect to meet because of his age.

As soon as we hear the word 'teen', it seems that anxiety is provoked and the expectation is that some form of trouble has to follow. The more we hype up the problems of relating to teenagers, the more we run the risk of sinking their entire ship of development with our expectations.

The teenage years (whenever they begin or end) are part of our long journey of development over our life. As such, these years need to be seen as a normal set of experiences for all involved. If we focus on aspects that are troublesome for us we run the risk of creating obstacles to relating better. We need to know as much of the context of their lives as possible in order to learn how to influence the relationship that we create with them and them with us.

TOP TIPS

1. To understand the world of the teenager, ask all of the 'w' questions – when, with whom, why, where, what.
2. But don't use them as accusations! Just build up a bigger picture.
3. Describe your teenager in ways other than her age.
4. Engage with your child as she is, not as you think she ought to be.

What are we really at?

A family is a system. It is made up of various people bound together by various connections that cause them to relate to one another in a way in which they do not relate to others. Because of the connections, what happens for one person has an influence on the others. A child does well in school and parents feel proud.

A row with a teenage son affects everyone in the home.

The connections are what make the family a system – everything that happens in the family is influencing everyone within the family. It is the big dance referred to in the previous chapter.

If we go a step further, it is possible to see that the family system is influenced by what happens around it. The world around the family is critically important if we are to understand exactly what is happening when we are engaging with teenagers.

Namely, we are helping to create, form and mould a person, an identity, a character, another human being.

So instead of asking the question, 'How can my daughter be fixed?' it may be much more illuminating for parents to ask these questions.

1. How have I prepared myself to be a parent of a teenager?
2. Do I know enough about how teenagers develop?
3. Am I too reliant on my own experience of being a teenager? Do I need other sources of information?
4. Am I ready to be challenged by the normal needs of my teenage child?
5. How do I look after myself in the task of forming this new person?

These questions are worth asking because research shows that puberty and all that goes with it is actually poorly understood by both teenagers and the significant adults in their lives. It is therefore critically important not to fall into any assumptions that with the onset of advanced education and the Internet, everybody knows what is happening as children continue their developmental journey into adolescence. This is not the case. Neither is it worth while looking for the 'one way' to raise a teenager. Thankfully there isn't one.

An idea that I object to is that there is a prescriptive method for raising a teenager in a manner that will guarantee some form of unidentified success. There is no doubt that there are key essentials to raising successfully any child. My list would include:

1. parents who are comfortable in their own relationships (and not just intimate, romantic relationships but also other key supportive ones with friends or family)
2. provision of food and shelter
3. provision of access to safe, stimulating and nurturing environments
4. provision of good social networks
5. freedom to be curious about emotions.

But a tick-box list of specific instructions simply undermines what both you and your child bring to the relationship. Provide the basic essentials and then let the natural pattern of your relationship develop on the basis of regular negotiation and compromise.

Teenagers' basic needs are little different from those of others.

My keystone to being a successful parent and a critical ingredient for an enjoyable adolescence for a child is the quality of the central relationships that the child is exposed to. Key indicators of that quality are:

- the flexibility that you allow in the emerging relationship with your teenager
- the type of care and love that you continue to give your teenager
- how you provide space for his emerging personality to begin to explore the world around him

- what values you explore with him as he makes sense of the world around him
- how you negotiate the difficult patches that you will both experience in the relationship.

These indicators cause us to ask what it is that we do with teenagers in ordinary day-to-day interactions.

In some ways, nothing more than what we were doing with that young person when she was an infant or a toddler. Think back to that time when the current teenager was but a 'babe in arms'. Look at the job description. It included:

- being an active communicator
- ensuring there was enough stimulation to keep the child entertained and to promote learning
- creating a safe environment
- being consistent and predictable
- observing and following patterns of cues from the child.

You did this in order to organise your own life. You also did it to offer predictable and consistent ways of relating with the child so that, for the most part, the infant felt safe and content in the world.

Parents created a space for the child to explore first the cot, then the kitchen and then the world outside. They introduced him to sounds, sights and smells in a way that both pleasured and stimulated him as he was eagerly curious about all that was around him. They watched him and allowed more and more space for him to fall over, scratch a knee, fall off a bicycle or have a tiff with a neighbour's child. They jumped in when things looked a little too dangerous and rescued him from potential disasters.

Now leap forward twenty or thirty years and ask the question:

what is it that most *adults* desire from their friendships and intimate relationships in adult life? They seek:

- a sense of connection to trusted family
- stimulating relationships with friends
- people who offer predictability and security
- people who can be trusted in times of need
- people who are there to enjoy times of fun
- people with whom they can share emotional and physical intimacy.

All of this shows us that young children have a set of needs that mirror the needs of adults, and vice versa. While the mechanisms for having these needs met changes over time, the core, crucial cornerstones upon which the potential for contentment is built are remarkably similar for older adults and young infants.

If this is the case, why should the group in between, the teenagers, be any different? Why is it that the core needs of human beings (food, shelter, belonging and connection) would be any different for a fifteen-year-old than a five- or forty-five-year-old? The needs of teenagers have numerous overlaps with the needs of the rest of humankind. It is curious, therefore, to waste time on trying to categorise them as being different, unexplainable, incomprehensible and generally out of touch with us.

And as a by the way, we are kidding ourselves that we interact with people in every other age group without difficulty. Relationships in all parts of our lives are both rewarding and at times difficult. We can have the biggest rows with two-year-old toddlers and eighty-two-year-old fathers.

Teenagers do not have a monopoly on being difficult.

TOP TIPS

1. Learn more about puberty and its effects on children. For starters, have a look at the last chapter in this book.
2. Put energy into improving the quality of the relationship rather than the quantity of things in a teenager's life.
3. Teenagers have much the same needs as everyone else – it's how we relate to them that changes.

So how have we got ourselves into a muddle?

I believe that many of our struggles with teenagers today emerge from the experience that we had ourselves as young children and adolescents. It strikes me that the parents of today's teenagers are not fully equipped to deal with teenagers because of their own teenage years.

I will outline more detailed reasons for this particular set of beliefs in a later chapter. For now, I want to acknowledge that many of the core needs of today's teenagers provide substantial challenges for parents because parents are still struggling with some of their own story of being a teenager. There is a lot of mental distress in the world of adults today and it is getting in the way of healthy relationships with teenagers.

There is no doubt that in today's world there are many more types of experiences and a pace of development that has produced a pressurised parenting environment different from that of thirty years ago. One example is that teenagers today are immediately influenced by events right across the world. Parents are no longer trying to exert control over good and bad influences in their own back yard but are also having to keep up with events thousands of miles away because those events are coming right into their sitting rooms. Gambling, violence, bullying and human distress can be brought into any sitting room, at any time, at the touch of a button.

The pace at which the world has shrunk to become the global village and the rapidity with which people are able to interconnect across communities from continent to continent without moving from their own homes is both astonishing and alarming. Astonishing because it is a tribute to human genius and invention; alarming because the timeframes for accommodating change have become so condensed that no sooner does a parent get an understanding of one new thing than there are a heap more waiting to be attended to.

The specific targeting of the younger generations as key sources of income for multinational corporations leaves many parents gasping for breath as they get caught in the whirlwind that seems to envelop the glasshouse in which teenagers live. It's like living in an emergency room for learning – busy, non-stop, over-stimulating and exhausting, with little sign of obvious reward.

It is no wonder, then, that parents struggle to keep up with the pace of development that goes on in the world around them. Many parents believe that they are unable to put into practice the strategies that will best meet the basic needs of their child.

However, inherent in this belief is an inaccurate assumption, which is that parents are in some way unable to meet the *core* needs of young people today. What parents need to be continually reminded of is that the core needs of a human being don't change substantially from one generation to the next. A quick glance at writings and art from thousands of years back will highlight how little changes over the millennia with regard to the fundamental needs of the person.

TOP TIPS

1. Slow down family life to a pace that suits all members of the family.
2. Use your own struggles as a teenager to give you precious insight into the struggles of your own teenager.
3. The basic but critical needs of people do not change that much over time – you do know what is important.

Looking out for love and the likes!

It strikes me that in some way it suits us not to become too concerned about how basic needs such as love, belonging and attention are actually met by parents today. It suits us because in our busy lives, these things require significant effort and time, both scarce commodities. Easier to buy jeans and shoes than work out how our teenagers feel about being loved or if they have a good sense of being connected to the people around them.

Many parents struggle with the pain of the loss of connection to their own mothers and fathers as they grew up in harsher economic and social times. Many parents today do not know how to create boundaries that are based on respect and dignity. They know that this is how they would like to set safe boundaries for their children but actually turning this desire into action is difficult. They are afraid that because the boundaries they experienced were often unfair or harsh, they will damage their own teenagers. And they made a promise that they would never do what their parents did to them!

This anxiety arises because the boundaries to which they were exposed as children arose out of an *authoritarian style* of parenting. Authoritarian parenting is based on control and rigid styles of communicating. It can be emotionally cold with little positive feedback. This style of parenting was itself immersed in a culture of top-down authoritarian decrees from Church and State. Parents of the 1950s were conditioned to look for direction outside themselves and to believe that they had little influence over their destiny. As a result, the children of those times, who are the parents of today, carry a message inside them that is based on the notion of what they should and should not be doing. These 'shoulds' and 'should nots' are often based on teachings that they never fully critically evaluated to see if they are actually any use.

SOME COMMON 'SHOULD' AND 'SHOULD NOT' STATEMENTS

1. I should have all the answers, right here, right now.
2. I should never be angry.
3. I should love my child at all times in all circumstances.
4. I should not ask for help.
5. I should not be dependent on others.
6. I should be at the top of my game at all times with my children.
7. I should not shout, scream, or cry out of sheer frustration.
8. I should be a fount of all knowledge and wisdom for my children because I am a parent.

If these statements are the basis of your parenting, it is likely that you will regularly feel overwhelmed and stressed. The danger is that then the 'should' and 'should not' statements will trigger guilt in you. When this happens you will want to overpower your child to try to get control back into a situation.

If this was done to you as a teenager you may find it difficult to prevent yourself doing the same to your children. Key steps to overcoming this include the following.

1. Make a list of your 'should' and 'should not' statements.
2. Work out which are genuinely your own and which you are simply repeating from other people.
3. Question whether any get in the way of expressing the love that you feel for your children.
4. If they do, create a list of alternative statements. For example, 'It's okay to ask for help', 'I don't know everything about being a parent', 'It's okay to be angry.'
5. Regularly check that you and your teenagers do something that maintains the special connection between you, e.g. planned time alone, a shared interest, you asking for a bit of help, etc.

Many parents will describe to me that they know *what* they wish to do with teenagers but they do not know *how* to put this into operation on a day-to-day basis. Sometimes I think that we opt for an easy way out when we know in our hearts what is the right and good thing to do but our heads do not have the same conviction.

That way is often to pretend that basic needs are not that important or are too difficult to deliver. We can kid ourselves that they will be met by someone else. We can even go so far as to deny that they exist and focus instead on what is easier to give to a child or teenager (which can either be the stuff of materialism or just plain old 'giving in').

When I carry out interviews with parents in order to try to get a picture of how the family system functions, I often follow a standard format which includes questions about the nature of the problem, any obvious triggers, what helps to alleviate the distress, what makes it worse and so on. This is good routine practice and helps parents clarify certain issues. It's not enough.

I also include questions like the following.

- How does the teenager know that he is loved?
- How often does he get hugged?
- How does he know that he is an important member of the family?
- How often does he get compliments?

These questions open the door into the world that exists deep inside us all. This is the place where we truly see ourselves in terms of how we interact and relate with others. This is where we work out how important we believe ourselves to be in life and how important we are to the people closest to us.

Our answers to these questions indicate what messages we hear and see being communicated in our direction, how we make sense of these messages and how we put them into the beliefs that we already hold about ourselves.

Teenagers need families.

It is a mistake to think that teenagers do not engage in thinking about their place in the family or that music and make-up are their primary concerns.

Teenagers look for love, warmth, support, tenderness and connection.

I have worked with young people in all sorts of settings and am regularly struck by their interest and ability to engage in the types of conversation that underlie issues fundamental to human nature. Such conversations tap into the most basic of desires and needs to do with being connected to others. They are also the place from which we are transformed from isolated individuals into energetic, dynamic and revitalised 'partners in living'.

Teenagers are up for this. Fifteen-year-old Sarah, who has problems with her body image and refuses to eat, also has significant problems with accepting who she is and finding a place for herself in the world. Give her a safe chance and see if she can respond to an offer of help.

Thirteen-year-old Tommy, who is out all hours of the day and night, may well be looking for connection to someone or something that is just not available to him at home. When he's at home he fights with his younger sister to relieve frustration; when he's away from home he has peace. Sometimes it's that simple.

Teenagers are working out how the world operates and fitting themselves into it. No different from the rest of us.

TOP TIPS

1. Rules based on 'should' and 'should not' need to be examined for how useful they really are.
2. Love and belonging are as necessary for teenagers as they were when they were infants.
3. Work hard at finding even the most ordinary, smallest connection with your teenager – it will stay with them for ever.

It's all about relationships

I have been repeatedly taught by young people that the core of the vast bulk of psychological distress is based on confused, compromised or cold relationships. Even when there is psychological illness or disorder, teenagers will still hunger for a bond or connection to somebody close to them. In other words, teenagers 'don't work' when viewed in isolation from their relationships, regardless of whether or not those relationships are working out to everyone's liking.

The power of relationships to significantly influence our mental health should not be underestimated. Remember that in the family system, what happens to one person impacts on the others. If Tommy's mother is depressed she will not be able to meet his emotional needs. Her mental health directly affects him and so he acts out (e.g. by fighting) and gets out.

The power of relationships carries an extra dimension when applied to teenagers, who are still in the process of forming aspects of their personality. They are still learning, still soaking up the hidden and unhidden messages that come from the many relationships they are involved with each day. Each day another layer is added to who they are as people.

Relationships are about emotional experiences

For me, at the heart of relationships, both positive and negative ones, is how emotion is managed by the people in the relationship. By emotion, I do not mean the kind of emotion that is only associated with the sulkiness, tears or door-slamming often described by both young performers and their adult audiences: I mean the full range of emotion from joy to sadness, despair to hilarity, guilt to contentment, irritability to anger. What is worth reflecting on is this: given that it is so central to our lives, why do we struggle so much with emotion?

Emotion provides us with information about how we are with people and situations, yet we seem to downgrade its importance, preferring to focus on behaviour as the key to how we develop. The word 'emotional' has a negative tinge to it. In everyday speech we use phrases that show how we deny emotion, repress emotion, or show too little emotion, too much emotion, high emotion and low emotion. It would make you wonder if we actually know what we are talking about. More important, do we know how to teach children how to experience their emotions in a way that is safe and useful?

It seems unusual that when parents or teachers of adolescents complain that teenagers have emotional problems, it is the emotion that is seen as a problem. Why, if a teenager is angry, is that seen as a problem as opposed to a justifiable response to a trigger that has greatly upset something within them that is very important to them? Strong emotion is deemed to be negative in some way.

Surely emotions are real ways of responding to a trigger in the person's environment. Emotions tell us whether something is safe, dangerous, upsetting, easy, joyous, understandable or threatening. They are natural, but it is rare to hear parents of a teenager standing back and taking time to try to work out what might be happening for the child. More often, parents will become defensive, react to the emotion, feel exhausted by doing this and forget to find out what is underneath it.

The shadow of emotional history

As a further challenge I would ask the following questions.

1. Why do we expect that adolescents should always be able to 'control' their emotions as if that is something that we are all able to do?
2. Why is it that emotions have to be seen to be controlled, anyway?
3. How much better would it be if there was general permission to experience and express emotions?

We have become fearful of emotional expression because when we see it or hear it, it reminds us of times past when emotional expression was not pleasant.

Many of us still carry the scars of irrational emotional expression, especially if we were brought up in an environment where free expression of emotion was frowned upon. We believe that there is something wrong with the *emotion* when in fact it is more likely that what we are actually afraid of is the possibility of some harmful *behaviour* after the emotion.

So Sarah, who does not like her body image, focuses on her body as the problem when in fact it may be that she is unsure of her emotions around accepting who she is. It seems easier for her to manipulate her body image than to deal with the sadness related to a feeling of not fitting in. It is easy to focus on her body image, but it is really her fear of being emotionally overwhelmed that is the fuel keeping the body image issue alive. Somewhere Sarah has learned or been taught that emotion is not safe – this will cast a very long shadow over her life.

Lighting up the shadow

One way to begin watching out for emotions is to remember that parents of teenagers have an expertise in observing their own child. *Your* expertise has been developing for over a decade. You have a range of useful responding skills but often get too caught up in the fear that the adolescent will win out in some argument or power struggle that is 'bound to happen'. This prevents you using some of the skills that you have built up over the years.

Parents can very quickly see, hear or sense the emotional state of their child and can tell whether something is right or wrong for them. This isn't mind-reading – it's using a store of knowledge built up over time. What is mind-reading is when you think you know what is going on when you pick up on something. Check out what you have sensed and give feedback to the child. With a teenager this needs to be done in a caring, clear manner so that she knows that she is being looked out for.

In forgetting their own abilities to troubleshoot many of the potential difficulties that might arise for the child, parents often choose to try to exert control over the emotional world of the teenager as a means of making themselves feel in control of a situation. This is a complete waste of time and energy and a useless way of trying to interact with a teenager.

None of us can control the emotional world of a teenager, any more than we can control when they will feel a hunger pang, or a surge of pleasure from a flirtatious look. What we can do is help them to understand the particular events, people or surroundings that trigger specific emotions for them so that they can understand themselves better. Therefore we need to have the maturity to engage in this process of naming and feeling emotions openly; and we should not be too frightened to do it for ourselves too. A big ask, but so vitally important.

If we do not possess this maturity, we will simply revert to attempts at controlling and become victim to the frustration that results from that particularly useless exercise – none of us bends easily to being controlled. It is a lose–lose situation – the adult trying to control someone who does not want to be controlled and the teenager reacting to avoid being trapped by someone else's desire to control.

Having an insight into your own emotional world can be scary and exciting. But in real terms it gives you another way of examining how you interact with your teenager, especially during the tricky moments of the relationship. The following questions will help you to begin building this insight.

DEVELOPING A PROFILE OF MY EMOTIONAL CAPACITY

1. How comfortable am I with the expression of emotions?
2. What do I do with my own strong emotions?
3. How do I differentiate between my emotions, my thinking and my behaviour?
4. How good am I at distinguishing between small changes in emotion, e.g. from irritability to frustration to anger?
5. What do I teach my child about emotions?
6. How do I stimulate myself when I am emotionally flat and how do I calm myself when emotionally charged?
7. How important is control of emotion for me, and why?

Just another step in how a personality is formed

Maintaining a sense of belonging for the child is what parents and other significant carers need to be mindful of when working with teenagers. The task for the teenager is one of identity continually evolving. More significantly, the task is also one of allowing her the opportunity to use newly acquired thinking, emotional, moral and behavioural abilities to develop her sense of herself. This allows her to create an understanding of what does and what does not make her an individual in the world. Part of her individuality is how she belongs to her family.

She is moving towards an identity that is being described and defined by herself and not primarily by family expectations and descriptions. She will accept some family labels and will reject others if they do not fit with her view of herself. She will even accept or reject some of the labels that she applies to herself as she grows and learns new information about herself. This is normal and healthy but challenging to be involved in: you are never quite sure who will be sitting at the dinner table with you.

Of course, it is very important to bear in mind that while involved in this process, the teenager is also an observer of it. Those long hours of listening to music, locked away in a bedroom with friends are not wasted. Teenagers use this time to come to the realisation that they are the owners of a few personality traits that remind them of their father and mother. That often does not sit comfortably and needs a lot of working out.

The capacity to deliberately observe ourselves becomes much more finely tuned during the teenage years. It opens up all sorts of curiosities, possibilities and conundrums and actually needs a fair amount of time to sort out. Sorting it out can involve lots of thinking, lots of texting and, when the learning gets too much, lots of irritation.

Looking in the mirror is difficult

During my work, I often sit with parents who are at their wits' end because their son or daughter is particularly selfish, stubborn, lazy, etc. I will ask if either of the parents is like this or was like this in the past. Usually there is agreement that this is or was the case. Of course, parents can offer reasons and justifications, some of which are perfectly reasonable – but they are just as reasonable for teenagers to use. If I'm fourteen and have just had sexual feelings for my best friend, I'm not going to have much interest in helping out at home. And I'm certainly not going to tell you why!

What is surprising is parents' inability to see how asking the teenager to change a particular feature of her personality is as big a task as asking them to change this same trait.

I challenge parents who see a trait in the child that they feel is problematic to put the shoe on the other foot and ask themselves what it is like for the child to have to be exposed to that particular trait in the parents themselves. And then to imagine what it was like in the years when they were unable to express their response to it or were confused by it. Needless to say, there is a softening of many a cough!

TOP TIPS

1. Emotion is natural, but each person has different tolerances for different emotions.
2. You already carry an expertise about your own teenager – use it to teach him about how you experience him and about how he can regulate himself.
3. The unfolding personality of your teenager offers opportunities to learn as much about yourself as about your child.

What's happening for the teenager?

The process for the teenager of letting his own view of his personality take precedence over how his parents define him began years earlier. However, with the onset of puberty the teenager is coming into a phase in his life where he can start to recognise, acknowledge and directly influence this in an independent way. This is quite an exciting development for him.

Up to this point he has most often been identified as an extension of you. He is seen as having likenesses with one parent, the other or both. He has also probably been defined by a certain role that he plays in the family system. As teenager, though, he can deliberately separate himself from the identities of other family members and get a clear sense of the unique aspects that make up his personality. He can separate himself to the point of actually allowing himself to become a member of other groups, sometimes to the exclusion of the family for a while. He also has the ability now to separate enough to be able to see that his parents are not the idols of perfection that he might have once thought as a younger child. This can be both a relief and a burden. A relief if he hears that parents do not have to be right all the time and a burden if he hears that it's better to 'talk it out'!

The need for belonging to a group other than the family is an important developmental milestone for the teenager and if it is blocked this can lead to distress. In other words, the safe separation from family is something to be supported and encouraged. Interestingly, research shows that the need for this is more pronounced in the early teenage years. It's like a flight into freedom.

However, by their mid-teens most teenagers will have a good sense of balance between their need for family connection and their need for peer group connection. This leaves a useful space for negotiation by parents. Early on they can highlight the importance of family time without the fear that they are causing serious damage to their child's self-esteem.

In other words, allow the sense of freedom to develop but be assertive in asking for family time because that's actually what your child will want ultimately. They just don't know that yet.

What's happening for the parents?

One particular angle that I have on the process of separation by teenagers may seem a little unusual, but I think it is highly relevant in managing successfully all the change that is going on for all family members. I am a strong advocate of the notion that 'what happens to you impacts on me' and vice versa.

It strikes me that as children grow up, reach developmental milestones and move on, there is an element of loss and grief built into the process. As parents we are a little saddened at the passing of babyhood, innocence and cuddliness. This often gets hidden in the excitement of change or the frustration of the continuous problem-solving that can accompany such change.

The teenager who moves into second-level education is definitely no longer a little boy or girl; the thirteen-year-old who does not want to be picked up outside school is evaluating what is important for her in the world; the seventeen-year-old who announces she has a boyfriend is giving a very clear signal about her separation from family.

These examples and hundreds more have the potential for dual meaning: there is the obvious evidence of growing up; but there is also the less obvious reality of an experience of the loss of the little son or daughter. I don't mean by this the need to be in hysterical tears of grief, just that there is an emotion associated with things that are moving on and will never be the same again.

I sometimes ask parents to write or talk about their teenager's development as a 'loss' event and it is powerful what parents will generate in terms of their reactions. They express ideas related to:

- how quickly their child has grown
- fear that they have not done enough for the child
- shame at disliking aspects of their child
- the depth of their love
- envy of the life their teenager leads
- and many other responses.

Interestingly, when I engage in whole-family work, the theme of loss is not confined to the parents. Adolescents, especially in times of vulnerability or distress, will express a desire to be like a young child because 'it's easier'. Or 'at least it's okay to ask for help when you're younger'. In other words, at times like this, young people yearn for a time that has gone before that was easier to manage.

Neither is this experience of loss confined to teenagers – just think of the amount of tears and 'nearly tears' that adults shed when the young child heads off to school for the first time. This despite the fact that most children will by that age already have spent time at childminders, a crèche or pre-school.

I use this example because it serves as a reminder that one of the truths that parents have to grapple with is that in bringing up a child, there is both the essential desire to support their growth to maturity but also the memories of the little bundle that came into the world all those years before.

There is absolutely nothing wrong with this, but it does need to be acknowledged. I cannot begin to count the number of angry, irritable, angst-ridden teenagers who have melted as they listened to their parents' wishes for them alongside the sense of sadness their parents also feel as their 'little one' sets out into the world. Bringing this out into the open is healthy, energising and enriching.

Such conversations can be the stuff of the real world of being in an adolescent–parent relationship.

Look at what the process teaches the teenager.

1. It shows him how important he is to you.
2. It teaches him how to acknowledge emotions.
3. It shows him some of the realities that you experience every day.
4. It brings all concerned into that private family space out of which come stronger bonds, calmer minds and easier households.

It just requires a little courage, some perseverance and a commitment to doing it.

I am not a great believer in the 'let's sit down and have this chat' approach with teenagers. It is much better to bring these types of conversation into the normal, everyday, routine events that happen around the home. There are usually plenty of opportunities, but we do tend to either miss out on them or overlook their potential by thinking that their ordinariness is too bland for such meaningful conversations. Nonsense.

Our lives are mostly made up of ordinary events, from which we derive satisfaction or distress. Every so often there is a peppering of extraordinary situations which can lift or depress us, but waiting for these moments is, in my view, a waste, as there is much more potential for development in using what is in our lives right now. The row in school, the best friend who lied, passing an exam, buying new clothes, the content of the 'soaps' all offer opportunity for comment, questioning and discussion.

How parents engage with the whole process of the teenager securing their sense of identity is critical. The next developmental milestone to occur will be when the child finishes secondary education. By then she will be deemed to be ready to 'fly the nest' and a critical phase of parental responsibility will have come to an end. (Watch out for the experience of loss here too.)

TOP TIPS

1. Take delight from the work you are doing to help form your child's character. Stop waiting for a good 'end result' when it's all over!
2. Allow teenagers to ebb and flow with regard to how they connect with the family.
3. Take note of your 'loss' moments and just let them happen. Take extra care of yourself when they do.

So what is this loss stuff all about?

This is the psychological process that is sometimes referred to as 'individuation'. We move slowly away from having our identities completely linked to and explained by the connections to our parents and family members. We work to a position where our own, unique personality and identity is perceived by others as being *separate* but *related* to our parents and families.

It is a journey that began at birth. But there is a speed during adolescence that forces us to take notice. It is also during the teenage years that it is perceived to cause most difficulties. So what was once lauded with, 'Isn't it great to see her becoming more independent with her friends?' becomes, 'Who does she think she is, hanging around with that lot at all hours of the day and night?'

The theme of this chapter poses a few very big questions for me.

1. What is parenting really all about?
2. What decisions do men and women actually make when they decide to become parents?
3. How do they think about these questions as they engage in parenting responsibilities on a daily basis?

In my practice, these questions are among the first points of discussion when I meet parents. The response is highly informative since it can reveal how much thought parents have given to the work of being a parent. How many parents would get the job of being a parent if they actually sat an interview for the job and had to answer questions like these?

*   What are your long-term goals for the project?
*   How will you bring those goals to reality?

- How will you seek help during times of struggle?
- What are your particular strengths?
- How can you be sure that you'll be around for the eighteen years that the substantial part of the project will take?

As I have written earlier, at the most basic level parenting is simply about providing food, shelter and safety to give children a fair chance of long-term survival so that they can go on to reproduce and maintain the natural cycle. All pretty straightforward.

However, with the human intellect and capacity to create values, attitudes, expectations, desires and beliefs, we have layered the most basic tasks of parenting with complex interactions, hopes and aspirations for our children. We want them to:

- experience pleasure and joy
- explore similarities and differences in their environments
- initiate contacts with others
- receive education
- make the world a better place through their presence
- earn a good living
- find good partners
- and a whole host of other noble, abstract and often unexpressed notions.

Fine so far, but how do parents prepare themselves for the epic journey that will be required to bring these aspirations to fruition? Much preparation goes into the preliminary functions of creating a relationship with a partner and securing accommodation, but where and how does the education and learning for parenthood come into the picture?

The answer seems straightforward – it is based on a philosophy of learning on the job, flying by the seat of your pants, or living on a wing and a prayer. This is not necessarily in itself a bad philosophy, but it does contain one significant flaw.

As any parent will confirm, once the child arrives, time for thinking about parenting or adopting new styles of communication or interaction becomes very scarce. Yet such thinking is a key strategy in effective learning on the job. It sets in place a skill of being able to reflect on what you are doing. Without it, the philosophy of the 'same old, same old' sets in.

Is reflection a fancy name for thinking?

No, although thinking is a key element of it. Reflection is more about working out where and how changes need to happen and then putting that thinking into action. Reflection needs to be a critical tool in how a parent understands how their parenting style develops over the years.

A classic example highlights its usefulness. Parents often express surprise or shock at doing something that they swore they would never do, or hearing themselves sound like their mother or father. If this becomes a pattern, it signals that they have not had the time to reflect on how they are doing the job. If they had this, they could work out why they said what their father used to say or did what their mother used to do. Reflection highlights the way we do things.

In terms of describing what reflection is, I use the image of being able to 'helicopter' above yourself to observe yourself carrying out a particular role in all its detail. That allows you to decide if you are happy with it and where you can make changes that would make you feel happier in your role. It will also increase the probability of your teenager being more confident in you as a parent because you will be showing that you don't necessarily always know best.

It is generally a really useful strategy with teenagers to

highlight why reflection works.

1. It lets them see that you are not always right about things.
2. Taking time out to evaluate what is happening can be useful because it gives breathing space around contentious issues.
3. It conveys that you are taking the job and them seriously.
4. It models for them a way of problem-solving in their own lives.

So a question for parents becomes: do you need to reflect on the legacy that you want to leave to your child in terms of how you solve problems?

In order to help with the task of forming the character of our teenagers we have to use as many tools as possible to support the work. Good relationships, asking for help, 'shoulds' and 'should nots', knowing your own story, understanding emotions, knowledge of your own story, and reflection are just some of these tools.

What I am pointing out here is that being a parent requires the time, effort, patience and willingness to engage in a very long-term project. This project will have a variety of outcomes: some desirable, others undesirable and many unexpected. The project will definitely produce many negatives, will cost a fortune and will be used by all around you as a measure of how successful you are as a member of society. That is one very tall order by any standards and therefore one that requires as much support as possible.

Why bother?

In undertaking the task of forming the personalities of the next generation, look at why we need to invest in this. Teenagers of today will:

- build our houses
- manage our money
- repair our cars
- replace our hips
- police our streets
- make our clothes
- steal from our homes
- corrupt the planning system
- marry our sons
- have children with our daughters.

Therefore we need to be aware as possible of what it is that impacts profoundly on the characters of these individuals as they pass through our hands in their vulnerable, formative years. We will be exposed to the result of our work with them, for better or for worse.

The project of being a parent has many inbuilt rewards: most parents will recall their children's first smile, sound, walk, song, party, etc. We need to hold the same reflections about our teenage children. I often wonder how many parents hold the memory of the first time their teenage son asked to go out with friends to a disco, or the first time their teenage daughter asked mum to collect her but to sit in the car down the street, away from the intense gaze of her friends.

These are also key moments that need to be cherished as a young person's positive step, as much as the infant's first 'da' or 'ma'. Indeed, catching and holding these moments can even be more important in the case of the teenager because they also have to capacity to share them in real time with their parents. Shared experiences with parents are very important for the developing teenager, even if most parents don't get to hear this until about ten years later, when the young adults are relaying stories to friends about their wonderful youth.

It is too easy to forget that, for all teenagers' swagger and ability, they are still children and they are still in the care of adults. This is not to demean them but to acknowledge their lack of experience of the world and their continued need for support and guidance. No amount of make-up or stony silence can remove their need for love, understanding and compassion. This does not undermine their intellect, strength and determination. It serves as a reminder that the process of bringing about the formation of a new person is a huge undertaking with great potential for joy and hardship and one that continues to evolve well into adulthood.

From minder to mentor

There is a need to change our perspective on how parents relate to teenagers in order to respect their ongoing development as well as to continue to have a strong influence on how their character is emerging. I sometimes describe this as the 'leap from minder to mentor' for parents.

A minder is someone who has the responsibility of looking after all aspects of a particular situation or the needs of a particular person. There is something all-encompassing about the word that suggests the minder is dealing with a vulnerable and needy person who is in some way unable or not fully able to exert influence over that vulnerability to ensure that they remain safe and cared for.

A mentor, on the other hand, is someone who has a vested interest in the welfare of a person, without the minute-to-minute responsibility for each detail of that person's life. The mentor carries responsibility for guidance and support but also has the freedom to allow space for the character of the individual being mentored to flourish.

In years gone by, many aspiring artists, musicians and writers had the benefit of a mentor who would guide them in the ways of their chosen path without curtailing the unique talent of each individual. And so it is with being a parent to an adolescent.

Parents need to tap into the qualities of the mentor that involve creating a growth space for teenagers to allow their character and personality to unfold. Then both parties can enjoy the 'creative project' that is actually unfolding.

A parent cannot have all the qualities of a mentor: this would require a type of emotional distance that is usually too difficult to maintain in a parent–child relationship. But here are some things parents *can* do.

1. Use the power of encouragement.
2. Use the skill of critical thinking.
3. Hand on worldly wisdom.
4. Set challenges to foster growth and development.
5. Give a slap on the back when all goes well.
6. Supply the hug of resuscitation when all is not well.

All done to guide the young person on their path through the life experiences that come their way.

When children get to the teenage years there is also a need for parents, teachers, neighbours and other significant adults in their lives to change. That change needs to move towards a position that resembles the way of the mentor. The responsibility for the safety and well-being of the individual teenager still rests with the adult, but it can be nurtured, shared and negotiated with the teenager.

The objective is that she can generate the space in which to learn about who she is and what is the best way of interacting with her world. She needs this so that a satisfactory level of psychological contentment becomes the hallmark of her experience of being a teenager.

For me the goal of any successful relationship is to produce satisfactory levels of contentment for those involved in it. It is not about how much pocket money, how many parties, what type of clothes or where holidays are taken, all of which are indicators that are fickle and subject to the whims of time and fads.

Psychological contentment is not subject to such whims. A sense of belonging, social acceptance, achievement, fun and the resources to cope with life's challenges have been the mainstay of human aspirations for thousands of years.

Mistakes are just 'takes' that were missed

For parents, who are responsible for leading the way, the shift from minder to mentor is of major proportions because they often do not have a map in their head for how this works. Yes, they have ideas, bits of information and observation of others. But they do not carry a tried and tested storyline that they can put in place that will calm their anxieties. Even parents of more than one teenager are surprised by how they are taken off guard when the next child is entering the phase but in a completely different fashion from the one gone before.

For most parents there is a strong sense of trial and error coupled with the anxiety that goes with that. However, I hold the line with parents that it is highly unlikely that they will do something so catastrophic that it cannot be rectified.

In making a film, directors will have to go through many takes before the final cut is called. Things get missed along the way, however good the story line and the actors. Things that were at one time incredibly important become almost irrelevant as the story line develops. Small things become central.

After all, regardless of the age of the child, parents still hold a vast store of knowledge about that child, even if they are not quite sure what to do about it. Also, in this age of political correctness, statistics and news stories that constantly remind us of how awful things can be, I ask parents to give themselves permission to make mistakes in their own lives.

It is funny how, with most things, if you actually encourage someone to try to make mistakes, the probability of them doing so decreases. Even in such an enormous task of helping to form the character of the next generation, mistakes can be made, will be made and need to be made, because it is from the mistakes that change and learning will emerge.

With teenagers, along comes the opportunity to share this learning with them. They have a vested interest in their own upbringing and therefore need to be central to how the story of their lives will unfold. This is just as a mentor would advocate.

TOP TIPS

1. Create time to review your work as a parent.
2. Think about a mentor who guided you – remind yourself of what was good and use this.
3. Let mistakes become an ordinary part of who you are as a parent.

And finally . . .

If learning, reflection and negotiated family experiences become the hallmark of being a parent to teenagers, the idea that they need things to be done to them in order to fix them becomes redundant.

Parents can learn that they are highly important partners with their children in the formation of their personality. They can then work towards bringing about a set of experiences for the child that not alone will help him through this particular phase of his development but will stand to him in the continuing years of development that are to come.

CHAPTER 4

History and Teenagers: Where do We Come From, Where are We Going?

In this chapter we will explore how different types of history can influence the work we do as parents. By history I mean the various experiences that make up our own story, for example what type of childhood we had, whether we enjoyed school, if our parents were strict, if we had access to money or not, etc. All of these things help to create our attitudes and beliefs and these in turn help to determine what we pass on to our children.

History has a story to tell

Psychology can be used in a number of ways to make the task of being a parent of a teenager easier. For example, it can focus on the here and now, on the past or on a mixture of both. It is invariably useful to have an understanding of the history out of which a particular problem has emerged. This allows us to get at more than just the surface issues. We can learn about what lies underneath the behaviour of both the teenager and the parent.

However, it is more important to have a clear understanding of the context from which good, healthy behaviour arises. This is because it is this context that we want to repeat in order to maintain a content and happy existence. Knowing what works is as valuable as knowing what does not work. History can shed light on both.

History does not serve the purpose of excusing inappropriate or unhealthy behaviour. Nor does it serve to offer rose-coloured memories of better times. What it does in psychology is to highlight the core beliefs and attitudes of a certain time period.

Once we have understood these we can learn about the rules and regulations in society that helped to maintain these beliefs. For example, there was a time in the recent past when society deemed it acceptable to use regular physical punishment on children. That attitude is now regularly challenged, and many people are totally against the idea of hitting children.

The use of history is a healthy device. It can:

- highlight current strengths and weaknesses in a given situation
- trigger questions and tease out the facts
- serve to promote a fuller understanding of a situation.

This is all useful because the ability to stand back from a given situation, question its component parts, weigh up the whys and wherefores and decide what is really happening is critical to effective parenting.

In standing back we might ask these questions.

1. Why, after thousands of years of human life, do we not fully understand the group of children who fall into the thirteen to nineteen age range?
2. Is it unusual that you would struggle to remember your parents or your grandparents describe their 'adolescent' years (as opposed to the years of their youth)?
3. Would it be interesting to ask them to describe what the problems of adolescence were like when they were growing up?
4. How were these problems managed when they were growing up?

Our elders do not believe in adolescence

I ask the questions above because of conversations I've had with older adults. What is unusual by today's standards is that there seems to have been no such thing as a 'teenager' prior to fifty years ago. They simply didn't exist.

The popular use of the term 'teenager' as a description of a distinct group of the population was not commonplace. When researching ideas for this book, I used the term 'adolescent' to trawl through some databases. As I reversed through decades the number of written articles with the word 'adolescent' or other similar terms started to decrease significantly. In the early 1900s it is used in American literature, but in terms of trying to understand the problems of 'this youthful age'! The following quotation is from the 1930s and holds nuggets of truth for today's parents.

> Problems the boy must solve are the questions of masturbation, homosexuality, prostitution, petting, venereal disease, and alcohol. Besides these sex problems there is the necessity for vocational choice. The boy of average intelligence often suffers because too much is expected of him.

How little changes through the generations.

My point here is that as little as fifty years ago, in the daily lives of ordinary people, teenagers were not singled out for particular mention in terms of development – this despite the thousands of years since humankind began to roam the earth. The idea of a distinct group of children with

- distinct psychological features
- different social drives and motivation

- individual moral values
- particular sets of needs and wants

would be alien to parents before the middle of the last century.

Children were children until they stopped going to school, and then they became young adults. They were for the most part working on farms, running kitchens and tending to fields, so that households could maintain their basic needs and requirements. A very select few went on to second-level education, fewer still to third level. A very clear class system operated and had done so for as long as oral history could recall.

So no hanging around on street corners, no discos, no big birthday parties, no competition over clothes, friends and holidays, no trials for hurling, soccer and rugby, and absolutely no hope of getting away with slamming doors!

Now we know that, psychologically, development continues well after the age of eighteen. We know, for example, that the front parts of the brain that look after how we understand many of the rules of social interaction do not fully mature until the age of approximately twenty-three. That's why some conversations end in tears – sometimes your teenager is struggling to know what is going on or how to respond appropriately. They simply get overwhelmed, particularly in heated situations where there are lots of things being said quickly in an emotionally charged environment.

We therefore don't want our teenage children getting married or working in the fields because we know that they are still in the process of maturing. So we support their interests in sport, friends, music or whatever in order to help their development progress as much as possible before they move on from the family environment.

Where did teenagers come from?

The lack of a distinct teenage phase only three generations ago is important to bear in mind. It means that we are in fact dealing with a relatively new concept in the history of our evolution. And new things take time to get used to.

Some might argue that this phase of development is not a natural phase but one that we have artificially constructed. The argument goes that people are just people, whatever their age.

Another, more cynical, opinion is that adolescence is a creation of consumerism and did not take hold in society until after the depression of the 1920s in the USA and the end of the Second World War in Europe. After these events economic stability resumed. Wealth became more widely distributed than before, giving rise to a phenomenon known as disposable income. This is the stuff that you want to hold on to for a rainy day when your teenager believes he is standing in the middle of a thunderstorm right now.

The multinationals think it's raining, too. They in turn reinforced the notion of a distinct group of humans called 'teenagers' by producing products specifically designed to be consumed by teenagers. These products were music and fashion – sources of much of the fun and games of the parent–teenager relationship!

It may also be worth considering that the artificial creation of this age group really indicates that as a separate psychological concept, adolescence does not exist at all. We have simply created a new word in order to name something that has naturally existed for thousands of years and then, in our joy over creating this, have hyped it out of all recognition into something that older generations would have to wonder about.

This argument may seem a bit extreme, but by holding on to the notion that something extraordinary happens between the ages of thirteen and nineteen, what we are in fact doing is separating young people from the rest of us. By seeing young people as being different, we are in some way excusing our struggle to meet their needs. And in looking for this excuse we keep them at a distance from us.

TOP TIPS

1. Adolescence is a new concept for us – be patient with yourself when you struggle to understand it.
2. See your teenager as just another person and relate to him accordingly.
3. Looking for difference between you and your child will make the work of being a parent difficult. Maintain a focus on the connections that you have.

Are there dangers in seeing teenagers as different?

In human nature, one of the things we do very easily is picking out the aspects of someone that are different and then using these as a way of victimising the person. Sure, we look for similarities in people but it's the differences that turn on our safety and threat radars. It is by the differences that we often decide what their character is made up of. Similarity is safe, difference is dangerous.

So much of what is written about teenagers is based on how different they are from the rest of the population, and I find this attitude worrying. Would it not be better if we viewed young people simply as that – young *people*?

It seems to me that by seeing teenagers as being different, we have in some ways weakened our own potential to interact with them. Once we see them as being different we struggle to support them using the ordinary communication mechanisms that we employ with people of other ages. We lose sight of patience, the importance of negotiation and accepting difference of opinion.

By examining them only on the basis of their differences, we make teenagers vulnerable to being picked on by us. We also blind ourselves to the positive values and additions that they contribute to society.

Worse still, by constantly referring to how different they are from the rest of the population, we make them scapegoats.

- Scapegoats for anti-social behaviour – but who taught them their morals and values in the first place?
- Scapegoats for alcohol abuse – but what about the massive abuse of alcohol by adults?
- Scapegoats for drug abuse – but what about middle-class users of so-called 'recreational' drugs?
- Scapegoats for irresponsible sexual activity – but do we really believe that the massive increase in human trafficking for the purposes of prostitution is being driven by the boys and girls in secondary school?

Scapegoating is as natural a part of the human condition as eating. It is also a sign of psychological immaturity, an inability to take responsibility for ourselves. We must be pretty immature as a society when we have gone to the trouble of creating a scapegoat of such massive proportions that we need an entire age range to support it. Teenagers are not equipped to deal with that particular role and it's not a role that supports their development.

Starting from scratch

However adolescence has come about, it is here; and, as with anything new, it takes time to acquire understanding of it, let alone to build up the knowledge base needed for managing it.

There are no long-standing traditions for what is supposed to happen to us as parents of teenagers.

Those that have evolved in recent years have not had the tests of time applied to them. The result is that parenting teenagers can often be reactive. It is rarely planned, and for parents much of the interaction with teenagers looks and feels like crisis management.

In other words, there are few parents with a solid knowledge base of teenagers that has been handed down through multiple generations and filtered through the experiences and wisdom of those who have gone before.

The 'newness' of this generation also means that we do not have a legacy of knowledge and skill in general society as to how best to understand it. So, as often happens when faced with the new and novel, parents look around for guidance and assurance and find that there is little to be obviously seen that has a solid track history.

This is particularly true if we look to state agencies, which are themselves made up of people of a generation struggling to come to terms with appropriate governmental agendas for children. It is only in recent political history that that the first Minister of State for the Office of Children was established in Ireland – a country that has had the concept of family enshrined in its constitution since the foundation of the State. This is not a criticism of those who are carrying out solid work in this domain – it is simply arguing that their work is truly emerging from a new knowledge base that will not have stood the tests of time for some generations to come.

Another consequence of the new generation is that today's parents of teenagers do not possess well-practised ways of interacting and communicating with young people. By well-practised, I mean passed down through the generations for hundreds of years. What know-how they do have is what they experienced from their parents, who were the *first* generation to have to deal with the phenomenon of 'teenagerism'. Let's look at it in more detail.

You are the pioneers of teenage parenting

The parents of today's teenage generation are most likely to be in the forty- to sixty-year-old age range. This means that they were born in the years from 1950 onwards. It was at this time when the first generation of teenagers was beginning to emerge in western culture. There are sound historical reasons for why this was happening.

Of greatest importance was the economic success experienced by significant areas of Europe as a consequence of stability following the end of the Second World War. Items such as clothing, music and other paraphernalia of popular culture began to emerge as being *necessary* as opposed to *desirable*. This was the start of the 'disposable generation'. The parents of today's teenagers were born on the crest of a wave of this new generation, the first to experience the phenomenon of the 'teen scene'.

Go back one step further. The grandparents of today's teenagers offer answers to the struggle of understanding how adolescence works. These grandparents were born into the times of the First World War, the civil war, the Second World War and food rationing. It's their parenting skills that were given to the parents of today's teenagers. Yet they had never even heard of a teenager.

The suddenness of the onset of the teenage generation has left many current parents at a loss. They struggle to generate strategies to keep up with their teenage children, strategies that were not and could not have been modelled to them by their parents. Today's parents are operating in a historical vacuum.

There is simply no long-established historical precedent for dealing safely and appropriately with independent-minded, idealistically motivated and change-driven young people who are seen as having sets of needs that are different from other people in the population. We don't yet know how to work and relate with teenagers.

That is not to argue that many parents cannot do this with their teenage child. Most parents get along fine but don't have the confidence in what they are doing. It is when relationship problems arise between teenagers and parents that the lack of long-held knowledge bases, with associated tried and tested skills, becomes obvious.

This is not simply referring to what has popularly become known as the generation gap. I'm not sure that this notion is useful as its basis is more likely to exist in the stuff of urban myth than real world evidence. There is not a gap, there is simply a lack of long-held knowledge. In other words, we are still in the process of constructing the know-how that will lead in future generations to smoother relationships with teenagers. Once we get the knowledge in place, we then need to practise it and refine it until we have a deeper understanding of how to relate to teenagers.

TOP TIPS

1. Reactive parenting will tire you out – think ahead about possible scenarios that will come your way with your teenager.
2. Teenagerism is new – it's okay to make mistakes. It's how you manage the mistake that is important.
3. You're not on your own – all parents are learning hard and fast.

Blame the grannies and not the mammies?

Why the focus on the grandparents of the current generation of teenagers? Primarily because it is this group of people who modelled directly to current parents what being a parent was about. They showed them the pitfalls, the strategies, the knowledge pool and the wisdom, however much of that was available. But how could they transfer such information about something that actually did not exist in their day?

In our grandparents' and great-grandparents' generation most children left school by the age of ten, but even for those children still at school, attendance was sporadic: from spring to autumn, children were often taken from school by parents in order to engage in seasonally available farm work. Therefore being in your teens was different from being a child, simply because you could work.

There was no such thing as peer group pressure relating to buying shoes, jeans or Wiis. There was no such thing as language college, grind schools or trips to Europe to learn about different cultures. A night out meant a night in with family, neighbours and friends, and anything exotic was served up by family members returning home from the UK or USA. The priest held power, the doctor was an authority and if you stepped out of line, a crack on the ear was the order of the day (and it could be delivered by a broad range of people).

This was the time of the grandparents and great-grandparents of the current generation of adolescents – a time impossibly impoverished to provide the parents of today's teenagers with more than the basic plans to manage their children. A time when there was a struggle to maintain basic needs and when the language of 'I want' got little or no attention. So what's so different now?

Navigating the noughties

Today we use specific indicators to judge progress in a teenager's development. These include:

1. increased ability to think and act based on moral reasoning
2. increased intellectual capacity
3. socialising with peer groups other than the family group
4. increased use of independent leisure time
5. experiencing short-term romantic relationships.

Thinking of young people in this way would have seemed strange to the generations of parents before us.

The parents of today's parents did not interact with teenagers as such – they just related to young people. Therefore they were not in a position to pass on the specific ways and means to make being a parent of a teenager a pleasant, rewarding and eagerly anticipated experience.

Psychologically, the absence of this has left a generation of parents of current teenagers to their own devices. This is not necessarily a bad thing. However, it is one that is without socially accepted, time-tested benchmarks that have proven to be safe and reliable and that can guide the parent reasonably safely. Hence, our rabbit in the headlights reaction to underage sex, alcohol use and even relatively benign occurrences such as boredom.

TOP TIPS

1. There can be no experts – we all have to learn from each other.
2. Work to your strengths as a parent – seek support for the rest.
3. History is giving you a chance to be compassionate to yourself – there is a ready-made reason for not knowing what you are doing.

Compassion for the parents

I want to make it clear that I do not hold the opinion that the current generation of parents I am writing about are incompetent, stupid or ignorant about the needs of their children. I am simply making the case that they have to carry out their parenting responsibility without the security of being able to draw from information that is deeply engrained in their own skill set. Furthermore, they have to do so in the context of a society that is also struggling with a lack of long-held know-how about the needs of teenagers.

Parents are, in a sense, winging it, flying by the seat of their pants and living on a wing and a prayer. Normal parenting of young people is therefore one big gamble comprised of a multitude of smaller gambles. Each gamble has the potential to generate feelings of euphoria or heartache, despite parents' best-intentioned efforts to take into account all the factors that will impact on the final result.

Of course the suddenness of the social, economic and cultural changes over the last three generations has at least taken place across a few generations. This has allowed for some consolidation of learning about adolescence, much of which has taken place in the UK and USA.

However, there have also been substantial changes *within* the current generation of parents.

A time of turbulence: but don't blame the teenager

As outlined above, Europe experienced significant social shifts from the late 1950s onwards. Ireland did not share in this experience until the latter part of the twentieth century. Parents with teenage children in Ireland today are not just trying to consolidate newly acquired knowledge about a 'new' phenomenon; they also have to deal with the fundamental cultural, financial, technological and psychological leaps that have defined the development of Ireland over the last fifteen years. These have impacted hugely on one generation of teenagers alone.

The significant majority of Irish teenagers today have never experienced poverty or anything like it. For this majority all basic needs are met. Many 'wants' are also met, to the point where few teenagers have been taught the difference between a want and a need. Sometimes I am not sure that many adults know the difference either.

Expectations that they have a right to all sorts of educational, material and social opportunities are at levels undreamed of even two decades ago. The rapidity of the pace of change in some way reflects the very experience of adolescence itself – fast, exhilarating and sometimes with an edge of danger to it.

Ireland itself was the poor *child* of Europe, having basic needs met by subsidies, loans and grants from parental figures in Brussels. Then it surged into adolescence with the Celtic Tiger. Along came the 'can do' attitude, the swagger of independence, self-assuredness and self-drive. Also came the evidence of destructive behaviour in the form of alcohol misuse, the cocaine epidemic and living on credit.

It will be very interesting to see how the adolescent identity of the country manages to limp into maturity in the face of economic weakness, and more interesting to see how individual teenagers cope with the loss of Dior, Diesel and D&G.

End of entitlement-based teenagerism

Parents are pressured into entitlement thinking by two key groups. There are the teenagers with ever-increasing, want-led expectations. Then there is the state, which did little to dampen expectations about the feasibility of wants becoming needs. The end result is that we have produced a society that is strongly built on the notion of 'entitlement'. That is, if I want it, I have the right to it.

This creates difficulties for parents, such as:

- how to limit behaviour (spending, demanding, wanting) when all around them the opposite has been encouraged by state policies
- how to motivate teenagers into reflecting on the importance of social and community values
- how to reduce the influence of values based on shallow self-progression, self-gratification and a philosophy of 'I and my needs are at the centre of the world'.

Parents are not just struggling with the behaviours of their teenage children, they are also faced with a much more substantial struggle in trying to make sense of their own personal value system. This is difficult work because there is now a robust but shallow value system that has been generated by the fads of the IT bubble, the property bubble and the Celtic Tiger. Everybody feels entitled to something and few people ask why or how this can be achieved.

Making sense of personal life stories, personal experiences

and personal value systems is a healthy, mature psychological exercise. It dilutes the power of entitlement and increases the capacity for responsibility. It helps to focus on what is actually important in our lives. We need this now because we need to clearly define how best to relate to our teenagers. The ways of the past can only bring us so far.

Modern ways have emerged out of a consumer-based value system and are not comprehensive enough. While we try to work out the values of the past against the needs of the present there is a lack of clarity in our interactions with teenagers.

- We remain unsure how to communicate with them – are they children or mini-adults?
- We struggle to avoid labelling them, and the labels we use are generally negative.
- We are lost in how to act in the role of support and guide to them.
- At times of crisis we scapegoat them.

You are still responsible for teenagers

The current status of adolescence seems to be one where we have assumed that the typical teenager is more or less a mini-adult. We hold high expectations of them, encourage them along the established path of education towards work and then hope for their safe journey into adulthood.

Teenagers engage in romantic relationships, many engage in sex, many drink alcohol and a substantial number have at least tried illicit drugs. Most will assert their right to full independence, most have access to disposable income and a social life that is the envy of many a hard-working woman and man.

But they are not adults. Teenagers are still children.

You need to be a strong authoritative figure able to warmly engage with your child while at the same time holding important boundaries to ensure his development is as content as it can be.

Treating adolescents as mini-adults gives them free rein with regard to many of the basic common-sense rules that help keep our society together. Danger lurks when we remove the protection of clear boundaries that children actually require in order to be able to explore social limits using common sense.

We are not proactive enough in teaching young people self-restraint and how to manage themselves so that their full potential can be reached. They need to be guided in order to learn the joy of being able to derive satisfaction from *within* themselves. We must teach them:

1. how to recognise their talents – by naming these for them and regularly reminding them of their talents
2. how to see what they have to offer to the people around them, be it as good listeners, active helpers, having a sense of humour, etc.
3. to recognise that at the centre of a fulfilling life is a set of solid relationships
4. that satisfaction also comes from learning that we do get it wrong from time to time and that the mistakes we make are opportunities for growth.

Teaching teenagers all this will also point out our responsibilities as parents, which might include the following.

- It should be neither socially acceptable nor justifiable for parents to allow teenagers wander the streets of towns without any knowledge as to their whereabouts.

- It should not be acceptable for a teenager to warn his parents that they cannot check who he is with and where he will be going.
- It is correct and proper for parents to know about friends and to seek out information that will help them make decisions as to the company that their child keeps.
- It is absolutely responsible to upset a teenager by holding your own ground on a range of issues, provided that you are willing to be clear, fair and reasonable about your reasons.

So, for example, despite our history of alcohol use and abuse, it is not desirable for gangs of teenagers to fall up and down the streets of our towns, drunk, disorderly and placing themselves in all sorts of potential danger. Equally, with our history of denial and turning the blind eye, it is not responsible of parents to think that their child would not do this. Somebody has to shoulder the responsibility for the thousands of teenagers who engage in this activity weekend in and weekend out. History teaches us that denial and turning a blind eye are dangerous ways of coping.

TOP TIPS

1. Identify your wants and your needs and teach your teenagers the difference between the two. Needs are few, wants are many.

2. You are not entitled to respect from your child – you earn it.

3. Teenagers need parents to lead the way on developing useful value systems. Conversations about the difficult issues that influence us today are central to the healthy moral development of your teenager.

The roots of relationship rules lie in our personal history

Perhaps an answer to the issue of poor parental responsibility lies in what it is that drives our psychological make-up in general. Specifically, we need to know what it is in our personal history that continues to influence how we live our lives today.

Relationships influence how we think, feel and act. I believe that the primary rules about relationships that we carry around were set down early in our lives. We continue to live by these rules fairly automatically unless for some reason we make a clear, deliberate decision to change them. Or unless some significant life event comes our way that forces us to change our thinking. So our history and relationships are directly linked together. This does not turn us into robots – it simply saves us having to learn new ways of relating every time we meet somebody new in our lives. Our history provides an inbuilt natural efficiency device that allows us to get along with each other.

Our relationship rules are open to regular minor changes when we hear a new opinion that we like or come across some new experience that we need to make sense of. They allow us to be categorised by other people in terms of our stable, regular personality traits that define us as being trustworthy, quiet, funny, or whatever else it is that makes us us.

So where do these relationship rules come from? If they are so important, understanding their history is crucial. The story of their development will guide us in how we can work to our best with teenagers – they will tap into these rules on a daily basis, because there will be similarities between their development and the story of our own development.

Born to belong

Rules about all human behaviour come from socialising with other people. Therefore our parents (or those who played this role) are the source of the rules in the first instance. If we examine very early infant development we see that infants are born with the capacity to recognise people in order to be able to socialise with them. For example, we know that very young babies can use their mother's hairline to recognise her face when they are five days old. We know that infants can match specific voices to specific faces from three months old. We know that newborn babies will imitate tongue and facial movements from birth and that they can initiate emotional expressions in adults with ease.

We are natural born relationship-seekers.

In terms of psychological development we know that there is a direct link between the mother's mood prior to birth and infant behaviour in the womb. Furthermore, a range of studies have shown that there is a link between a mother's anxiety and stress levels and later thinking, behavioural and emotional problems in the child.

Unfortunately, less is known about the impact of fathers' psychological profile on the developing child. There is some evidence that shows that if a father experiences the type of low mood that is associated with depression, the infant is more likely to be fussy.

In other words, research supports the theory that infants in interaction with the people they are immediately surrounded by are very strongly influenced by these people in a way that has long-term consequences.

It also highlights that sensitive and responsive parenting in infancy is related to more favourable patterns of behaviour and emotion in children in the longer term.

Moreover, it is possible to summarise the best conditions for a child to be exposed to during the formative years, as highlighted in the following table.

BENCHMARKING HEALTHY PSYCHOLOGICAL DEVELOPMENT

1	Safety/sustenance	Having a protector, nutrition
2	Stimulation	Play, entertainment
3	Socio-emotional support	Healthy, responsive relationships
4	Structure	Consistent, predictable parenting behaviours
5	Surveillance	Watching out for children

Safety and sustenance can begin before birth, with prenatal care, and continue throughout the child's life.

Stimulation is also a lifelong pursuit but is especially important in the early phases of development, when neural development in the brain is under way.

Socio-emotional support spans both economic and emotional supports that give the child a sense of belonging and worth. This support also teaches the child about the norms and expectations of society.

Structure involves setting appropriate limits for the child, as well as managing parental expectations so that they match with the child's developmental ability.

Surveillance is keeping track of a child's whereabouts and ultimate safety. It is the watchful eye and the listening ear, the mechanism that parents need to use constantly in order to make assessments about potential dangers for their teenagers. It is knowing where they are, how they use their phones and who sends them what sort of material on the Internet.

Each of these benchmarks points to one overarching factor that unites all of the forces into delivering the desired outcome; that a child has received the best possible opportunity for psychological development that will enhance his life and bring him to reach his full potential. That factor is relationships.

Effective parenting lies in effective relationships

As can be seen from the five headings above, the key relationship is the child's relationship with parents, because they are the only ones in enough contact with the child to tap into all these headings simultaneously on a regular enough basis for them to have an impact on development.

If relationships are such a key tool in promoting the development of the child, your own experience of being a child (your personal history) is critical. You need to learn about the messages that you received from your parents and the role models that your parents offered to you. This will point directly to how you will relate with your own teenager.

In other words, if you find it difficult to tell your fifteen-year-old how proud you are of her, it would be useful to take a look to see what message or rule you picked up from your own parents about feeling proud, or about how this was shown to you. Chances are, you are repeating a difficulty your own parents had.

Equally, if you live in constant anxiety that your daughter will come home pregnant but you cannot engage in sex education because of that anxiety, you might find that sex and sexuality in your own upbringing were associated with guilt and shame. If this is the case, you have yet to learn how to understand this fully. You need to recognise that you feel shamed about a part of yourself, to talk this through with someone you trust and to learn whether you are passing this feeling on to your teenager.

It may be useful to consider that the intent in examining your personal history is not to lay blame on the generations that went before us. I do not believe in simply laying blame on people or events in our past. This has the effect of disempowering us and playing out a victim role that only serves to undermine our psychological well-being.

However, it does not make sense to try to explain any type of human behaviour without having information about the context from which the behaviour emerged in the first instance – the history.

Your understanding of your own history will free you from blaming yourself or thinking that you are, in some fundamental way, flawed as a parent. It will indicate the areas that you need to work on to improve your skills as a parent and highlight opportunities for personal growth. Once this is done, you then have to choose whether you want to change or stay the same. Your history is generated by many people, but this choice is yours alone.

TOP TIPS

1. Your own experience of your parents is crucial to developing an understanding of how you act as a parent.
2. Seeking out connection is natural – don't get isolated in your work as a parent. Talk to other parents, share the frustration and joy that you feel and use others as an opportunity to further your learning.
3. To become more effective, try to change one small thing at a time. Build up small successes and regularly remind yourself of these.

Why don't I even realise what I'm doing?

In psychology there has been a debate raging for years about the influence of what has been called the 'unconscious' on ordinary day-to-day human behaviour and thinking. That is, there is something in our brain chemistry that influences our daily lives but we don't really know when, where or why.

Complex advances in brain research now show that there are brain activities that manage information in a way that fits with the idea of an unconscious influence. This influence is triggered by ordinary life events and it colours our view of the world and the particular interactions that we engage in. This influence is full of the detail of our unique personal histories.

Such groundbreaking research is of tremendous importance in understanding how we manage relationships, particularly those relationships that take us by surprise or are very intense. Relationships with teenagers spring to mind. What this tells us is that when we are interacting with teenagers, key memories from our own experience of being a teenager will become part of how we react and respond to our teenage children.

So for example, let's take David, aged forty-eight and the father of a teenage son. When he was a teenager, David's parents suffocated him with over-protection that did not allow him to develop his own sense of identity. He was not allowed to express his own opinions clearly without fear of being undermined. In addition, his parents tried to pre-empt all his behaviour, so he learned little about his capacity to influence his life. His personality was melded into his parents' personality and his identity was really who they were. He simply became 'other people', unsure of who he was himself.

This will play havoc with his ability to interact with his own son. His son, through his thinking, attitudes and behaviour, will trigger old memories for David. David will react to these memories and his reaction will influence how he deals with a situation that is happening in the here and now. His past becomes his present.

So if his teenage son is having a particularly bad day as a result of a falling out with a friend, David will feel equally unhappy because he is unable to stand back from his son's experience and disentangle his identity from that of his son. David repeats the message that what happens to another happens to him. The rule becomes 'I cannot be happy unless you are happy', and this is quite obviously a recipe for many years of psychological distress, longing and neediness.

Consider another example. If as a young person your parents taught you the message that your primary purpose was to meet their needs, the rule that you would have placed deep in the recesses of your brain is 'I am second to others – others have right of way over me.' If you come from this type of background you will struggle with teenage demands and will not be able to differentiate between those demands and your own needs. You will get caught by the logic of the teenager that is based on 'I have a right to this' as you will not feel strong enough to assert your needs as a parent.

This might sound daft – surely a parent knows what he is doing? Well, if a belief is one that is central to your existence, it is also very powerful. That power may be positive or negative. If it is positive, contentment and joy become regular parts of your life. If it is negative, you will end up in psychological turmoil each time the belief is triggered. And children trigger parents' beliefs all the time.

A final example also shows the difficulty when past messages are brought to bear on current situations. If as a child you were exposed to a style of parenting that was rigidly based on an authoritarian, overly disciplined and highly regulated approach, as a parent you will automatically adopt the notion that you must have rules to control everything and everyone. Given that one of the tasks of a teenager is to test rules in order to learn who they are as a person, your experience as a parent is going to be one of turmoil. You will want everything governed by rules at the same time that they seem to want all rules destroyed. A match made in hell, the end result being a frustrated child and a frustrated parent.

History is as alive today as the day it was made

What each of these examples highlights is that today's teenagers are influenced not just by the social and political history that has coloured the society they were born into but also by the personal histories of their parents. A fifteen-year-old daughter who demands money for music and make-up will clash with her 'tight' parents who still remember a time when money was scarce. These examples also show that the direction of the influence is not just one way. In other words, you can progress through life relatively content with less than useful messages in your psychological make-up. How vulnerable you are made by these messages does not become clear until a particular trigger in your environment activates the messages. That trigger can be your teenager.

It is not because he has a well-thought-out plan about how to derail your stability and happy existence. It is because the he will engage in natural styles of thinking and behaviour that, unknown to him, will plug directly into the socket of the memories that you carry around with you every day. That is how you and countless other parents can be taken so unawares by teenagers.

Your own past, hidden story of being a teenager is activated by your own child: the past and present ebb and flow in the day-to-day routines and interactions of parents and teenagers.

This helps to explain why what are perceived to be innocent remarks, trivial statements and irrelevant behaviours on the part of the teenager can provoke a most surprising and intense response from their parents. A thirteen-year-old who screams at his father, 'you're a fool' may get a volcanic response if his father was made to suffer that message all the way through school.

Such reactions to the past also explain why many parents find themselves at a loss to explain their own intense (and mostly unwanted) reactions to what they know are just the normal highs and lows of interacting with teenagers. Because they are not aware of the existence of these messages, or think that the past is in the past, they get caught out.

So history is not just the stuff of books about past events, faraway places and exotic people. Your own personal history:

- is a dynamic and powerful force in how your life unfolds on a daily basis
- is alive inside you, bursting to get through when it can
- determines the intensity of your emotional responses
- creates the content of your speech and language
- influences the lifestyle you live
- influences the types of relationships that you choose
- feeds into your understanding of what it means to share your world with young people.

TOP TIPS

1. We experience our history in our current relationships. Do not be afraid of your own story. Allow it to teach you about how you are today.
2. Teenagers can tune into your history without realising it. They don't always do it deliberately!
3. There is much to be learned from your own story, even if that story has hurt in it. Learning lessons from it helps you to bring more to the relationship with your teenager.

And finally . . . history of the future?

I wonder how history in the years to come will assess the current parental and societal attitudes to adolescence. I am left with a series of questions that may be answered in due course by our children.

1. Will history emphasise the freedom and potential that was encouraged by a stable education system?
2. Will it capture the creativity of youth, demonstrated in young scientist competitions, football teams, community concerts and projects?
3. Will it bear witness to the abundant energy and frivolity of thousands of young people at huge concerts in wind and rain?
4. How will it present the vomit-stained, designer-labelled girl and boy abusing busy health professionals in the accident and emergency department on a Saturday night?
5. How will history interpret the weak responses of parents and others unable to ensure that their son and daughter have a basic set of manners?
6. How will we be judged on the lessons we taught them to successfully negotiate their way into society so that they too can give back to those that have nurtured their uniqueness?

It strikes me that in a country where history has played such an important part in the development of how we see ourselves as a nation, we have much work to do. Work to ensure that as contributors to the history of this particular moment in our evolution, we will be judged favourably in terms of how we met the needs of the young people who will sustain us in the future. Work to ensure that when our children write the history of today, we would be proud to read it and proud to tell our grandchildren about the part we played in it.

CHAPTER 5

What's Important? Achievement and Success

I n this chapter, I focus on the concepts of achievement and success – the move to adolescence seems to sharpen the focus on these for parents involved in supporting the development of their children. I believe strongly that because the teenager is still developing, there is the potential to impact on that development in a way that will facilitate the experience of healthy long-term psychological contentment and success.

Why is achievement important?

It is important for all of us to experience the afterglow that comes with achieving a particular goal. It is central to the normal development of identity and esteem that we collect memories of being successful so that we can draw on them to facilitate future learning. More important, we can use these memories when things go wrong in the future: we can tap into them to remind ourselves that in terms of who we are, we are more than just one particular moment or event.

I emphasise repeatedly this message to confused parents and set up exercises with them in which they can learn how to experience reward and success in a step-by-step approach. One focus is to gather evidence from the ordinary daily activities that they regularly do easily and well and to use these as a learning opportunity for other areas that they would like to feel competent in.

We look at conversations that went well with teenagers, meals that were pleasant to share, trips that were enjoyed, situations that didn't end up in a row. We break these down to see what it was that worked and then look at how we can use this in situations that create problems. Consider the following example:

Poor outcome	Successful outcome
Parent: Why did you come home late last night?	*Parent*: I think you were in a bit later than we agreed.
Teen: Cos . . .	*Teen*: Ya . . .
Parent: How many times do I have to tell you about coming in on time?	*Parent*: Having a good time, then?
Teen: I dunno . . .	*Teen*: No, Jane got locked out so we waited till her Dad got home.
Parent: Can you never do what you're told?	*Parent*: I was a bit worried about you.
Teen: S'pose . . .	*Teen*: No need for that.
Parent: Just learn to read the clock.	*Parent*: Suppose not. Still, drop me a text next time.
Teen: Yeah, whatever.	

The poor outcome came about as a result of a serious of questions that really sounded like accusations. The successful outcome comes from the open statement at the start that led to useful information for the parent, who still got his point across.

By success I do not mean being first in the class, captain of the team or young person of the year. Our psychological world exists on a moment-to-moment basis: we are constantly taking in information from all of the senses, organising this in our brains and then placing it in storage for future reference. It is through these ordinary experiences that achievement, mastery and success can be achieved.

So coffee with a friend is not just the coffee, it is a representation of the ability to sustain a friendship, share a joke, offer a shoulder to cry on and a whole host of other factors that symbolise being successful at friendships. It is, in some ways, incredible how many sad, angry or confused people there are who do not know how to draw sustenance and energy from the ordinary stuff of life in order to boost their own self-worth.

Therefore it is important that we educate young people to be able to recognise internal, personally meaningful goals. Goals such as:

- being able to ask for help without being embarrassed
- accepting that I cannot be good at everything
- accepting that I have as much to offer as others
- understanding how I am different from others
- knowing what upsets me and what fills me with joy
- building and keeping up good relationships.

These goals are as important as external, society-appointed goals that may or may not be relevant to the person, such as doing well in school or behaving according to unclear rules.

The question for parents then becomes, 'Can you support these goals in order to create for the young person the types of opportunity necessary to increase the probability that they will achieve them?' How to do this includes:

- being a positive role model for your child in your own relationships
- being clear about the rules and boundaries that you create and the reasons for them
- offering hobbies and interests that will help to foster independence
- accepting that he will make mistakes and that this is not the end of the world
- balancing his need for study and school work with the need for 'play time'

- not judging his friends negatively all the time
- being willing to engage in debates about the rights and wrongs of situations, without needing your opinion to win.

For most parents, when their child is born, there is also the birth of dreams and aspirations for the child and for themselves as the guardian, protector and educator of the child. Parents who live in the comfort of stable social and financial circumstances wish that their child will develop the skills to maintain this standard for themselves. Parents from deprived circumstances aspire to wealth and opportunity for their children so that they can have a better standard of living and more opportunity than the parents themselves experienced in their life.

All told, parents aspire to achievement for their children, and by extension for themselves.

Achievement is lots of things to lots of people

Society places a high value on success and achievement and it is worth noting how these two variables are understood in current social values. Not surprisingly, the economic identity of the nation has a strong influence. In the 1980s, with an economic recession biting hard, achievement and success were measured in no small way by the ability to secure relatively stable employment or income. There are two useful pieces of evidence to support this notion.

First, the vast number of people who emigrated to seek employment and economic security; second, the huge number who had to stand in long queues to sign for unemployment support benefits. Television footage and photograph archives of both groups show the desperate misery and depression on the faces of many as they came to terms with their failure to achieve a societal standard in their own country, through no particular fault of their own. We are now witnessing this again.

Family values are equally important measures for people to judge each other with regard to success or achievement. Family stability, relationships, marriages, births and deaths are all topics of conversation that serve the purpose of knowing where people fit into social hierarchies. Comments such as, 'Hasn't he done well for himself?' or 'She married well' are not that long out of common usage.

A related idea here is the change that has been observed in religious beliefs and practices and the faith placed in religious institutions. These changes have emerged from the traumatic experiences of the dominant Roman Catholic faith in its acknowledgment and handling of various child abuse cases. Traditionally, family and Church values were closely linked, so it is not surprising that both have undergone fundamental change in recent times. Parents still want children to develop sound value systems and, for many, religious faith remains an important legacy to hand on.

There is no doubt that it is during the age range that covers second-level education when the notions of achievement and success become a dominant force in the lives of the teenager and other significant people in his life. Quite quickly, and in a relatively dramatic fashion, the emphasis seems to change from one of the child as a passive receiver of learning to one of him being in control of learning and performance, particularly in matters pertaining to school.

This is a big shift. We expect that because they are growing quickly, teenagers will also have a corresponding ability to automatically take control of the learning environment at school. This shift is rarely teased out with the child by the parent: it is just expected to happen. The impact of this change should not be minimised – the move from primary to secondary school and the high demands that are part of this change can be distressing for teenagers.

Exams and school performance are dealt with in more detail in Chapter 9 and so will not be covered here, apart from noting that they have an important impact on teenage development.

The changes in all of these measures of success have been extraordinary over the past ten years, in terms of both quality and quantity, but, more important, in terms of the speed at which they happened. It is my firm belief that this is having significant negative impacts on our teenager population.

TOP TIPS

1. Achievement is many things but it can often be best found in the ordinary experiences of our lives.
2. You have more influence over achieving goals if those goals are yours and not imposed on you.
3. Just as with young children, teenagers need ordinary simple achievements to be noted, praised and celebrated.

All is changed, changed utterly

The Irish economy at full employment generated an experience of wealth that was unprecedented. All the indicators of economic success show that more people had more money and a higher standard of living than was imaginable twenty years ago. The rapidity of this change, in my opinion, has not allowed for the time to reflect and discuss what has been the impact on society beyond the price of a house or the cost of education.

For example, why is it that parents believe they have to buy a pair of jeans for €100 as opposed to €30? Who is experiencing the peer pressure here? How have parents in particular taught their children about the value of money and the value in spending power? Or is it simply a case of 'if you want it, I'll buy it'?

I am not arguing that teenagers should not have choice in their spending or that parents should not spend on their children. I am advocating for using the intelligence in the teenage population to ensure that they learn that success cannot be solely defined by clothes, make-up and holidays. It is much more substantial and exciting than that.

Teenagers need to learn that the ability to purchase and enjoy material objects is the by-product of:

1. success at exams, or
2. success at training, or
3. success at becoming part of the workforce, or
4. success at becoming a valued member of the community, or
5. most likely, a mix of all of the above.

The bottom line is: how do parents ensure that teenagers, whose first experience of their spending power is often one of meeting wants rather than needs, learn that society does not automatically bestow this fortune on them? Well, they need to highlight that for the vast majority of us it comes from hard work, money well earned and little sense of entitlement to an easy life. Much of whether life is easy or difficult is down to the choices we make and our responses to what comes our way.

I have worked with teenagers and adults whose backgrounds are perceived to be stable, secure and often held up as a benchmark to others and watched their despondency, depression and lack of knowledge about how to value their ordinary daily experiences in life. How might this happen?

Sabotaging the ordinary

- The joy of a coffee with a friend becomes the obsession of 'How will I look while having the coffee?'
- The sleep-over with friends becomes 'Who has what brand of make-up for the morning?'
- The success at exams becomes 'Who will arrive drunk at the celebration in the back of a stretch limo?'
- Meeting family members becomes an opportunity to gossip about largely unimportant issues in others' lives.

The danger with looks, riches, drunkenness and gossip is that the focus gets placed on these as if they were an achievement in themselves, not on the value of the real achievement. The value of the friendship gets lost, the fun of the sleep-over gets lost, the exam result gets lost and the connection to family gets lost. So teenagers lose out on the opportunity to feel pure and simple pride and to learn that this of itself is enough to be content. How can we counteract this?

Creating compliments

Understanding compliments and how we give and receive them provides an insight into how we can instil pride in young people. This ability acts as a way of communicating to a teenager that they have successfully achieved or completed something in a way that you genuinely appreciate. I am not convinced that many people can receive a compliment about themselves or their actions without in some way devaluing it in their own thinking. This is not a lesson that we need to pass on to teenagers.

For example, you compliment someone on the way they look

and their response is to highlight what they think is wrong with them. This has the effect of both dismissing the effort that you made to compliment them in the first place and suggesting that your perception is actually inaccurate. So your compliment to them becomes their insult to you!

Many parents of teenagers were brought up in the culture of 'being careful not to get too big for your boots'. This was a subtle but powerful dynamic that undermined success and achievement. It has the effect of guiding people to attribute their achievements to outside influences or to say that they were 'just lucky'.

The handing over of pride is very often found in depressive styles of thinking and is compounded by the flip-side of this thinking, which is to take on too much responsibility for when things go wrong.

Because we do not compliment teenagers regularly, we have developed an over-dependence on materialism as either a substitute or as a way of fending off the guilt for not catching teenagers doing the 'right things'.

Parents often say they struggle to praise their teenage children because of embarrassment, fear of getting it wrong, fear of exhibiting their own pride and joy or simply not knowing how to do it. This cannot be judged too harshly. Many of these parents have emerged from a parental atmosphere that was not conducive to modelling this type of interaction between adults and teenagers.

Yet the ability to teach a teenager how to receive a compliment openly and without minimising it is critically important in how that teenager creates his esteem and self-worth. Parents can struggle with teaching this. One less than useful way of overcoming this struggle is to substitute the art of relating through praise and compliments with the mechanics of buying things.

The whole basis of praise and complimenting each other is founded on the concept of relationships and how two people interact with each other. Let your interaction become more nurturing and praise-oriented. It's an easier way for a teenager to live with you.

PROMOTING PRIDE

- Give teenagers compliments. They need them.
- Don't devalue compliments with a 'but', e.g. 'Well done, but next time try it this way.'
- Don't dismiss compliments that you receive – this teaches teenagers that there is something wrong with praise.
- Limit the amount of things that you contribute to luck. Instead, note how you create opportunities for yourself.
- When things do not go according to plan, accept responsibility for what you are responsible for – no more, no less.
- Do not substitute material gifts for the spoken compliment. If you are proud of your teenager, say it very loud and very clear.
- If your teenager gives you a compliment, say thanks.

Community over individual

In looking at economic success and achievement, I cannot but feel somewhat deflated by how a culture and a country that was so rooted in the tradition of building communities in close relationship has in such a short period of time diluted the notion of community principles and community values. Our need to come together every so often in order to achieve what is good for the community has been moved into second place behind the individual materialistic need that drove economic success in the early part of the new millennium.

It strikes me that in the past twenty years one of the things that people have become particularly skilled at is devaluing the importance of shared experiences and shared values.

Margaret Thatcher, when she was prime minister of the UK, reportedly said that there is no such thing as society, there is only the individual. Undoubtedly the influence of these words very quickly crossed the water, for in these words lies the value system in which many of our teenagers are currently being brought up.

Parents of teenagers today seem to want to throw away old-fashioned values simply because these values are old, and this needs to be challenged. Many old-fashioned ideas were a sign of their times and have outlived those times. However, many others reflected values that are noble, virtuous and worth holding on to, regardless of how modern and technologically advanced we think we have become. Courtesy, honour, respect, good manners and acceptance of difference could all do with being placed on parents' agendas again.

It strikes me that a key to sustaining our communities lies in what we hand on to the next generation in terms of core values and principles that go way beyond those that are represented purely by materialism and wealth. There is a place for Google, Twitter, iPods and designer outlets but they will never be able to replace the currency that binds people together in relationships. We need to look at promoting family and friends as the key to real success and achievement.

TOP TIPS

1. Work at making courtesy and compliments part of your daily interactions with your teenager.
2. Work out with your teenager the things about herself that she can be happy about.
3. Material things bring happiness, too, but they are useless without meaningful relationships in our lives.

Parenting the next wave of 'family'

Family and all that goes with it is at the centre of the teenage experience. Without doubt this has undergone seismic change in the last twenty years and with this change has come vagueness about exactly what family values parents are expected to deliver to the next generation.

It is only in the last twenty years that contraception has become freely available, that homosexuality has been decriminalised, and that divorce has been introduced. It is only twenty-five years since the Kerry babies were front page headlines and since Christy Moore was prompted to write a heart-wrenching song about the death of Ann Lovett.

In that time, families have been formed outside either church or legal marriage in a way that has become a norm. Families that were formed in one or the other were dismantled through separation and divorce. New family units were formed by new partnerships and the joining of children from different parents.

As to whether any of this was and is good for individuals or society is a matter for continuing debate. What is clear is that an impact has been felt by the generation of teenagers currently being prepared for some form of family life in the future. If success within the family has traditionally been determined by being married and then having children and subsequently staying within that particular family, what exactly is the definition of success with regard to family life today?

Well, being married is definitely still part of the equation. The rate and number of marriages in Ireland is as high as ever. This poses the question of how teenagers are being taught about what marriage is. That is, in what manner and with what content are teenagers being prepared for future married and family life?

This is relevant to how teenagers are brought up in our families. Look at the functions of being in a family. Teenagers learn:

1. about the operations and functions of family life
2. about the roles of men and women and how they are acquired and operated
3. how women treat men and men treat women (which they then go on to practise in the outside world)
4. to see in action such important factors as intimacy, emotionality, power, respect, dignity and discipline.

So at a time in their lives when they are for the first time physically and mentally able to monitor and form some understanding of what family life is about, the scripts that they will act out in later years are being well and truly cemented into place. Having successful scripts in place is absolutely fundamental for success in later relationships.

Parents need to address the type of relationship that they want to model to their teenager. If you primarily want to control, harass and give out, this is what he will do in due course. If you take time to negotiate, empathise, listen and create agreed solutions to difficulties, this is what he is likely to live out in later years with you and others.

Promoting peer groups

Research shows us that parents are concerned about the social contexts in which their children participate. This refers to the types of friends that they engage with and the types of relationships that become part and parcel of their daily life.

In particular, parents analyse and manage as best they can the relationships that teenagers develop because they have an eye on their future development. There is a reasonable but unspoken message that current social relationships influence the outcome of future development.

So, for example, parents will engage in some form of unspoken competition to have their child on the best football team, enrolled in the best school, or linked with the best private tuition. They become involved in various types of social groups so that life for their children is made as smooth as possible with the greatest probability of a positive outcome.

Of course, in doing all this they are also ensuring that their teenager is engaged in minute-to-minute interactions with children who are most likely to do well, according to standards set by them.

It is as if each parent is engaged in monitoring the development of young people from other families as a way of benchmarking the pace and content of their own child's development. This works to ensure that there is a good fit between the hopes and aspirations of the parent and what the children in the peer group have to offer. If this works out it is more likely that a positive outcome will occur in the future in the form of a psychologically healthy adult.

This theme continues to run through adulthood, with parents very quickly forming opinions on the 'fit' between their child and his potential marriage and life partners.

All of this points us to the conclusion that achievement and success as defined by parents is hugely determined by the social relations, friendships and partnerships that their offspring initiate and maintain.

This is good because the peer group is important for teenagers and parents can play a role in influencing it. You can do this by having friends around, chatting to your children's friends, linking with the parents of friends, having sleep-overs and taking teenagers to matches, competitions, etc. In other words, bring the peer group into the family environment, don't keep it on the periphery of family life.

Down with religion does not mean down with values

Traditionally, family values have been strongly influenced by religious values. There is a general perception that young people are just not religious. However, they do have the capacity to maintain strong sets of values.

It is worth exploring this idea because my sense is that people in society who lead successful lives from a psychological point of view have a strong set of values that underlie their lives. These do not necessarily have to be religious in nature but they often have a connection to religious teachings which are based on particular sets of values.

There is absolutely no doubt that the traditional understanding of religious practice needs to be overhauled when discussing this in relation to today's young people. That is primarily because they do not live in fear of the authoritarian teaching of the Church in the way that previous generations did. They are also more exposed to a variety of sects, churches and religions through media coverage and as such are not bootstrapped by the idea that there is 'only one way'.

What religious beliefs and practices offer is:

1. a framework and structure for one aspect of psychological development
2. a mechanism for promoting mental health by recognising that young people develop much more effectively in the context of structure
3. a connection and a sense of belonging, not just to the family but also to the wider community that shares in similar beliefs and practices.

There is another important aspect of religious experience which taps directly into the idealism that is found in young people. Psychological contentment also comes from being involved in social action that works to alleviate poverty, injustice and social abuses. Involvement in activities to reduce these problems gives teenagers both internal and external rewards. This is in turn a powerful reinforcer of self-esteem and a source of pride.

Much social conscience work is either funded or organised by religious-based institutions and offers young people the opportunity to act on their natural sense of idealism while at the same time creating a distance from the more formal expressions of religious belief that have 'fallen out of fashion'. Research shows that more young people are engaged in pro-social activities than they are generally given credit for.

Pro-social activities have very significant positive effects on long-term psychological development.

Such activities also have positive effects on community-oriented identity and offer a much-needed break from the philosophy of 'I am the centre of everything'. Religious involvement and commitment in young people has been shown to increase the types of behaviour that society actually values. Indicators such as

- school achievement
- school attendance
- anti-social behaviour
- substance use
- sexual permissiveness

are all positively impacted on by having a clear set of religious values which are then turned into practice. If parents have clear religious beliefs and values, these can be communicated to teenagers with the clear knowledge that they are good for them.

I'm not saying that a teenager cannot develop a sense of mastery or achievement in the absence of religious beliefs. But it does serve to remind us that the abandonment of traditional values simply because they are traditional or because it is not fashionable to practise them could also remove a valuable psychological tool for the developing teenager.

What young people react against is being forced to accept particular sets of religious beliefs and practices.

To make religion a useful developmental experience for young people, it is better to allow them freedom to explore their own relationship with both religious institutions and the particular god that forms the basis of these.

Religion offers the opportunity for a set of relationships with others who share the same beliefs, with the institution itself and ultimately with the particular god that inspires it. No relationship works if one partner is forced into it.

In promoting well-being and self-esteem, it is important for adults to recognise the important role that organised religious beliefs and groups can continue to play in helping to foster pro-social, community-oriented and value-based achievements in young people. It is also a reminder to parents that not all of what they were brought up with was necessarily unhealthy and that some of it may indeed be useful to hand on to the next generation.

TOP TIPS

1. Remember that how you relate to your children is most likely how they will relate to their families in the future.
2. Peer groups are hugely important for teenagers. Support them, but do not be afraid to monitor and judge their influence on your child.
3. Values and morals appeal to teenagers. Don't be embarrassed by your own faith, spirituality or belief system.

Sport

Given the obsession with sport in most countries, perhaps it is opportune to examine how achievement, mastery and success in adolescence are channelled through this particular medium. I chose to write about this area not just because of the massive influence of sport but because sport tends to do something that reminds us of achievement. Earl Warren, the Chief Justice of the United States once said, 'I always turn to the sports page first, which records people's accomplishments. The front page has nothing but man's failures.' In a world so full of dread, doom and gloom, sport can be a reminder to the next generation of what is possible and achievable.

As always, there is not a one-size-fits-all package and not every young person will enjoy sport, but every young person will enjoy some activity if they are not conditioned otherwise.

Participation in sport can be a significant factor in the development of a young person's identity, self-esteem and competence. Sport can be seen as a platform, a structured environment, from which to learn the skills associated with personality values, such as:

- responsibility
- conformity
- perseverance
- risk-taking
- courage
- self-control.

We know from research that a wide range of skills that are important in maintaining healthy social relationships can be learned and practised in sporting activities. Such skills include:

- goal-setting
- effective communication
- dealing with conflict
- problem-solving
- expressing and regulating emotions
- providing and receiving feedback
- identifying a role in a team
- managing stress.

These are all core components of sporting activities.

Sport in all its guises and whether played for fun or profit is ultimately about relating and relationships.

We know that of all the positive aspects of being involved in sport it is the engagement in a structured environment that is most significant in preventing young people from becoming involved in either anti-social or health-compromising behaviours.

Structure provides a very significant platform for successfully accomplishing goals that is both satisfying to the teenager and has wider social gains associated with it. One of the advantages of using sport to symbolise mastery and success is that the goals in sport are usually easy to see, short-term and easily measured. Equally, when things do not go right, when games are lost or injuries are sustained, young people get to learn about and practise resilience, patience and the idea that not all effort receives gratification in the form that we initially expected.

It is worth reflecting on the words of the founder of the modern Olympics, Baron de Coubertain, when he commented:

Sport plants in the body seeds of physio-psychological qualities such as coolness, confidence, decision etc. These qualities may remain localised around the exercise which brought them into being; this often happens – it even happens most often. How many daredevil cyclists there are who once they leave the machines are hesitant at every crossroads of existence, how many swimmers who are brave in the water but frightened by the waves of human existence, how many fencers who cannot apply to life's battles the quick eye and nice timing which they show on the boards! The educator's task is to make the seed bear fruit throughout the organism, to transpose it from a particular circumstance to a whole array of circumstances, from a special category of activities to all of the individual's actions.

If sports programmes have the potential to significantly contribute to the psychological development of our teenagers and, in particular, to enhance their sense of achievement and mastery in their lives, it is critical that the education and skills picked up on the training field or in the team-building work can be transferred to non-sports settings.

A range of strategies have been highlighted that help to promote the transfer from the playing field to other social environments that the teenager will find himself in.

USING SPORT TO ENHANCE SOCIAL RELATIONSHIPS

1. Clearly identifying the links between the sporting activity and other areas in life at the beginning of the activity, e.g. importance of planning, obstacles to achieving desired goal, available resources, etc.

2. Providing opportunities to practise transfer of the skill while the activity is actually being learned, e.g. showing what happens when a team doesn't play by the rules and seeing how this also works in the home.

3. Providing opportunities to reflect on the experiences, e.g. what worked, what was useful, what didn't help, etc.

4. Involving other young people who have already completed the activity and are in a position to comment on its usefulness.

5. Involving other significant people in the learning process, e.g. coaches, mentors, teachers, friends, etc.

6. Providing follow-up experiences that reinforce the learning that occurred and that will help to consolidate this learning into the behaviours by which other people will judge the teenager, e.g. asking a teenager to lead a team and then asking her to lead the family for a day!

What these suggestions teach us is that young people can be active participants in their own development. They need the support of significant adults in their lives to take the time and energy that is required to create the atmosphere and environment from which optimal psychological growth can occur.

Somebody has to train the team, organise the travel arrangements, wash the jerseys and support the team on the day. Parents who ferry teenagers around to training, who stand on sidelines on freezing December days and sit reading endless newspapers at swim meetings are sending countless messages of support and nurturance to their child. If you want proof, ask a teenager who doesn't get this.

Work – can he, should he, will he?

The importance of developing a portfolio of successful experiences during the teenage years is highlighted by the general agreement that one of the main tasks during adolescence is to become prepared to contribute to the social and economic functions of the state at some stage in the future. In my experience teenagers themselves are most interested in their future education and occupation. This is likely to be linked to the idea that securing employment and receiving regular income is a very powerful and symbolic statement of independence, autonomy and, ultimately, adulthood.

However, during the teenage years the experience of the workplace can play an important role in the way young people define themselves. Many parents struggle with the notion of sending their children out to work and can see both the positive and negative aspects of this.

There is a wide range of arguments both for and against sending young people to work and my conclusion from listening to the stories of parents, teachers, youth workers and teenagers is that they can benefit from part-time work; but only if they are also able to maintain their commitment to their education, their peers and their family life.

This is quite a tall order and one that requires careful monitoring by parents, as young people themselves may not have the ability to be objective about their own resources and the strain that part-time work can place on these resources. Parents must ensure that in general the experience of part-time work brings *added value* to the life of the teenager beyond that which is measured by take-home pay.

ADDED VALUE FROM WORK EXPERIENCES

- Learn how power is managed.
- See how conflict is resolved.
- Observe how assertiveness is practised.
- Learn to be a team player.
- See how money is managed.
- Understand the concept of hard work.
- Learn to balance a number of commitments in daily life.
- Understand authority and how it can be used both fairly and unfairly.

Early experiences of work relationships are crucial in helping the young person begin to form that part of their identity which is based around work life. This is particularly important when we remind ourselves that many individuals seek meaning in their lives through activities associated directly or indirectly with their work.

The power of others in teenagers' development

The area of work experience brings us to another important domain in the life of a young person, which is centred on how teenagers create relationships with adults who are unrelated to them.

Historically the workplace was the place where young people met unrelated adults. However, this has changed in recent decades, with many of the jobs that teenagers are employed to do now being supervised by people not that much older than they are themselves (for example in the catering and leisure industries).

Another important dynamic to note is that the number of families in which all adults work has left more teenagers unsupervised after school than ever before. This obviously has a range of consequences, but one often not considered is that in addition to making young people less likely to spend time with their own parents, it is also likely to decrease their contact with the parents of their friends.

This is quite a substantial cultural shift in the experience of young people. As mentioned in Chapter 4, fifty years ago young people spent most of their time engaged in strong family- and community-based units within which all members of the social group operated and interacted on a regular basis. Even regular attendance at school and the separation from family that this involves was sporadic for most individuals.

Back then, people of all ages usually socialised together. In the work situation, many young people engaged in apprenticeships, which lasted a number of years and placed them very firmly under the watchful eye of unrelated adults. Not today, though.

Now we are more than well-informed about the potential dangers and threats to the safety and well-being of our children. We are accumulating a wealth of evidence to show how breaches in trust in the adult–child relationship can have devastating psychological consequences. We have had to become more questioning of the people who come into the lives of our children. This is correct and proper, given what we now know of how abusive relationships are generated.

However, it strikes me that we must be careful not to destroy this potentially useful avenue of influence in the life of a young person. There will always be abusers, but we are now armed with more information and we can use this to protect our children. At the same time we can give them the opportunity to learn from the vast majority of people who care for their welfare.

Being able to take the social skills that have been practised within the family unit and transfer these into developing relationships with peers and adults is important. These are the people who will continue to offer a platform for learning for the young person in the future.

Unrelated adults can offer different perspectives and a sense of objectivity to the life of the teenager.

They can also act as resources for issues that the teenager may not be comfortable communicating to parents. Such adults have skills and knowledge that may not exist in the family unit, e.g. how to handle a death in the family, what to do if you're left off the football team. Importantly, they do not carry the emotional connection that would draw them into power struggles over relatively trivial incidents that occur as part of daily living for family members.

Unrelated adults can be powerfully positive influences on teenagers and can bring added value to the work that you have already completed with your child.

Alliance, affiliation and companionship are all roles that unrelated adults can add to the repertoire of the teenager to help them accumulate experiences related to mastering social interactions and social values. And it is indeed an achievement to be able to relate successfully to someone who is older (and hopefully wiser) while at the same time drawing inspiration for personal development, which is exactly what young people do when regularly in the company of safe adults.

In other words, unrelated adults offer a role that is different from those of peers or parents in that the role is seen by young people as being *instrumentally* based rather than *emotionally* based.

These adults become instruments in the process of bridging the need for security with the need for experimentation. This will build up the types of life experience that help to generate beliefs such as 'I'm good at that', 'I did well there' or 'I've got that cracked.' Such people carry a different sense of responsibility from parents and can therefore relax boundaries, which gives a sense of freedom to the young person from which they can continue to be curious about the world around them. They also share stories about their own lives, and young people will readily pick up learning from these, which they can use at a later stage.

Unrelated adults can act as a bridge between teenagers and family as well as between teenagers and society at large, which is why their role can be so powerful. Abuse of that power has been too evident in recent history. Equally, we have to acknowledge the thousands of adults interacting every day with young people in clubs, choirs, teams and projects who have genuine positive impacts on their development that have very long-term effects for society.

TOP TIPS

1. Enjoyment and fun must be at the heart of hobbies and interests. Don't turn everything into a league table or medal opportunity.
2. Carefully managed work experiences are excellent learning opportunities for teenagers and their parents.
3. Unrelated adults – teachers, friends, neighbours, coaches, mentors – still have a vital role to play in the successful development of teenagers

Achievement – whose need is it anyway?

I want to conclude this chapter by differentiating between the need for achievement and mastery in the teenager and the need for achievement in a parent. In particular I want to focus on when parents mix up their own needs with the needs of the child and manage to create a pressure cooker of confusion based on unrealistic demands and not enough compassion.

Parents with high expectations of achievement for their children and who do not take into account the capacity and resources of the child to fulfil these expectations are liable to do harm to the esteem of the child. Sending her to extra tuition to secure a higher grade or a place on the football team is only of benefit if the child is motivated to do this and finds the tuition of benefit to their own well-being.

Leaving school with a string of A grades is pretty useless if the teenager does not know how to enjoy life, or has had their social activities curtailed to the extent that they cannot function in a group of peers.

It is a natural drive in parents to want to open the potential of the child as fully as possible, but the process of how that is achieved is important. Teenagers should not become pawns in the internal need of the parent to feel good about themselves. They should not be seen as the currency in the judgment of others as to whether you are a successful parent or not.

Teenagers do not exist solely to perform the roles and secure the opportunities that did not come the way of the parent. And no amount of good grades or goals scored will ever make up for the loss to the young person if their natural personality has been dampened, trodden upon or completely stolen from them by the needs of others, particularly their parents.

Being open and honest about expectations and demands will allow a teenager to see where a parent is coming from and will also allow her to inform and educate the parent as to her analysis of her capacity, competence and resources. This may result in a compromise for the parent that is uncomfortable to wear and it may also produce results that the teenager did not foresee and is not happy with.

This is the stuff of life, though, and parents have to learn to live with choices that their children make that do not work out for them. Comfort needs to be drawn from the fact that very few teenagers make choices that produce catastrophic results, and if they do make such an obvious poor choice, parents still have the right and responsibility to step in and apply their worldly wisdom to the situation.

And finally . . .

Achievement is one of those areas that definitely benefits from very clear feedback loops between the young person and the parent so that the conditions for the right learning environment are maintained.

Too high a demand with not enough personal coping resources produces a burnt-out teenager unsure of who they are, trying to live out a life that is the making of someone else.

Too low a demand with too much protection produces a bored and frustrated person who views themselves as having little to offer, sees threat in every challenge and so withdraws as a means of protecting themselves.

With regard to how teenagers perceive their own sense of mastery over the many swings and roundabouts of life, there is only one way to find out and that is to directly engage them in this conversation. It highlights your interest, makes evident your continuing care and attention and occasionally shows the wisdom that you have acquired from a multitude of life experiences.

Most important, it makes you a source of support at times when the hard realities of life hit home for the developing teenager; and if there is one guarantee it is that there will be plenty of these.

CHAPTER 6

Where am I Going Wrong? Snags, Traps and Pitfalls

I n Chapter 2 we learned about some myths regarding young people and how they experience their lives. In this chapter we take a look at a range of snags, traps and pitfalls that many parents find they repeatedly fall into as they try to work out a smooth and efficient format for relating to teenagers. I use the phrase snags, traps and pitfalls because they simply stop us from getting on in life. They hold us back, make us tired and often make us work hard at going nowhere.

Know your rules!

Rules are a greenhouse for snags, traps and pitfalls. We know that such is the human condition that for every rule, there is an even larger number of loopholes. The reason that we have rules and regulations within families is to ensure that certain family attitudes, beliefs and values systems are upheld. This creates a sense of order and organisation for people, which allows healthy development to flourish. So far, so good.

However, it is often the case that these rules exist in families simply because they have been handed down from one generation to the next. Usually they are handed on without much thought being given to their usefulness or value. Not knowing where rules came from or if they have any value will lead to a head-on collision with your teenager. Teenagers are loophole experts because they are bright, intelligent and inquisitive. Be prepared!

If you don't know much about your rule book, then an assessment of rules and values that are core to the family system is useful in determining which rules need to be changed, which are useful and which need to be thrown out completely.

Of course, all rules and regulations are bound by the fact that there is a certain outcome that is aspired to by the people in charge of rule enforcement. In other words, you apply rules because somewhere you have an ideal picture of how you would like things to turn out for your children. While there is merit in this, it is also problematic. Rules demand that you pay attention to whether they are followed or not. The end result becomes a focus of how you interact with your teenager. You become an outcome obsessive!

Omit outcomes – there are no league tables for parents.

One of the snags for the parent of a teenager is that they often get very caught up in what the outcomes of their interactions with teenagers will be. So, for example, parents get concerned about the outcome at school. They get anxious that if their daughter has a boyfriend an outcome may be an unwanted pregnancy. Parents are concerned that in being involved with their peer group, an outcome might be the risk of using alcohol, smoking or getting into trouble.

While these outcomes are important in terms of protecting our teenage children, it is also important to be aware that if we become so concerned about potential outcomes that exist in the future we can lose sight of the potential of the 'here and now' interactions with our teenagers.

One of the strategies that I use with families is to try to reduce the focus on some type of potential outcome that may or may not happen in the future. This allows us to re-focus on the current relationship that exists between them. Ultimately it is the current relationship that you and your teenager have the strongest influence over.

If, for example, in an argument, both teenager and parents were able to engage in a here and now conversation and were able to remove the power of whatever outcome they both think *might* happen, the chances are that the argument would not escalate. This is because they could stay dealing with the issue in hand and not waste energy either dragging up material from the past or getting into crystal-balling the future. Then they would both be able to at least hear the opinion of the other side. When both sides believe that they are being listened to, the need to win the argument is weakened.

Outcome-focused argument	Here and now-focused argument
(parent wants to stay in charge of teenager by the end of conversation)	(parent wants to stay influencing the conversation now)
Teen: I'm not a child any more, stop trying to control me.	**Teen:** I'm not a child any more, stop trying to control me.
Parent: I'm your mother – you'll listen to me when I'm talking to you.	**Parent:** Look, I just want to see if we can get some agreement on meeting the lads later. What do you think?
Teen: Ya, go on, make me.	**Teen:** Just feels like you're always at me.
Parent: Don't speak to me like that again, you're always doing that.	**Parent:** I suppose sometimes I am, but if we agreed now then we could leave it.
Teen: So bloody what? You're always trying to stop me from meeting my friends.	**Teen:** You mean I can meet the lads.
Parent: This is my house, so I'll decide what's good for you.	**Parent:** Ya. I'm just concerned right now that I don't know what your plans are. When I do, I'll tell you what I think of them and then we can work out something that works for us both.
Teen: As if you'd know …	**Teen:** S'pose. But only if I can tell you what I think of your thinking!

Most parents, once their children reach adolescence, get very caught up in the power of a potential outcome and lose track of the here-and-now strategies that they can use. The desire to 'win' each row, to be seen as 'in charge' and to 'face down troublesome teenagers' becomes the target. Big pitfall!

It is my experience that if parents devote energy to the here and now with their children, the probability of negative outcomes down the road is decreased significantly. Both sides abandon the pretty useless mind-reading games that are necessary when trying to predict future happenings. They also catch potential problems early on before they become tricky issues. (There is a list of strategies for staying present in the here and now later in this chapter.)

It is very easy to think back to when the teenager was a child and remember times when he was easier to manage and to get on with. Equally it is very easy with a teenager to think forward into the future and become concerned about educational possibilities, employment possibilities, relationship issues and a whole host of other potential influences that in fact parents, teenagers and others have little current knowledge of.

This is one of the costliest snags of all – being caught up in cravings for the historic parts of who the young person was or being caught up in anxieties about futuristic possibilities of who she might be – the price being that it makes the present redundant. I want to nail this in some detail in the following section because this snag can do so much damage.

Parent in the present

I use an idea from the field of sports psychology whereby skills are practised to ensure that not a lot of energy is put into trying to 'crystal-ball' the final outcome.

When we become overly obsessed about the final outcome

and trying to make sure that it is in our favour, all of our attention and concentration gets future-focused and we increase the probability that we make errors in what we are doing in the here and now. That is because that part of our brain that is engaged in future thinking is consuming chunks of the psychological space that we have available to sort out a problem or a challenge that is actually facing us in the present.

It is interesting to note from the biographies of many successful sports people that at critical moments in major sporting events their concentration was solely focused on what was happening for them in that moment, rather than on what might happen at the end of a particular move or game. Likewise with parenting. If our focus becomes completely targeted on an eventual outcome, that attention is using up our psychological energy, physical energy and emotional availability to our children in the here and now.

That is not to say that we cannot have our dreams and aspirations for our children and work towards these. But it is better to channel our energy into making relationships better now rather than getting caught up in what the future might or might not hold. So statements like 'You *will* fail exams', 'She *will* get you in trouble' only serve to raise fear in both parent and child. When we feel fear, we get defensive, feel irritated, withdraw or have a row. Sound familiar?

But what about 'How can I help you with your study?', 'What does the friendship with her mean to you?' These questions are less judgmental, show your interest and highlight a tone of support. They also guide you to being more respectful to your teenager by recognising what is going on in her life now.

This approach makes sense because if our attention is focused on nurturing the relationship in the here and now we become available to the teenager as they make their way through their own development. We become able to spot potential for trouble for them and we can work with them on learning how to trouble-shoot events in their own lives. We have the space and time to be able to sit back and reflect with them on what it is that is actually happening for them in their lives.

There are many external influences on outcomes that we either have little control over or whose existence we are unaware of until they pop up in the life of the teenager. Therefore worrying and being overly concerned about an eventual outcome on a day-to-day basis is, from a psychological perspective, not a useful or efficient way of managing the relationship between you and your child.

TOP TIPS

1. Outcomes happen because of the road to them. Focus on the journey, not the goal.
2. Here-and-now relationships are the key to healthy living.
3. Mind-reading, future gazing and crystal-balling the future will undermine what you and your teenager have to offer right now.

The key is here and now

It is much more useful to focus on the process that is currently unfolding. By process I mean the events, interactions, feelings, thinking and behaviours that are currently happening between the parent and the teenager. We carry an enormous capacity to influence these. That influence can ultimately bring about outcomes that are similar to those we would have wished for.

So, for example, if an outcome that is desired is success at passing an examination, being concerned about that outcome does not produce that required result. However, if energy is channelled into the process that leads up to the examination –

learning at school, carrying out projects, reading, relaxation, good food and fun, study time – the likelihood of success is increased.

This activity is the part of the process that a teenager and parent have a lot more influence over and can change on a day-to-day basis if necessary. Equally, if we are concerned about being successful parents with our teenagers, worrying about whether that will actually happen will waste real time and energy that could be more usefully invested into how we interact with them right now.

Strategies for staying present in the here and now

1. Listening to teenagers without trying to judge the outcome.
2. Challenging teenagers gently when you are unclear about their thinking.
3. Stimulating their thinking by asking open questions that allow them to reflect on their line of reasoning, e.g. 'What do you mean I'm still not clear?', 'Can you help me a bit more?'
4. Giving them their own time and space to cool down in an argument.
5. Acknowledging their opinions and their right to have those opinions.
6. Agreeing with what you agree with in their opinions. Disagreeing with what you don't like.
7. Empathising with them, e.g. 'I can see you don't like what I'm saying', 'You look mad at me for doing that.'
8. Naming their difficulties for them, e.g. 'You're struggling with school', 'Friends seem to be causing some problems for you.'

---

9. Highlighting and being clear in your thinking.
10. Naming the emotions that you are experiencing in your conversation with them.
11. Searching for a compromise situation that you can both live with.
12. Not being afraid to say clearly that your teenager was right about something you disagreed with.

All of these elements can become part of a daily routine that will ultimately lead to a robust and well-honed relationship that will become the foundation for the long-term project that is involved in bringing a child to adulthood.

Research consistently tells us that safe, predictable and consistent relationship patterns will help to develop proper and appropriate social behaviour in all children. Such relationships help to develop and promote high levels of emotional awareness in the child. This helps him to empathise with other people and step into their shoes to see how they see the world.

Teenagers exposed to safe relationships have a much better ability and capacity to be able to express what they feel about positive events that occur in their life. They learn not to be shy about their talents and not to undermine their capacity to live out their full potential. They also have much less need to express negativity.

Emotional intelligence

Equally, we also know that a range of teenage issues such as drinking alcohol, engaging in sexual activity and belonging to a peer group are related to the amount of emotional intelligence a teenager has. Emotional intelligence is the ability to acknowledge, identify, manage and express our own emotions as well as being able to empathise with the emotional responses of others. It is developed from safe relationships where parents attend to the needs of children, do not use fear and power as a way of dominating children, and stay focused on managing the present. Emotional intelligence is a key protective tool that teenagers can use in order to be able to sustain themselves in their daily contact with others. It enables them to realise their own individuality while at the same time experiencing a sense of being connected to their family, friends and general community.

Given the complexity that is involved in all of this, if attention is focused solely on future outcomes, we will not be able to sustain the energy to maintain the focus on the various interactions that need to occur on a day-to-day basis in order to promote emotional well-being and emotional health.

TOP TIPS

1. Watch out for words like 'will' or 'might' and statements like 'I'm telling you' – if you are using them you're in the future.
2. Be careful about using fear as a way of motivating teenagers – it only makes them and you afraid.
3. Encourage emotional expression in your teenagers and don't take it personally!

Loop-the-loop thinking leads to lopsided parenting

Another common trap is to get caught up with your own thoughts in a manner that just loops them around endlessly in your head and prevents you getting into any form of useful action. For example, thinking that:

'Johnny might fail his exams,

so I had better help him,
but I didn't do his subjects in school,
so I'm not much use,
so how can I help him,
but without my help,
he might fail his exams,
and if he fails his exams,
how can I help him?'

Lots of thoughts, lots of predictions, no action – lopsided. The simple way out is to ask him what help he needs and see if you can provide it. If you can't, see if you can find someone who can.

Teenagers have a way of triggering this thinking in parents by their curiosity and exploration of the world, which panics parents. Obviously there is a need to think about both yourself and your child in terms of working out what is best for them and how best to achieve that. However, when thoughts paralyse you into not taking any action you feel well and truly trapped.

We tend to engage in this type of 'looping' thinking when we are under stress, and it is also interesting to note that it is when we are under stress that we are most likely to remember experiences that were negative. This makes us feel either depressed or anxious. Either makes us fearful. In turn this triggers other negative thinking patterns, which produce more of the same, which keeps us looping around this negative thinking cycle. Then we lose all sense of perspective on a problem. This builds up, preventing us from moving into any sort of action phase that would allow us to sort out the issue that is causing the distress. It's the classical case of arguing in circles and achieving nothing but exhaustion, irritated parents and grumpy teenagers.

One of the things I do with parents when they get into this cycle of looping is to ask them to keep a record of actions they have taken during the day with regard to their child. It is interesting to note how little *productive* action they engage in. Sure, they have been busy and feel exhausted by the amount of action in their daily lives. But the quality of the action is not very uplifting. Parents don't get energised by it.

So there is a fine line between taking the time out to think about your teenager but ensuring that this doesn't get you into a cycle of simply being caught up with your own thoughts and with the worry that is produced from these thoughts. Looping the loop is best kept at the amusement park!

Teenagers are right – we're all bad parents!

Oftentimes we use the thinking outlined above as simply a way of stopping us from engaging with somebody in a relationship out of a fear that we are not good enough or that it may all go wrong. All relationships, including those of parents and teenagers, carry a large element of gamble and risk in them.

Daily gambles when interacting with teenagers

1. I will appear foolish in front of my children.
2. I will appear old-fashioned in front of my children.
3. They will show up weaknesses in my parenting style.
4. I will be judged by my children.
5. I will make lots of mistakes.
6. I will have some regrets.
7. By the end of the day I will consider myself to be the worst parent in the world.

If you could gamble on each of these, you'd never have to work a day again! Any of these factors can help to trigger off a looping thinking cycle in you because they tap into natural vulnerabilities about how you think about yourself. These then prevent you engaging in the type of thinking that would show you that in fact most of the time you do a good enough job in engaging with your children. Accepting this will let you deflect away the more negative messages that come from either yourself or your teenager.

Any one of these ordinary, normal daily gambles is also evidence for a teenager that you are a 'bad' parent. So be it. I wouldn't bother trying to defend myself against the accusation that I am normal and ordinary and I cannot possibly get everything right all of the time. Teenagers need to learn about the real world of parents too.

You don't need to be God's gift to parents – stay ordinary

Parents tend to get straitjacketed by a belief that in some way they do not have the skills to be parents of a teenager. This is indicative of having fallen into the trap of believing that adolescence is something quite extraordinary and out of the range of normal understanding. Adolescence is as ordinary or extraordinary as we want to believe that it is or want to perceive it.

One way to counteract this is to reflect on your child and examine the types of experience that you see your teenager involved with. Think about how he is in school. Who does he see as his friends? Which parts of family life does he enjoy and which does he struggle with? Notice that much of his life is quite ordinary. It is about trying to be happy, seeking out help, being connected to others and being valued as a person.

Also notice how you can build up a picture of your teenager which will give you very clear insights into what is going on for him and how he is functioning in the world. You will see what it is that raises his anxiety before exams and what it is that helps to reduce this. You can watch out for the things that make him excited. You can learn what it is that makes him laugh and you can see what makes him sad. Almost all of this will be ordinary and almost all of it can be spotted any time, any day by the person best qualified to do this – a parent.

This is something that most parents do with their young children and it does not need to stop because the teenager is suddenly more mature. Generally, underlying personality traits do not to tend to change that much and the teenage child will have spent the best part of a decade or more exhibiting his personality. Parents are therefore in a position to put together all the various pieces and to connect them into patterns that they can be fairly confident in. Patterns will vary from time to time but will not fundamentally change unless there is some hugely significant event in the young person's life that causes him to completely re-evaluate how he presents himself to the world.

Even teenagers who 'go off the rails' will, if given a safe opportunity, exhibit previously held character traits that are more acceptable to those around them. So the trick is to remember that you know your child, and even if he forgets himself for a while, hold tight to the knowledge that what you have seen of him before will win through.

Young people need to explore the different parts of their personality. To the observer it is like watching a stage performance where different characters come and go, except that in this instance, it is a one-actor play and the stage and props are the home, school and peer group.

Clueless I'm not!

A thinking trap that parents can set themselves is when they start to believe that they simply do not have a clue about what is happening to their child as he matures. This is not true.

By the time a child reaches adolescence, you will have had up to twelve years of daily contact with him. You have observed how he interacts with the world and picked up on his habits, attitudes and particularly unique behaviours. You have collected an enormous store of information about your child which can be used to help you provide him with healthy guidance.

Parents are keen observers and have an expert knowledge base about how their child operates in the world. You have practised teaching your child how to engage with others. You have seen him find enjoyment in the world and you have soothed him when the world does something that makes him feel unsafe or creates pain for him.

It is often a sign of sheer frustration when parents report that they simply do not know what's going on in the world of their child. This notion needs a strong challenge as it can be a misguided short-term relief strategy. It only works for parents who decide that they don't have the time or energy to sit down and tease out slowly and carefully what is actually happening for their child.

I strongly challenge this notion because when I conduct interviews with parents they show how much information they have about their teenager. They can describe their friendships, their school, their hobbies, their likes and dislikes, what hurts them and what makes them happy. Parents are able to provide very detailed and rich accounts of the world of the child. Indeed, when we engage in a process of probing, parents can oftentimes be quite surprised at how much insight they have into the world of their child.

When I gather this information with parents, we sit down and try and put together a map of the child's life to see the areas where there are many strengths or opportunities for the child. We also look at the areas of weakness that need to be supported. There is no doubt in my mind that even the most distant parents have a sense of what's going on for their child. They have had many years of practice observing and putting together information in order to be able to generate patterns about how their unique child finds their place in the world. Parents can use this information just as much as professionals can.

TOP TIPS

1. Your thoughts are neither good nor bad – they are pieces of information that you can use to take some action.
2. Focus on the ordinary behaviours between you and your child – there are a lot more of them to work with – rather than waiting for 'big' events to happen.
3. Trust yourself that you know what is going on in your relationship – you may not know it all and nor may you need to.

The big, bad outside world – bring it in

There is one area where the idea that parents don't know what is going on for their child may have some element of truth to it. This occurs when teenagers are allowed out of the home environment in order to interact with peers. Not knowing what is going on only occurs when parents don't ask about it, don't take the time to check what friends their child is with or don't take the opportunity to check exactly where their child is at a given time. Careful and considered supervision of your teenage child is healthy and necessary, regardless of their objections.

While it is important that opportunities for independence and distance from the family are created by parents, it is even more important that this distance is monitored. It is in effect a process whereby parents generate a type of supported independence. And the *supported* bit of this is more important than the *independence* bit. Your teenager wanting all of their independence is not the same as your teenager needing it!

Frankly, I cannot see a problem with parents checking in on their child, checking in with parents of other teenagers, calling other parents to ensure that they have been given the full story of a planned evening. It is often a sign of lazy or tired behaviour when parents simply hand over pocket money to a child and allow them the freedom to head away with a group of friends for five or six hours to a specified place and not check that what they have given permission for actually occurs. It's a fingers-crossed approach to parenting that undermines your ability to influence how your child relates to his peers.

I've heard plenty of examples from young people who have told parents that they are heading up the road to spend some time with a friend when in fact they travel into town, head to a party or engage in an activity that, if not unlawful, brings them to the notice of the authorities. Of course there may be nothing particularly wrong in heading into town with a group of friends, but there is a lot wrong with the fact that parents don't bother to establish the truth about the information they are given.

Parents need to be upfront about how they will monitor the safety of their young sons and daughters – 'I'll call down to Jane's house to see that you are all okay'; 'I'll ring Tim's dad later to see that he is collecting you all at eleven.' Young people will not like this, but once you have established that in fact they are as safe as is reasonable and are taking responsibility for this safety, checking in can become a less stringent activity. It needs to be a negotiated decision between the teenager and the parent and it can be justified on the grounds of ensuring safety on all sorts of levels.

Love is never lost on children – particularly teenagers

Because parents get frustrated with their teenagers or cannot seem to get through to them, it's sometimes felt that in some way their love for them has diminished.

Handling this type of thinking is of course not a new experience for most parents. Many parents of very young infants and toddlers will often feel shame or embarrassment because they are so frustrated at being unable to interact with their child out of tiredness, exhaustion or lack of understanding. They start to question their own ability to be a parent and ask how they can find the resources to maintain indefinitely their love for their child.

Parents of teenagers are no different. Week on week teenage children will engage in thinking, language or behaviour that really will frustrate you and cause you to react in a way that you are not happy about. You may even get embarrassed by your child and in quiet times reflect on this. One of the doubts that will enter into your thinking is about how you love your child.

Even in clinical practice, where I have worked with a range of severe problem presentations, it is extremely rare to come across a parent who will say that they do not love their child. With teenagers who have become entangled with the law, most parents still have the capacity to love their child and support their child with love through very difficult times. Of course they yearn for a time when it was easier to express that love and easier to see the evidence for why that love exists in the first place.

The bottom line is that love for children is a very deep-rooted experience that weathers most storms.

There seems to be an unspoken awkwardness which can prevail around the love bond between parents and their teenage children. It is that parents of teenagers don't love them in the same way as they used to love the little newborn of earlier years. Almost without fail, parents I meet dearly love the child that they are sharing their life with. What often becomes a struggle for them is the expression of this love. This strikes me as a direct kickback to their own experiences of when they were teenagers and how their own parents expressed their love for them. We do what was done to us.

Young people's core needs are no different from the basic needs of an adult or young child. Young people need to experience love from parents in order to be able to develop in themselves the esteem necessary for robust psychological health. They need to experience love in order to maintain the bonds that connect them to people, particularly in their family, and they need to hear about, witness and experience this love on a regular basis.

Teenagers need to be physically connected to this love with hugs and touches of affection from parents and siblings (and no, this does not have to done with great drama in full view of a public audience). Most of all they actually *want* this to happen, but for some reason the expression of this type of love comes under strong pressure when a child moves into their teenager years.

A standard part of my interviews with teenagers is to ask them whether they know if they are loved at home. Most teenagers will reply that they are. I ask how they know this and this is where they tend to stumble out a response along the lines of 'I just know'.

Similarly I ask parents if they love their children and they generally say that they do, with the usual caveat that there are numerous times when they are fit to disown or throttle them. Again I ask how this is expressed by parents and there is a mumbled half-answer.

Parents have a responsibility to take the lead in how affection is communicated within the family: children will take their cue from them on this. While I am not advocating that every meeting between a parent and teenager has to be one full of hugs and kisses, I am saying that something needs to occur on a regular basis so that the teenager feels continually sustained in their relationships at home.

Adults I have worked with in therapy can clearly recall the coldness that crept into their family relationships when unspoken rules about touch and physical connection came into play once the innocence of childhood had departed. This is a lesson not worth repeating.

A message that I constantly give to parents is that it is extremely important that the sense of belonging that emerges out of physical contacts – hugs, a kiss goodbye in the morning, a slap on the back as he runs out to play a game – cannot be undermined simply because they teenager might shrug it off.

I'm not advocating that you should stand outside the school gate and do all of the above, but these things do need to happen. Physical contact is extremely important for us as children. Physical contact is extremely important for us as adults. It is equally important for teenagers. It reminds us that we are not isolated from others. Touch helps us to regulate our emotions. It can trigger a wave of tears that is required to relieve frustration or it can give us a high when we jump around together in celebration.

It is a very, very powerful tangible sign that we are connected to people around us, that we are still loved and that in some way there will always be a place for us within the family unit.

If your child shrugs off the hug or doesn't answer you when you say that you love them, it doesn't matter. The message will be remembered. If you have the patience to keep giving that message a time will come when the teenager will actually be able to send it back to you freely and openly.

The expression of love through touch is natural, it's normal, and it's human.

TOP TIPS

1. Be honest with your teenager that you will check out their whereabouts from time to time.
2. Experiencing family love is essential to healthy development in teenagers.
3. If you struggle with this, seek help with your own life story – don't hand it on to the next generation.

Teenagerism has to be difficult

Another snag that parents of teenagers tend to get caught by is the belief that they simply do not have the capacity to be good and effective parents of their teenagers because of the difficult developmental phase that they perceive adolescence to be.

This is a myth, simply because adults do have capacities to be as effective as they choose to be. However, this requires making time and space to engage with parenting activity in a way that is somewhat different from when children were younger. In some ways teenagers make obvious the need to model how to be an effective person in life. They throw you into your teaching role.

Teaching time by parents – lessons you give

1. Different communicating styles for different people and situations.
2. How to express emotional reactions.
3. How to talk about fears.
4. How to be happy.
5. How to be sad.
6. How to engage in conflict resolution.
7. How to engage in negative thinking.
8. How to be able to exist effectively in the community.

Of course there are countless other lessons to impart as well. You do these routinely and automatically. With a teenager you often need to stop these activities being so automatic; to break them down piece by piece in order to understand what areas of strength you and your child have and what areas need to be strengthened. You cannot simply assume that because you do it and do it well your child can do the same. All learning takes time, patience and practice: and both of you are in this learning process together.

Handing on your wisdom

Being effective parents is not about controlling behaviour, it is about the formation of character and personality. This requires handing on what you have learned that is useful in life. A lot of this can be automatic, but a lot needs to be made explicit for a teenager because they are able to understand the logic behind the things that you do. So telling him how you handle conflict at work, or dealing with an unpleasant neighbour, allows him to set up possibilities for how to deal with similar situations for himself.

While your child mirrors variations of who you are, he is also unique. His own skills, strengths and weaknesses all need to be highlighted so that he can learn his limitations and strengths in order to be able to function successfully in life.

Of course, while all parents have the capacity to be better parents that does not necessarily mean that they are currently ineffective parents. All parents make mistakes, all parents would like to change things that they have done with their children. However, most do well enough, most of the time.

If parents can let themselves off the hook that they need to be the perfect parents acting in the perfect way all the time, they will view mistakes as challenges that have arisen in the relationship with their teenager, which can help trigger new learning, for both the parent and the young person.

If they can share some of this learning experience with others, so much the better, as the general community of parents gets to benefit from new wisdom. Conversations about these mistakes with other parents actually helps to challenge the notion that we all need to know exactly how to be good parents all the time and that there is no room for error.

It is very rare that a single mistake in parenting leads to any significant impairment or damage to the relationship with the child. It is only when it is repeated and becomes part of the relationship that real damage is done. Think of some mistakes that you have made with your teenager. Most often they only lead to an argument or a bit of silence – not really end of the world stuff.

What happens in poor parenting is that mistakes are repeated over and over and become patterns of interaction; and it's the patterns that do the damage. For example, if your tone of discussion is one of constantly accusing a teenager, then you will be involved in regular arguments. However, if you are open to having this brought to your attention, you can learn very effective communication and relating strategies.

Teenagers have a voice

And what about bringing the teenagers themselves directly into these conversations? One of the things that parents do not do often enough with their teenagers is to say 'I got it wrong: I made a mistake. I'm not sure what that mistake has done to you but I'm open to hearing about it.' We must remember that teenagers, because of their stage of development, have a very sharp capacity to spot mistakes in what we do and also to spot how we manage these.

It is how we manage these errors that will allow us to become very powerful role models to the teenager as to how to negotiate his way through life. Put it like this:

- if we pretend that we have not made a mistake
- if we stand our ground even when that ground is very weak
- if we try to laugh it off
- if we try to displace responsibility on to another party

we are simply teaching the teenager to repeat this way of behaving in their later life.

If, however, we say, 'I got it wrong on this occasion but I believe that I can do better':

- we are we giving the teenager a clear message about our capacity for new learning
- we are also indicating our ability to change
- we are letting ourselves off the hook by saying, 'I don't need to be perfect about this all the time'
- and 'when I make a mistake I can engage in some learning for myself'.

Increasing your effectiveness

In encouraging parents to see themselves as being effective, I ask them to recall times when the teenager was an infant or a young child that were particularly demanding. This highlights to parents that in fact the developmental pathway that their child undertakes is one that is *often* challenging. It also shows that they have had years of experiences and skills which they can use to continue nurturing the development of their teenager.

I sometimes think that what parents mean when they talk about being ineffective is that they feel tired by the challenge of being a parent of a teenager. My suggestion is that often parents are trying to maintain the relationship with the teenager as if she were a young child. They are still using strategies that were once effective but which need to be adapted, for example telling her what to do, constantly advising but not getting her opinion, and demanding that you be obeyed.

Strategies need to reflect an appropriate response to the type of relationship that the young person is able for – clear, reasonable and fair parental thinking and behaviour which is based on the simple fact that there are two partners in the relationship, teenager and parent.

Just like any relationship, the needs of each person in it change over time. When this happens, discussion and agreement about how the new needs can be met is required. Having these discussions with teenagers will help them to understand their changing needs while also showing them how those needs can be met within the family, if this is reasonable. Investing in the time to do this with a teenager brings long-term reward and reduces the chance that you have to take a position of dominance when relating to them.

Others have it all sorted

Sometimes when parents hear lots of advice or read about how others manage their children they generate a pitfall for themselves by believing that others have it all sorted.

This is not the case. All parents struggle with all of their children at some stage because struggles emerge out of how we relate to people and out of the relationships that we develop with them over time. Believing that others have it all sorted out is just a way of kicking yourself and undermining your own ability to work out what's happening in the life of your child.

Of course there are parents who are more successful at

relating with their teenagers than others. It's interesting to know the types of behaviours and relating style that they engage in to produce this outcome. As mentioned earlier, the most effective parents are those who engage in predictable and consistent parenting behaviour. They provide a safe, nurturing, warm and loving environment for their children to grow up in.

However, successful parents are also not afraid to challenge the ideas that their children generate. This challenge is done in a way that respects individual difference but also allows for firm boundaries to be maintained that are appropriate, safe and allow for growth of the child.

Keeping up with the Joneses

One way of developing this style of engaging with teenagers is simply to speak to other parents about the concerns that you have. It is a useful strategy to normalise our experiences against those of others in the same situation as us. Social comparisons show what we do well as well as teaching us where we can improve.

It is comforting to hear how many parents will empathise with the story that you are presenting. In doing so it is important to respect the dignity of each teenager so that they do not become an item to be moaned about and complained about. See it as an opportunity to broaden your own skills at relating with teenagers, not as a chance to complain about your child.

It would be a great community response to see peer learning groups and peer support groups for parents of teenagers come together. Here parents could meet to discuss the strategies they use to nurture and promote the relationship between themselves and their child, and in particular to share information about how they can become better partners in that relationship.

In some ways this is like the old Irish tradition of a 'meitheal', whereby groups of individuals came together to form a team for a specific task over a specific period of time. The group effort and group capacity was made up of what every individual brought to it. It strikes me that in today's world of individualism there are too many parents caught in the trap of believing that they have to do it all themselves.

It does not have to be this way. Individual responsibility to bring about a community response to how best support the development of teenagers would indeed be a mature rebuff to the philosophy of individualism that has seeped into society.

TOP TIPS

1. Believe in your ability to be effective – look for what worked before and see if it can be adapted to your relationship with your teenager.
2. Use mistakes to take time out and learn something new. Repeating them will leave you tired and frustrated.
3. No one ever has it sorted – parents sometimes achieve and sometimes struggle.

I had nothing – I must give them as much as I can

There is another tremendous pressure on parents of teenagers today that is related to the more materialistic, individualistic society that we now live in. Many parents have described a belief that they will harm the self-esteem of their child in some way if they do not keep up with the child's friends in terms of activities, pocket money, meeting friends, going to discos, etc.

Using the teenager's friends as a benchmark against which to measure the development of your own child can be a useful strategy. We know from research that teenagers have a tendency to choose friends with similar interests that in many ways reflect their own individual personality. Therefore it is useful for parents to tap into that tried and tested method espoused in the saying, 'You are who your friends are.'

However, that needs to be balanced with the capacity to teach your own teenager that while their friends may be doing a certain activity or engaging in a certain way of thinking, you might not agree with this. This teaches your teenager that you are acknowledging differences between your way of thinking and others' ways of doing things. It also highlights that you want your thinking, your beliefs and values to be respected.

You are also teaching teenagers that sometimes it is just not possible to keep up with everything that is going on around you. It is okay to say to them that they are not going to a disco, wearing a certain type of clothes, going on holidays or whatever it is without having their self-esteem damaged for life.

Teenagers need to learn that their confidence in their rights can be matched by your confidence in your responsibilities. It will take a few years before a teenager is able to understand this perspective, however, so be prepared for a delay before you hear the thanks!

Relationships are central to the development of personality, but there are few ways of harming your child unless you undermine the quality of the relationships that your child experiences. The quality of relationships will not be substantially determined by how many nights out, how many holidays, how much pocket money, etc. they have. If only it were that easy.

I know him so well...

Perhaps the biggest pitfall that I come across is the one where parents describe that they believe that they do not know how to interact with their child – 'I just don't know how to relate to him any more.'

That message, and maintaining a belief system built on it, not alone undermines the very essence of what being a parent is about, it also undermines what you have to offer to the child. It can leave him with the message that in some way he is beyond being supported and nurtured; which is untrue. This is one of the occasions where it is useful to take a little look back into the history of your relationship and try to establish times when you and he were in fact well able to communicate.

These were the times when interaction and enjoyment were as normal as eating and sleeping. Being able to draw from memories of good and happy experiences and work out what it was that made the interaction at the time particularly good, positive and useful is something I regularly do with parents.

Once we have the ingredients teased out, the next step is to work on trying to bring those ingredients back to life in the current teenager–parent relationship. I use the term *back to life* because once a skill like this has been established in childhood it doesn't go away. It may become dormant or forgotten about by both parties, but it is not lost; it just needs to be reactivated by doing the same sort of things that were done before.

This exercise often shows how little time parents spend alone with their teenagers. This is time outside of rushing to school, heading to football training or other important activities. I mean just plain and simple time in each others' company without agendas and just seeing what emerges from that.

Look at what you have had to do so far as a parent:

1. hold so much information about his existence from conception onwards
2. watched so much of his development
3. observed how his personality unfolded over time
4. felt his pain and sadness
5. experienced his joy and humour

6. shared his achievements
7. monitored his growth and maturity.

You cannot have done this without knowing what it takes to interact with your child.

Fighting fit

When parents of teenagers throw their hands up in frustration and say that they do not know how to interact with their child, the message I hear is that they have forgotten about the ways of relating that will actually work for them.

So parents and teenagers who tend to fight with each other also tend to look for opportunities to engage only in that fighting style. They do not take up the opportunities to engage in a different style because of fear of losing face. They stay in fight mode in case the other might catch them out. Fit to fight but not fit for fun!

Fighting is about outcome and we often cannot control outcome. Maintain your energy and attention on the process that is happening between you and the teenager in a given moment, and increase the probability that the interaction will be useful to both parties.

And finally . . .

This chapter has outlined a range of possible traps that parents can find themselves in, often without being really aware of how this happened. Stopping yourself getting into these traps is an important step in balancing the relationship with your teenager. There are some steps to spotting these traps outlined below. You will need to be willing to spend the time teaching yourself about them and practising them.

Throwing away traps

1. Become aware of your responses to feeling trapped, e.g. feeling anxious, irritable, explosive, unable to think straight.
2. Ask yourself if you are thinking about the possible outcome of a situation.
3. Identify exactly what it is that is causing you distress within yourself.
4. Stop trying to see the source of the distress in other people.
5. Identify what you can do to reduce the stress.
6. Do it.

These steps simply act as a device that allows for time to think and feel about a situation or a person and increases the chances that you will be able to spot traps before they cause real distress. In other words, we often find ourselves in traps because we automatically repeat certain thoughts, feelings and behaviours in a particular situation. Stopping ourselves making this repetition gives us the choice of keeping or throwing away the traps and avoiding the pitfalls.

CHAPTER 7

You Can't Make Me – Rules, Regulations and Rows

N ow that some of the snags, traps and pitfalls have been highlighted and described, it is worth turning our attention to how it might be possible to un-snag some of those attitudes and behaviours that lead us into difficulty in the first instance. At the end of the last chapter, some steps were highlighted that can help when you find yourself in a trap. There are also other, more general, issues to be tackled that can help to steer clear of parenting problems in the first place.

Parenting style

A useful first step is to understand the style of parenting that you employ day to day. Just as we have certain traits that make up our personalities, we also have traits that when put together create a general style to describe how we do the work of being a parent.

Research shows that in general there are four main parenting styles that can be observed in how parents assert their influence on their children. It is not the case that you will have only one of these styles, but you will have a predominance of one style over the other.

1. Authoritative parenting

An authoritative style is characterised by a high degree of being responsive. This means plenty of warmth, support and nurturing behaviours as well as a high degree of demanding age-appropriate behaviour from the child. Feedback is given to the teenager in a helpful but firm way and the parent does not use force or dominance to control the child.

This is the style that most parents aspire to, but unless you have had this experience in your own childhood it can be difficult to carry out with your children. Most parenting courses aim to equip parents with this type of parenting style.

2. Authoritarian parenting

In contrast to this, an authoritarian style of parenting involves relatively low levels of warmth and nurturance. This is coupled with very high levels of demanding, which can trigger high levels of anxiety in the child.

The child learns that there is not much point in looking for comfort from parents. She also learns that the things being asked of her are often beyond her abilities, leading to criticism and her feelings of being worthless.

3. Permissive parenting

The third category is permissive parenting, in which there are high levels of being responsive to the child but low levels of demanding age-appropriate behaviour and thinking from the child.

The child gets indulged and is seen as 'getting away' with things. Parents give in to the child's demands and are poor at helping the child distinguish between needs and wants. It is like continually keeping peace with the child without looking for appropriate behaviour from him.

4. Neglectful parenting

The final parenting style, which is called neglectful, involves relatively low levels of being responsive to the child coupled with relatively low levels of demanding age-appropriate behaviour.

The child becomes unsure of where and when love is coming from and does not know what is appropriate or inappropriate to do. Essentially the child does not really know *how* she will receive care or, in the worst case, *if* she will receive care. Her needs are only partially met and she is not taught what is okay in terms of her thinking, feelings and behaviour.

So what's best?

As you would expect, the authoritative style is associated with the most positive outcomes for young people: they perceive their parents as supportive, perform better in school, have better social networking skills and cope with stress better. In other words, they are the most psychologically well-adjusted teenagers and they see themselves as that.

In contrast to this, teenagers who perceive their parents as having predominantly one of the other styles report more delinquent behaviour, more extreme dependency on parents, more psychosomatic illnesses and more immature behaviour.

It is important to reiterate that parents do not have only one style of parenting behaviour, but most show preference for a predominant style that the young person is exposed to on a regular basis.

Be your own flexible friend

Indeed, the best parents are those who are able to be flexible in choosing particular parenting behaviours in particular situations. So, for example, if my teenager has just experienced a row with a friend it is best to comfort and support the distress she feels. However, if she has deliberately caused a row with a friend it is best to offer clear feedback that challenges her to see her role in what she has done.

Obviously this can also sometimes mean choosing a style that causes some discomfort to a teenager (and I don't mean actually throttling them), as captured in the phrase 'love hurts'. The point is that parents are responsible for the guidance of teenagers and teenagers are dependent on parents to carry out all of those duties, even the ones that hurt.

TOP TIPS

1. If you want to change your parenting style, do it slowly. Pick one thing to work on and stay with it until it is complete before moving to another task.
2. Don't expect your teenagers to jump for joy while you try to change. There is a natural confusion when parents change how they do things.
3. Be patient and compassionate with yourself – change is hard work.

Automatic is not always accurate

The next useful step in keeping pitfalls at bay is to try to locate the automatic reactions that both parents and teenagers have when they get into difficult interactions.

Automatic reactions are simply those things that we experience, feel, think and say without giving any thought to their consequence. They are literally the words that jump out of our mouths without being filtered for the potential destruction that they might cause. They can also be the behaviours we engage in without giving any consideration as to their potential effect on the teenager or, indeed, on ourselves. They are automatic because we have practised and rehearsed them so many times that we do not even realise we are doing them. Usually the first clue we get is a physical reaction in our bodies (stomach tightens, throat feels dry, muscles tense, etc).

Interestingly, even though these words, phrases, behaviours tend to feel automatic it is clear to me that most parents, when they are out of a stressful situation and asked to slow down, can quite readily point their finger to exactly what it is they do in these situations that is distressing. They can highlight what it is that causes them to continue to engage in what are in effect pretty useless communicating behaviours. Some people have phrases that they use to keep arguments going, e.g. 'you never listen to me'. Others use body language to aggravate the situation further, e.g. turning their back on the teenager talking to them.

Time out ... for parents

In order to be able to firmly pinpoint automatic reactions, you need time away from the stressful situation. This gives some understanding of exactly what it is you do that may not be the most useful in a given row. The following examples show what can be learned with a little bit of 'time out' for parents.

Unchain yourself

Once the automatic reactions are identified, the next step in loosening the chains that might hold back a parent from being able to easily resolve a situation is to try and identify the chain of behaviours that happens once the automatic response has taken place. Take the following example:

Parent: You look grumpy, what's wrong with you? (Accusation.)
Teen: Nothing. Anyway, it's none of your business. (Defends himself, agrees there is something wrong but doesn't want to talk.)
Parent: Don't talk to me like that in my house – I said what's wrong? (Feels insulted, misses opportunity to acknowledge that it isn't any of his business but can see teen is upset.)

Teen: Nothing. And leave me alone, you never listen anyway. (Wants a bit of calm, matches the earlier accusation with one of his own.)

Parent: How many times have I told you not to talk to me like that? (Has now turned the conversation away from the original observation that there was something wrong into a pretty useless question about previous conversations.)

Teen: What do you care anyway? (Defends himself by attacking the ability of the parent to care.)

Any one of the phases in the conversation above could have been suspended with a few carefully chosen words or the ability not to attack in conversation – 'Sorry about that, didn't mean to interfere. Just checking.' The parent saw that something was wrong but instead of acknowledging this in the first instance, he came out with an accusation about the teenager being grumpy. It's a slippery slope from then on and both end up feeling annoyed by each other.

Pinpoint the patterns

Like most things that we engage in, there are fairly predictable patterns and consistencies in our reactions in any given situation. When I work with parents and teenagers we try and break down to the smallest detail the chain of behaviours that ultimately leads to an explosion of emotions, slamming of doors or harsh words being spoken. We work out the phrases, words, sighs and grunts that serve to escalate a tense situation.

In doing so, what we learn is that the chain contains lots of opportunities for one side to relieve the stress. But crucially, often neither parent or teenager believes that it is okay to do this. Often all it takes is for a parent to say 'okay, I'm happy to leave this for a while' or 'I don't know about you but I'm unhappy about how I'm talking to you now so we can pick this up later.'

In a situation that is already tense, it is a parent's responsibility to look for and take advantage of a way out of it. This is not a sign of giving in, backing down or being beaten – it simply shows that you know how to calm a situation without having to beat everybody up. Teenagers are still in the process of learning how to do this, so expecting them to be reasonable at all times is unfair.

Situation	Body response	Automatic feeling	Automatic thought	Automatic behaviour	Response from teenager
Request to visit friend's house.	Tense muscles ready for a fight; sinking sensation in stomach.	Fear, dread.	She'll come home late. She won't listen to me.	Telling her she can't go. Giving out that she can't be depended on.	Go anyway. Storm out. Tells you that you're responsible for her having no friends.
Poor exam results.	Knotted stomach; feeling hot; jaws clenching.	Anger, frustration.	That ungrateful child.	Using phrases like 'I told you if you didn't work, this would happen.'	Shut down; get depressed; feel ashamed; get angry; feel isolated.
She's got an older boyfriend	Surge of adrenalin throughout body; ready for a fight.	Horror, helplessnes, fear	Over my dead body!	Full-scale lecture on how you will not allow it.	Nothing you can do anyway; you're just jealous; I love him!

Hang up the habits

The importance of being able to tease out this chain of behaviours lies in the fact that because they are repeated so often in our interactions, they will become habitual. In other words, over time they become the only way we engage with the young person when there is a stressful situation. Once something is a habit, we start to feel that we have little influence over it, which makes it even more stressful. As alluded to in an earlier chapter, it is always better to focus on what you can influence and work on this.

The repetition of patterns is one of the main reasons why many teenagers will describe their frustrations at interacting with adults: they will use the oft-repeated line, 'I'm never listened to anyway.' They have actually seen it before in their parents.

We learned earlier that it is critically important that adults, when they interact with their teenagers, to suspend as far as possible whatever expectations they have of the outcome. This is underlined when we consider that the chain of habitual, well-practised reactions is more likely to be repeated when the outcome that we predict will happen is already set in our minds before we even begin to engage with the teenager.

This will usually happen with something that is either uncomfortable or likely to be highly charged, for example setting out new rules and regulations regarding behaviour in the home.

So the lesson is, suspend expectations regarding outcomes, catch your habits and mind your language!

TOP TIPS

1. Become aware of body signals that hint that you are getting upset about something – map out your own stress signature that tells you to take time out!
2. Instead of trying to change what the teenager is saying, influence him by changing what you are saying to him and how you say it.
3. Don't try to mind-read his intentions or the outcome of an interaction with him.

Respond rather than react

I often advise parents to try not to *react* to what is being said by a teenager because the word *react* often means to do what has already been done. It is literally a re-acting of what the teenager has just acted!

I advocate that parents *respond* to the messages their children are giving them. The difference between a response and a reaction is that the response is a more thoughtful and fully informed communication. A response tries to capture everything that was in the message coming from the teenager.

A reaction is much more immediate and tends to be more superficial in that it is being triggered by the obvious. It is more often acted out of an intense emotion such as being hurt. In this case, we want to put down the other person's view. In addition, we do not take into account all the contents of the message that they might be trying to deliver.

An example of this might be when, in a heated moment, a teenager, who feels completely over-stimulated or unable to handle the amount of information that is being delivered by angry parents, walks out of the room, slams the door and goes upstairs. The parent reacts by shouting out a series of orders about slamming the door but fails to respond to the frustration or the sadness or the fact that the teenager has been overwhelmed by the entire interaction.

Paying attention to everything that's going on in any interaction requires a lot of practice, a cool head and a very strong ability to be able to say, 'I'm getting this wrong and I need your help to be able to work it out.' But this is also a very powerful way of teaching and educating teenagers how to engage in meaningful and mature communication with people, particularly when both parties are in a state of disagreement.

Slow down, you're moving too fast

It helps to slow down the pace of what's happening for both parties and this in turn helps to keep strong emotion contained. Helping teenagers to regulate their emotional world is such a useful tool because there are times when they will feel overwhelmed by interacting with adults.

Slowing everything down helps to maintain the connection in the relationship by blocking the quality and quantity of hurtful things that might be said.

Choose wisely

Just like the strategy of reacting to every thought in your head, responding to everything that happens in a situation is also ineffective. Again, in the scenario where you and your teenager are in an argument, it is a much wiser approach to respond to only one or two things that are emerging from the interaction.

Better still if you can both decide on exactly what needs to be responded to now and what can wait. Most teenagers prefer problems to be solved in a task-oriented way. So:

- state the issue
- break it down into its parts
- show what parts are being focused on right now
- agree what both of you can compromise on
- decide on what each of you can do now
- leave the rest.

Many adults like to sort out problems using a mix of tasks and emotions. With emotion-focused problem-solving, you know when something is wrong because of the feeling you have and you keep working at it until the feeling is sorted out. Emotion-focused problem-solving is often too intense for teenagers. It is usually better to stick to specific tasks.

Remember that most disagreements do not need to be fully resolved in a given moment. They usually need time out for both parties to be able to reflect on exactly what it was that they were trying to get across and exactly what it was that the other party didn't manage to see or hear. Parents, because of their maturity, will have a more complete response to the actual interaction and can respond to more of it more quickly. Thus they want it sorted right now.

However, we have to remember that the teenager may not be able or ready for this: so it is important not to try and overload the situation, which can result in confusing the mix even more. Teenagers may need time away to reflect on things in order to make sense of them. They are not equipped with the worldly wisdom of their parents. Allowing for this models a powerful and mature way of communicating with a teenager. It shows that any given interaction has a message that needs to be delivered in the here and now but also that there are other messages that will emerge with time as the situation cools down.

Participating in an interaction with a teenager will be a much easier experience for both parties if the parent can show some leadership by how they respond. Much of the problematic interaction with teenagers is because of a reliance on reactions. Parents need to show the way by stepping back and attempting to bring calm. Respond rather than react.

TOP TIPS

1. Learn the differences between your reactions and your responses.
2. In responding, slow down the pace of your conversation and monitor the volume levels of your voice.
3. Give yourself permission to resolve a disagreement over a period of time if this is necessary.

Curiosity only ever killed the cat

Good responding is fostered by staying curious about lots of possibilities with the teenager. It is filled with comments like, 'How did that come about?', 'I noticed that you were a bit put out there' or 'That would make me feel upset, what did it do to you?'

I have taken this notion of curiosity from how parents tend to interact with very young infants. A lot of interactions between parents and infants is based on communication that centres on seeking out new information and asks lots of questions like, 'What are you doing now?', 'What is that sound for?', 'Where are you going?'

All these types of phrases link the parents and the infant into a world where exploration and curiosity become the mainstay of the relationship and where enjoyment and contentment result from how both explore the word around them. They let the experience between them unfold with neither person too concerned about the final outcome.

Maintaining this attitude of curiosity with all children right through the teenage years is a really useful way of finding out what is happening in the world of the young person – how they perceive themselves and the world, how they perceive others and how they perceive their parents.

Oftentimes we approach teenagers with the attitude that we should have all the answers, afraid to show some weakness in case they see this as a vulnerability that they can attack. We seem unable to apologise for something that we have done wrong and in general take a very rigid and tightly controlled interactive style into the relationship with them.

Get onside

Teenagers tend to interact better with people who make an attempt to empathise with how they see the world. People who are willing to explore the possibility that what teenagers have to offer is valid are respected. In professional practice the psychologist is able to offer a complete outsider's perspective on family issues because he is being exposed to the story for the first time.

First-time-perspective building is also a useful technique for parents and when combined with curiosity it can open up platforms for communication.

One of the things I try to guide parents into doing is to try to view the interaction with the teenager as if it is the first time they are experiencing it. This means dropping prejudices and biases and suspending trying to predict the outcome. This can trigger alternative perspectives that can help to move the relationship forward by keeping the communicating style between them clear, focused and productive.

In some ways this is a little bit like being able to sit down and watch a DVD of how you interact with your child over a particular issue. You can imagine that you are able to sit back in the director's chair and observe all that is happening and then generate new ways of behaving out of the observations.

Thinking doesn't make it so

I regularly challenge parents to examine their own relationship with their own thinking. An error that adults tend to make in their thinking style is a belief that because they were taught something it must be true, e.g. teenagers are trouble. Not always so. We tend to be poor at being objective about our own thinking. We don't like evidence that goes against what we think. The bottom line is that we don't particularly like changing how we think or behave.

Understanding this is particularly important with teenagers. If we get caught off guard and find that we engage in very defensive, rigid thinking about how we should interact with them, we might find that we maintain a lot of the tension that does occur in disagreements with teenagers. In other words, it's not about them, it's about us as parents. It's our rigidity and defensiveness that can be the problem, but of course it's much easier to blame the 'moody teenager'.

TOP TIPS

1. In your interactions with your teenager, stay open to the possibility that you might learn something.
2. Let teenagers see that you don't have answers but that you do have thoughts and opinions that might help a situation.
3. Accept that there are things you do that are unhelpful when disagreements take place.

A good start makes for half of the work

I am not a strong advocate of big 'sit down, let's have a chat' interactions between parents and teenagers. These tend to produce too much anxiety for both parties and also tend to be quite artificial. However, there are times when serious issues arise when this needs to happen. I am continually surprised by the fact that most parents go into these types of interaction without having fully prepared for what might lie ahead.

There is no doubt that you cannot read the mind of a teenager and that you cannot take account of all possible outcomes. However, preparation for the interaction will allow you to better manage your own emotional responses as you deliver whatever message it is that needs to be delivered.

Preparation means that you will have a very small number of points in your head that you want to communicate. This stops you from going up side alleys and culs de sac that will ultimately lead to a major disagreement.

Preparation also allows you to influence the process by which you will both engage. By having a strong sense of how you would like to engage with him you will offer a confidence, an assuredness to the teenager that you will not be distracted from what you want to say. This will also reduce the risk of you ranting and raving about completely irrelevant issues.

There are three core issues to examine in your preparation for the interaction:

1. **Know what your intention in the interaction is.** You need to make this clear to yourself so that you can remain focused on the issue. This prevents you and your teenager falling into the trap of arguing about something irrelevant or something old.

2. **Establish what attention you can pay to the interaction at the time that you choose to have it.** It often strikes me that parents choose the most inopportune moment to launch into a serious discussion with their teenager. This dilutes the chance that it will move ahead successfully. If you're not able to give your full attention to the issue in hand at a given time, abandon the idea and wait until a better moment occurs.

3. **Know what attitude you bring to the interaction.** Remembering that most of our communication is non-verbal, if you arrive into an interaction swinging a large sledgehammer in order to crack a small nut the teenager will spot this. They will put up defences and do everything to outsmart you. You'll end up feeling foolish and tired.

Lazy language leads to easy trouble

I have mentioned communication and conversation on a

number of occasions and at the heart of these are words, phrases and sayings. Language and its use lead to creating some of the biggest messes and snags for both parents and teenagers. The conversation example earlier highlights some trouble that lazy language can generate.

Lazy language is all about not saying what you mean, not meaning what you say and looking for a way to 'stay on top'.

In an ordinary conversation both parties try to come to terms with communicating clear thoughts in a way that keeps them clear for the receiver, without leading to all-out war. This is quite a skilled and complex task.

For me, language really is the stuff of thoughts, particularly when relationships crash, burn out or are in the throes of battle. Words and how they are spoken can offer delightfully clear insights into real emotion, passion and hurt, and can often offer a 'way out' for even the most entrenched position.

Words and how they are used are very important. What is said as a joke in one place can in another be heard as a racial insult that can provoke street riots. What is negotiated at peace talks can be heard as victory for one side and humiliation for the other. There is a massive difference to the listening audience between a 'war on terror' and a 'war of terror'. Language as a communication tool in relationships is both extremely complex and very powerful.

In the home or school, language is a tool laden with all sorts of pitfalls for families to fall into.

- A simple request is heard as a tyrannical demand. ('Please tidy your room.')
- A polite refusal is taken as a massive insult to intelligence. ('No, I'd prefer you not to travel on your own.')

- An offer of help is heard as an implication of stupidity. ('Would you like a hand with that?')
- A request for more information is felt as a lack of trust. ('Who did you say you're going to the party with?')
- An inability to understand is perceived as evidence of being a relic from the dark ages. ('I don't get that Twitter, Bebo thing, what is it?')

Language links us

I think that language gets us into more trouble at home than outside because somewhere deep inside us as parents, there is an unwritten expectation that because we are directly linked to our children by the deepest of deep bonds, in some way we must all be speaking the same language.

Or perhaps it is more accurate to say that we have to understand language we hear from each other in an identical way so that it marks us out from other families or related groups of people. It helps to hold our unique identity as a family unit. There is a lot of truth in this.

Families develop lots of unique ways of communicating with each other that are not easily accessible to people outside the family unit. Parents of toddlers derive great fun from hearing their youngest acquire family words or sayings that are not in the slightest bit funny to outsiders. However, the idea that similar understanding happens for everyone in the family is not, for me, shown in the evidence. This is particularly obvious during the teenage years, when teenagers bring their unique take on the world into play.

Going beyond words

Teenagers' ability to think abstractly and 'outside the box' becomes acutely into focus during this phase of their development. As with all new toys, they will want to engage with this new language skill and try it out until it becomes just another normal part of who they are.

With this skill comes not just the ability to use more complex words and arguments, but also a greater capacity to hear *beyond* words. They are able to pick up the underlying messages in language, to infer a message that was not actually said or to imply a message that was not actually delivered. They have been at this for years but they really get it now. See some of the examples below for what happens in teenagers' heads when they hear some parental orders.

FUN TIME WITH LANGUAGE	
Parent says out loud . . .	**Teenager says quietly to himself . . .**
'I forbid you to smoke.'	'You are forbidding me to do something I have already done – you're too late, thicko.'
'We need some more family time together.'	'You're kidding! Sitting listening to what happened in your boring work and how hard you work for this family? I never asked for that.'
'I will not stand for that rule being broken in this house.'	'Nothing to do with me – they're not my rules anyway.'
'You should study more.'	'You want me to abandon my friends and become a social outcast.'
'You're too young for a girlfriend.'	'You didn't get any until Mam took pity on you, you jealous sod.'
'Don't use bad language in this house.'	'You f****** hypocrite.'
'You need to do this right now.'	'So now you're an expert on my needs, you can read my heart as well as my brain, you're so completely clever.'

The teenager is able to go beyond the actual words used to both hear underlying messages and create their own perception of what you have been talking about. This becomes a bit of a mind-read game that in my experience is most likely to go wrong just when you do not need it to, for example in a disagreement.

Rows are a good example of where the norm is for both parties to end up arguing over something that bears no resemblance to what initially was the problem. An outsider would have little difficulty in hearing that the combatants are actually having two entirely different conversations – *at* but not *with* each other – at the same time.

Much of how we use language is actually not that direct: we tend to hide our real feelings, requests and desires out of an underlying fear of rejection or being ridiculed. Young people tend to ride over that particular habit because sometimes the only control they feel they have in conversations with adults is the power to trigger embarrassment and ridicule.

If you fall into the trap of responding to language alone, this offers the teenager the chance to wrest back some power into the relationship, albeit in a manner that might get them grounded for a week.

Experiment with the following strategies so as to generate a fully informed response about the language you use.

1. Try not to respond only to words in conversations.
2. Listen out for the underlying message.
3. Feel the emotion that goes along with the words.
4. Comment on the atmosphere that the conversation is generating.
5. Make explicit in a calm manner exactly what the conversation is doing for you and whether you are happy with this or not.
6. Use 'I' statements (I feel, I am, I think) – they will prevent you getting into accusations.

Pay attention, parent

There is a tendency not to pay full attention to all of what is actually happening in a given interaction. It is very easy in interaction with teenagers because of their verbal capacity and their increased thinking skills to focus only on what is being said.

To make a useful informed response, we need to pay attention to a lot but respond to a little.

We have to remember that teenagers are still in the process of evolving both physically and mentally and that, for all their swagger and confidence, they still do not have the same mental capacities as adults. Therefore, as parents, it is important in interaction with teenagers to pay attention not just to the spoken word but also to what is not said by a teenager.

Over ninety per cent of our communication is non-verbal. Therefore, when we get a hunch that a teenager might be trying to communicate a message that is difficult for them it is our responsibility as parents to act on this hunch and to check it out.

This is advice I try to put into practice with parents, particularly when arguments occur. In an argument the biggest mistake that both sides tend to make is that they react only to what is being said; they do not take into account the way the message is being spoken. They miss the underlying hurt or the quiet request for help.

The tone may be an indicator of underlying distress. It is important to check out if there are particular emotions being felt that might in fact be the opposite of what is being said. The classic example here is the answer to the question 'How are you?' The words say 'I'm fine', the tone says 'I'm not'. Listen to *how* things are being said to you and if you feel uneasy about something, name that unease and offer the opportunity to talk about it.

TOP TIPS

1. Just because you have said something doesn't mean it was picked up the way you intended.
2. Listen to more than your teenager's words – there are quieter ways for them to communicate.
3. If you suspect distress, follow up on it. You may have picked up on non-verbal clues that are as important as verbal signs of distress.

Attitude speaks louder than words

Having a reasonable attitude that is based on fairness and respect will ultimately lead to far more rewarding interactions. This will ultimately produce the type of calm interaction that parents desire.

You need to allow yourself to be patient while the teenager is trying to grapple with issues like rules and responsibilities, rows with friends, not having enough money, not wanting to study, etc. Moreover, you need to know when you have done all that you can to influence a given situation. Accept that ultimately the teenager can thwart your wishes for him.

If your child does not want to study, gets nothing out of the extra tuition you have paid for and couldn't care less about learning, no amount of arguing over this is going to change that outcome for now. Likewise, no amount of threats about sex is going to stop your daughter from having sex if that is something she chooses to do.

Part of the responsibility of being a parent to any child is living with the fact that you cannot control all outcomes, nor bring all desirable outcomes to fruition. This is so difficult to live out, though. And it is made more difficult because every so often your fears for their safety and well-being will materialise. She might get an STD or he will take up smoking. He will get questioned by the guards or she will fail exams. Life happens.

There is a strong need to be able to live with uncertainty. There is also a strong need to be able to accept that ultimately your child, regardless of their age, is a unique individual who may see things differently from you and want different outcomes. If you can accept this and allow yourself some patience you will create a space in how you communicate with the teenager.

Whenever there is a chance of communication there is a chance that they may be able to learn more about your perspective and why you want things to be a certain way. If your attitude is one of acceptance of them as a person they can always come back for help if things go badly wrong for them. Accepting someone does not mean that you have to like them – it simply means that you are not pretending about your feelings towards them.

Continue the connection

Ultimately the goal of getting yourself out of any snag, trap or pitfall is to be able to develop and sustain the connection with your child. It is therefore very important that once a particular interaction is completed, you take a lot of the responsibility for ensuring that there is connection with your teenager in the aftermath of it.

This is easy when the interaction was all fun and games but more important and more difficult when there was tension and disorder. Holding the connection reminds teenagers that you are there for them, that you do believe in their potential and that things move on in life. So try and make the conversation, don't allow silences to develop, change topics, don't look for every opportunity to start an argument and, somewhere along the line, say, 'I'm sticking with you anyway!'

Some history is best in the past

One of the things that happens to teenagers is that they become more self-conscious about who they are and how they are perceived. This is a relatively new experience for them. So a parent who reverts back to previous incidents or continually drags up past incidents in order to make fun or undermine the teenager is doing a lot more harm than might be obvious to the eye. Teenagers' feelings of awkwardness or self-consciousness are not something for you to use as a final put-down when you can't think of something more useful to say. Reverting to the past in this instance will rekindle the row and also make the teenager see you as unsafe. She will be wary of you and distrust you with important issues as she will fear that they might be used against her in the future. Leave comedy about teenage angst to the television sitcoms – it could really badly backfire on you if you do the DIY version at home.

Change what you can

One of the things that the adult will have to educate the teenager about is that there are only certain things in life in which you can effect change.

To make sure that you don't fall into the pitfall of becoming burdened with life and its challenges, it is important to be able to take responsibility for what you can change and to make this clear to the teenager. Equally, it is important to be clear for yourself about those things you have little or no chance of changing.

Parents need to set the example to teenagers that not everything in the world can go their way. Part of becoming wise is about living with the frustration or the sadness of this and then going on with what is open to you in life.

Ultimately, the point of highlighting traps and pitfalls and ways of avoiding them is to ensure that both you and your teenager learn to communicate with each other in a way that promotes self-respect and dignity.

Out of this style of interaction comes the opportunity for both of you to be able to engage in a process by which your beliefs, attitudes and values can be put up for discussion, teased out and amended if necessary. Such a process within the family leads to creating flexibility in thinking and in communicating. This will help to resolve many more issues than if there are very fixed and rigid procedures that everybody must abide by.

And finally . . .

Spotting your own snags, taking responsibility for what will help you undo them and teaching teenagers about this is highly important in terms of psychological development. This is ultimately about the ability and capacity to be able to sustain personal control in what can sometimes be very difficult situations.

As always, this requires much time, effort and patience but the rewards are valuable and long lasting. These rewards will flow outwards from the family into the community in which the teenager lives, goes to school and interacts. Snags and un-snagging them are all about how people communicate, and teenagers need both positive and negative interactions with parents to learn how to do this. Both are required to ensure that they learn to manage these normal human responses outside the home. Mistakes will be made and hurt will be felt, but this is part of the reality of living – and successful living is based as much on what we do with hurt as on trying to keep hurt at bay.

For the idealistic teenager it can be a bit of an eye-opener that much of what we do in our daily lives revolves around managing ordinary interactions with ordinary people. Knowing how we get ourselves into and out of such interactions is valuable knowledge. Handing this knowledge on is priceless.

CHAPTER 8

Know your Game: Getting out of the Traps

During the teenage years the spoken and unspoken rules of the household, school, club or peer group suddenly explode into daily life in a manner not previously seen. In this chapter I will examine the daily dance that goes with trying to keep order in the family. In particular I will look to see if parents can avoid making confrontation a normal part of their interacting style with teenagers.

Why all the friction?

Until puberty, you led your child into some acceptance of the power imbalance that exists between children and adults in the home. With the teenage years, questioning, challenging and rejecting this imbalance seems to become children's very reason for living. It's important to understand a range of issues before deciding that the teenager must have some form of rare undiagnosable condition that has them hell-bent on disturbing the lives of all around them.

Rules, regulations and boundaries make a significant contribution to either successful or unsuccessful family life. However, the management and negotiation of these often leave a lot to be desired in most families.

As we have seen, there are a range of snags, traps and pitfalls that both parents and teenagers can fall into in their engagements with each other. If parents can spot the slippery slope into a negative interacting style with their children (which could make the five or six teenage years very difficult indeed), they may well be able to halt the progress of that style. So what do you need to watch out for?

The criticism camera

There are a number of behaviours that begin to appear in the relationship between parents and teenagers around the time of puberty. These can indicate that a problematic pattern may emerge in the interaction style between them. Chief amongst these is criticism. It is telling to note how criticism seeps into the ordinary day-to-day language between parents and teenagers. After a while it simply becomes the norm.

Normally parents are quite clear that criticism of children is not healthy. Most work hard at trying to sustain positive, affirming and constructive interactions with their children. However, something seems to happen with the onset of puberty and in many families criticism becomes a normal, familiar daily occurrence.

While constructive criticism is very useful, it has been my experience that this is often in poor supply in families where there are teenagers. As teenagers develop quickly and their mental capacity increases, one of the things they are able to point out is the flaws in the arguments that adults make to them.

When this happens adults automatically get into a defence position to try to preserve their own authority as parents. That defence can quickly become a criticism of a teenager's opinion simply for the sake of trying to win an argument or save face.

The message given to the teenager is that what they have to offer is only of value as long as it doesn't threaten us. If it threatens us we engage in criticism, which is a deliberate put-down of the teenager simply for the sake of it. When we don't perceive a threat we are more likely to engage in critical evaluation, standing back from a situation and offering an opinion on the good and bad in it without the need to put down the teenager.

Constructive criticism	Destructive criticism
'There's good and bad here, let's try and break them down.'	'That'll never work, it's stupid.'
'You're doing well and I think if you do this, it'll help more.'	'Now, the way I would have done that is . . .'
'You seem to struggle a bit with that, how can I help?'	'Will you ever learn? How many times have I said . . .?'
'When you used that angry tone with me, I got really annoyed.'	'Don't you dare use that tone with me or I'll teach you . . .'

When we perceive a threat we often do not listen to what is being said to us. We simply hear that we are being attacked and we then move into a counter-position in order to defend ourselves.

Hearing that we are being attacked and actually being attacked require two different psychological processes.

- The first requires us to turn on a camera that only watches out for our own safety and is blind to all other possibilities.
- The second allows us to evaluate what someone else says, decide whether it poses a threat to us and then find an appropriate course of action.

Choosing the first psychological process closes off the possibility that the criticism that is coming our way might actually be valid. We only hear the threat to our authority and fail to spot any other message that is in the criticism. This prevents any useful review of our particular attitude or behaviour, which in turn might cause us to shift our stance somewhat.

The second process requires of us not to react in the first instance but to wait and see if we can listen fully to what is being said in the criticism. **It is very rare that *all* the content of any given criticism is inaccurate.** We tend only to react to what is wrong in it and miss the opportunity to consider what might be useful. Just because the delivery might be poor doesn't mean that the content is poor.

I am often surprised at the capacity of many teenagers to name, clearly and accurately, genuinely poor parenting behaviours that they see in their family. I'm even more surprised that parents do not have the capacity to let this evaluation seep into their way of thinking about themselves as a parent. After all, many parents bemoan the fact that they couldn't have this type of conversation with their own parents. They could then use such evaluation to become better parents. This would require a way of parenting that is built on maintaining a process of reflection on their own parenting skills. That philosophy is not one that is traditionally the way of parents in much of modern culture.

Useful critical feedback questions on being a parent

1. How did I handle that particular situation?
2. What did I do that worked well for you?
3. What did I do that did not help the situation?
4. What do you think I'm good at as your mother/father?
5. What do you think I struggle with in being your mother/father?

If parents can hear critical evaluation from their children and turn it into useful learning, they are also teaching teenagers how to receive criticism. This is part of my explanation for why many of us simply revert to what our parents did to us – parents of today's parents did not live in a time when you offered critical feedback of the job being done to you. Few, if any, parents were taught how to make use of the questions listed on page 223.

Creeping from criticism to contempt

In families where there is a lot of argument over rules, criticism can become a normal part of day-to-day interactions. In times of crisis that criticism often deepens to become contempt. Contempt is a real feeling of dislike with a condescending edge to it. It is at these times that phrases such as 'I hate you', or 'You have nothing to offer', or 'I never wanted to be part of this family anyway' become part of the common language of the interactions between teenagers and parents.

I call this 'lazy language' because it is simply a way of deflecting from something important that is not expressed by the teenager (either because they do not know how to or are afraid to). Equally they may not be being accurately listened to by the parent (because they are tired, angry or do not know how to).

If parents respond to lazy language with lazy language, then contempt takes over and both struggle to respect each other's point of view. This increases the likelihood of triggering rage circuits in the brain, which fuel the argument further, cause hurt and leave little energy for sorting out the whole mess.

Contempt has an added danger because it is based on disrespect and a complete inability to be able to see any perspective on the world other than your own. It causes emotional chaos within a family if there are a number of people engaging in this type of interaction. Equally, contempt is draining on the resources of other children in the family who are also going to be caught up in the friendly fire that goes with family fallouts. What affects one affects all.

Digging in the defences

Contempt reinforces the need for people to protect themselves and use all sorts of defences to protect their sense of dignity. Teenagers show one way of protecting themselves when they withdraw from interactions so as not to let them develop into any meaningful conversations. This is simply a reaction to their perception of very strong negativity in the family atmosphere. They need to reinforce the defences in case more contempt will be aimed at them.

Parents need to lead the way at trying to keep negativity at a minimum because it introduces a layer of anxiety and dysfunction that can lead to a breakdown in respect, trust and communication. Keeping negativity at bay means:

- naming an issue clearly
- stating what emotion you are feeling
- making it clear that you have observed the feelings of others
- asking what can be learned from a situation
- taking responsibility for your part in creating the negativity
- offering compromises
- saying 'I was wrong'/'I don't know'.

Stone walls are hard to hear through

Not keeping negativity in check means that the communication style takes on a hard-line, emotionally cold profile, often referred to as stonewalling. This happens when people simply freeze each other out. This is an extremely negative, draining and useless obstacle to healthy family functioning and will require a lot of persistent work to try and break down. It is usually a sign of hurt and pain which if left unattended can lead to the type of psychological distress that really gets in the way of the development of the teenager. It also exhausts parents.

Overcoming it really does need both parties to accept responsibility for the hurt that they have caused. However, the level of hurt that is being felt means that it is easy for emotions to overrun any negotiations or ceasefires. Oftentimes it is better to offer and accept simple tasks or behaviours that can show an apology rather than insisting on hearing the words 'I'm sorry'.

To increase the likelihood of a successful outcome it might even require you as a parent to put the issue on the long finger and let feelings settle. Only then might it be useful to sort it out.

If stonewalling is left to fester between two people, it might be time to call in a negotiator to help break the ice. This role can be filled by the other parent, a grandparent, a trusted family friend. Ultimately, though, the warring parties will have to negotiate their own way forward and usually they do this.

TOP TIPS

1. Cut out criticism and contempt and encourage helpful evaluation.
2. Just because you don't like it doesn't mean that all negative feedback is inaccurate.
3. Lazy language leaves lousy leftovers – be clear and honest about what you are really saying or hearing.

Defusing the crisis

An important element to note in these linked communicating behaviours of criticism, contempt, defensiveness and stonewalling is that at each stage they can be defused. It just takes one person to reflect on the situation and offer some conciliatory noises around responsibility and apology. Or one person to leave the scene in order to let the tension subside.

Sometimes that means having to withhold your own sense of

frustration and hurt in order to buy some breathing space. This is better than having to clean up after an all-out, over-the-top assault. Besides, as adults we can hold on to the fact that hurt and pain can be dealt with a little later without the world coming to a standstill, but this is something that teenagers have yet to learn.

At times when criticism and contempt behaviours are triggered another brain capacity kicks into play, which is not particularly useful in a row situation. This is the process of selective attention.

In selective attention we tend to only allow information into our thinking system that confirms the beliefs or attitudes that we already hold.

For example, if we are having a row with a teenager whom we believe is awkward and disobedient, the only information that we allow into our thinking will be information that confirms this. So we may not pay any attention to the fact that his complaint may be accurate or genuine.

The difficulty with this process is that we will not be able to attend to any signals from the teenager that show that he is offering a lifeline, a white flag, or some sign that he is willing to negotiate on the difficulty in question.

Sometimes those signals are small to us but feel really big to them.

Selective attention is something that all adults will fall foul of at some stage, and it can be very difficult to catch yourself doing it. The best indicator that it is likely to have been triggered is actually in monitoring how your body responds in an argument situation. If your 'blood is boiling' or you would love to hear the sound of all your favourite mugs, plates and glasses hopping off the wall, the chances are that the selective attention party is in full swing.

Getting out of the immediate physical environment and calming down your physical responses is a must in this situation so that you give yourself the chance to reflect on what is *actually* happening.

Groups, groupies, peers and parents

All groups of people have expectations with regard to the behaviour, thinking and emotional lives of the individuals who make up the group. Most of these expectations are transferred through the generations by word and action. Some seem to move through the generations in a more discreet manner – they are learned by observation.

Generally changes tend to happen at a pace that the group is capable of managing. If change is too quick there is a risk that the group might fall apart or not be able to sustain itself. If it is too slow, irritation and frustration can set in and bring disorder to the way the group functions. The limits to change can be challenged from time to time, which reminds individuals of how far the group can be pushed. The challenge can also show that there is spare capacity for new learning or action.

Peers are positive

Group membership is very important for the normal development of a teenager and it is generally accepted that the influence of peers during the teenage years is both positive and constructive. Critically, if by mid-adolescence a child is not actively part of one group or another, this may indicate more serious mental health problems for him that may warrant further investigation by parents in the first instance and, if necessary, professionals. This does not mean that he has to be the life and soul of the party, but being isolated from some form of group membership can be an indicator of distress that is worth investigating.

If you can bide your time, it is also worth noting that strict conformity to group expectations and pressures actually lessens from mid-adolescence onwards as the teenager starts to really assert their own individuality on the world.

The long-held belief that the peer group wields so much pressure that it can push each child into all sorts of trouble simply does not hold up. Teenagers have the ability to hold a strong sense of self-determination. They also have the capacity to choose friends with similar interests to themselves. Like all their evolving personality traits, this needs to be nurtured and guided by the significant adults in their lives. They are still learning how to be group members outside the family group, a complex skill that requires much practice.

Teenage thinking rocks the boat

With adolescence comes a direct challenge to the group that is the family. A key element of change for a teenager is the increased capacity to use logic and reason in a manner similar to adults. This is often at the root of the debates, rows and ructions that seem to come with rules and regulations in the family. Teenagers don't understand the illogical rules that bind the family together. So they offer their opinion and with it a chance for you to outline your reasons for the rules.

The natural thinking style of teenagers can often be described as idealistic. They have the mental capacity to know what the world 'should' be like but lack the concrete experience that teaches that the word 'should' is generally a pretty useless one. It doesn't really say much – 'I should do that' doesn't mean that I will or won't do it.

I advise parents that over-use of the word 'should' is likely to be an indicator of the lazy language that I referred to earlier. It is an interesting experiment to try to set aside a day when you deliberately try not to use it. You will find that you have to become much clearer in how you express yourself and that others will understand you better and more quickly.

It is as adults that we have gathered enough knowledge and experience to teach us that the world is a more complicated place than the idealised fantasy we created as young people. When that idealised style of thinking is turned to the rules and regulations that make up family life, what teenagers often experience is a bit of an eye-opener to reality. Consider the following examples.

Rule	Reality	Realisation
Respect for all members of the family.	Listening to parents complain viciously about their own family members.	There is no written charter that can be logically followed in all instances.
There is to be no smoking in this house.	Teenager has been caught smoking again, and family friends who drop by can smoke in the house.	Adults often generate rules after something has happened and then try to enforce them as if they have been written in stone since the beginning of time.
Don't lose your self-respect by hanging around with people who get drunk and act foolishly.	Mothers and fathers do this all the time with a range of justifications.	Adults often have a set of guiding principles that are completely at odds with some of their behaviour.

Teenagers also learn that many regulations are set in some vague, abstract view in the mind of the adult that is not made clear to the teenager (be home before 10.15 or else there will be trouble – means what exactly?). Of course even teenagers accept that a very few are just about liveable with (you need to save some money if you want to go out to the cinema at the weekend).

TOP TIPS

1. Lead the way in calming the storm – it improves your sense of influence.
2. Expect your child to ebb and flow in and out of various groups in her life, including the family group.
3. Accept that some of your rules may not be that useful and that your teenager will spot this and let you know. Use the opportunity to update your own thinking on your rules.

Celebrating change – a new arrival in the family!

Few families with teenage children have sat down and explored plans for how the family will manage itself as it changes due to the presence of a teenager. In many cultures there are initiation ceremonies for boys and girls in which the elders in the community demonstrate in concrete fashion the transition from one developmental stage to another. Ceremonies are often accompanied by a handing on of the rules, laws and behavioural expectations of the community to the teenager. There is often a feast to celebrate the arrival of a new generation of young men and women who will maintain the existence of that particular community.

How is this managed in our culture? I think it is difficult to be sure. Girls have conversations regarding the onset of their monthly period and the requirement to maintain appropriate personal hygiene. Boys get to buy a razor. There is, in many cases, a change of school, which is itself a useful symbolic gesture. Religions may have special celebrations to herald a moving on in terms of spiritual growth.

But what do families do to celebrate the onset of adolescence?

How do parents prepare themselves for the new arrival? Compare the preparation, or lack of it, with preparing for the arrival of a newborn baby, which is heavily loaded with big gestures over the course of the pregnancy and in the aftermath of the birth. Where are the preparations, little rituals, and other symbols that mark the fact that something uniquely important is happening to the child who is entering adolescence? This is something that is also very important for the family system.

One argument as to why there is a lack of any celebration of adolescence is because many parents maintain the notion that teenagers cannot on the whole be enjoyed. There is almost an unspoken wish that somehow if all involved can get the teenager to eighteen years of age, a collective sigh of relief can be breathed. This mindset can paralyse parents into a self-fulfilling prophecy whereby they batten down the hatches for the so-called inevitable war. And of course when we look for trouble, we often get it. So we go rule-making to try and avoid it.

Rule profiling – where did they all come from?

Little thought is given to sitting back and exploring what are the rules and regulations within the family and deciding how these can be discussed with a teenager. She will now have the intellectual capacity to spot the flaws and hypocrisies that make them up. She is also the person who will feel the impact of them on a day-to-day basis. She is a stakeholder with a voice that needs to be heard.

Of course this does not happen because it is not the type of communication that happens in busy households or between partners who have lost – or never had – the experience of this type of communication.

It also doesn't happen, in my experience, because many parents do not actually know the reasons for the family rules.

This means that they run the risk of producing rules out of a hat, rabbit-like, at the most inopportune moments, usually in the middle of a row.

Communication with teenagers requires a commitment to stand back, analyse, reflect and learn about the many rules that people accept in their lives without question. We don't do this easily. That is why parents will often hear the voices of their own parents in certain situations – without their parents' voice there would not be anything at all.

Simply accepting what has gone before is lazy thinking. This laziness haunts us in the presence of teenagers who are more than well equipped to spot a weakness in an argument or a flaw in the logic of a particular rule.

Or even more critically, they will spot that the particular rule does not belong to us – it has been borrowed, handed down without any attempt on our part to mould it into something that is relevant to today. Therefore is open to all sorts of teenage spears being thrown at it.

If our laziness of thought leads us to accept the attitudes and opinions of others as a defence for our own behaviour, a teenager with the sharpened powers of perception will be able to tear this defence down with ease and derive a lot of fun from doing it. I am reminded of young children in a shop pulling the box at the bottom of the pile, not to cause the inevitable chaos but to see the hilarious reactions of their poor parents. Teenagers like fun too!

So simply doing or thinking something because some authority figure in our past life did it is a recipe for frustration and despondency, even if that something is useful and positive. A young person needs to know we have a claim to ownership of a particular rule. They need to see that we believe in it for some meaningful reason and that we are willing to live it out with them rather than force it on them.

You need to have your own clear understanding of your rules and regulations so that when your teenager's curiosity as to their origin and worth is raised, you can feel assured in standing your ground.

Profiling the roots of our rules

1. Where exactly did a particular rule come from?
2. Why are you happy to have it in your home?
3. How happy are you with the way that you operate a particular rule?
4. When do the rules not work?
5. What do you do when rules need to be changed?

If you engage in a critical evaluation of your rule book, you can then be confident in applying the rules and confident in outlining your reasoning for them. And remember, it's not about making teenagers like the rules – it's about highlighting that you have given consideration to them and believe that they are fair. And that you own them but that they are not so precious that they are irreplaceable.

Teenagers will not be always able to fully understand where you are coming from with your rules. They have never been parents of teenagers. You need to allow them some leeway with trying to grapple with your rules. You've had the benefit of being a teenager.

Paradoxically, your sense of assuredness will also allow you to accommodate more challenges to the rule. When we are confident about something, we can be more open to hearing evaluations of it because of that confidence. Such evaluation may well bring about a change to a rule which will have the positive effect of involving all who are affected by it. All of this is powerful modelling of mature, adult discussion and negotiation as well as a preventative for door-slamming (although the odd door slam is hardly the end of the world).

Talking the talk but not walking the walk

One of the issues most difficult for parents to accommodate is that their teenagers are capable of having adult-*style* conversations but not necessarily adult-*type* conversations. Style because they have all the words and phrases, but not type because they don't have the depth of knowledge that comes with experience.

So the often-used technique of talking down to a younger child or engaging in logic that is beyond the brain capacity of the younger child fails miserably soon after the onset of adolescence. The capacity for abstract reasoning through complex problems is not beyond the ability of the average teenager.

That is not to say that you are dealing with a mini-adult. Generally teenagers can best apply their newly acquired intellectual capacity to situations that actually have relevance to their lives, and particularly if they have some experience of those situations. However, teenagers generally do not have access to a large store of broad life experiences and this can bring some of their lofty, idealistic thinking back to earth with a bang every now and then.

When this happens, it is important for parents and teachers not to fall into the tempting trap of making fun of the teenager. This is just part of the learning experience for them and if any of us had fun poked at us while we learned, we would soon run for cover.

Making fun with teenagers can also be a delicate exercise because the very changes that produce increased thinking ability also have the effect of increasing their ability to think about themselves. This raises their self-consciousness, which is why they sometimes react quite furiously when 'harmless' fun is aimed in their direction.

However, if you think that you can win debate and argument by relying on the parental power of logic or adult authority alone, the teenager is not the only one about to come down to earth with a bang.

It is absolutely reasonable for a parent to use their life experience to point out the flaws in the argument of a teenager. It is not reasonable to do so in a manner that belittles or shames the teenager into submission. This is authoritarianism and one of the worst ways to live out parental responsibility. It is also so easy to do it for the very short-lived relief that it might seem to bring.

Longer term, it is more useful to bring your real life experience to the table of discussion. This is a way of showing the teenager that you do not simply make up these rules to be awkward and to highlight that you do possess some wisdom. It also shows that in interaction between you, your views need to be respected as much as the opposing views of the teenager.

Respect is a crucially important concept for idealistic-thinking teenagers – they need to learn that they have a right to expect it and a responsibility to use it.

TOP TIPS

1. Do celebrate the ordinary ways that teenagers mature.
2. Learn all about your own rules – know their history.
3. If you're going to have fun at anyone's expense, let it be your own.

Using their thinking to teach teenagers

The capacity to think and reason is also the very capacity that parents need to use in order to maintain reasonably good relationships with them. Teenagers love to talk, debate and argue. It is being done in a new way, a novelty of performance which was until now the preserve of the authority figures in their lives. They need to be affirmed in this new role so that their curiosity about life and how it does or does not work lets them learn new ways of not just surviving but enhancing the world they live in.

As people on the way to adult thinking, teenagers have a lot to offer. They can point to the fact that some of our thinking may be outdated, illogical or idiotic. We can benefit from the type of questions they put our way. The freshness and innocence of some their thinking can be a reminder of the powerful role we play in protecting them from some of life's harsh lessons. They also offer us the opportunity to pick up the pieces when things go wrong and this makes us feel good.

Brain power – not all there yet

In responding to them it is important to remember that teenagers at different ages will have different capacities to reason and remember. The ability to attend and concentrate on material improves as the child progresses from early to late adolescence. Short-term and long-term memory improves as adolescence unfolds. So we need to adjust our communicating style to take into account the amount of time we spend in conversation with them and how much of that we expect them to remember. How?

1. Don't overload younger teenagers with heaps of questions or directions.
2. Use the better memory capacity of older teenagers to solve problems based on their previous experience.

3. Allow younger teenagers the chance to rehearse and repeat experiences in order for them to fully understand the world around them.
4. Check whether they actually remember what you said yesterday or why you want something done in a certain way.
5. Remember that tiredness affects concentration and memory ability. Teenagers feel a lot of tiredness because their bodies are changing. Cut them some slack!

There is another biological change that goes unnoticed and is a very significant influence on parent–teenager communication. That is the fact that from early adolescence to late adolescence there is a substantial increase in the speed at which the teenager's brain can actually handle information.

This is critical in communicating, especially about rules and regulations. Too often adults, particularly in stressful situations like a row, will offload a load of information in the form of opinions, conditions, directives and orders and just get a mouthful of abuse in return.

This abuse may have nothing to do with the content of the adult's opinions but it may have a lot to do with the teenager being unable to make sense of it quickly enough. In order to save face and rescue themselves from the adult, they take on a fiercely defensive stance.

I have learned this from asking teenagers what actually happens to them when they storm off into another room and so many times they describe a need to be away from what I call the 'noise and stimulation' of the interaction. It all becomes too much so they need to be out of it. This is normal and natural. Infants do it by falling asleep or crying; adults do it by taking sick leave; teenagers do it by storming off.

Parental communication profile

Having a good understanding of your communication profile is one key to regulating your interactions with your teenager. Creating that could be based on asking yourself the following probing questions.

Communication style profile

1. What is my capacity to handle a different style of communication from my child, who is now a teenager?
2. What if I was never listened to as a teenager – how have I learned to challenge an authority role in a useful manner?
3. Where did I learn conflict management strategies that can be used when people who live together inevitably disagree?
4. How, as a parent, do I resolve issues in general?
5. What happens when a teenager triggers a reaction in me that is more appropriate to a younger age?
6. How would I respond to the accusation, 'you're acting like a child'?

Of course there is an assumption in all of the above that the people the teenager has to live with are actually adult parents. I am not referring here to the age of the parent but rather to a pattern whereby the parents of the teenager are behaving as if they are teenagers themselves!

In other words, the parents exhibit immature thinking and communicating skills. Imagine the scenario, then, in which a relatively mature teenager has to contend with parents incapacitated by their own psychological immaturity – there are now three teenagers in interaction, but only one of them has the capacity to see this.

Investment in communication channels makes sense

Essentially, given the teenager's new-found capacity for logic and argument, I think the safest way to educate them about the rules and regulations is to bring them into the process by which those rules are actually made. Like much of what is in this book, this process holds far better potential if it is started in early childhood rather than on the crest of crisis in early adolescence. However, it is definitely not too late to begin or make it more of a central dynamic in the parent–teenager relationship, as this way of doing things will also start to happen naturally in the newly formed peer groups.

Within the family, you can invite the teenager into the conversation when new ideas about appropriate and acceptable family behaviour are openly discussed. Bringing the child into this process has the advantage of educating him about how rules are arrived at and letting him know that you are not setting rules 'just for the sake of it'. Crucially, if he has actually helped to make them he gains some sense of ownership of the rules.

This also takes you off the hook of having to come up with absolute rules that are foolproof in every situation. This is an impossible task and an utter waste of time and scarce energy. Trying to second-guess any child is perilous but it can be made easier if he is part of the process where he can tell you whether a rule is useful or just plain daft.

Seek and ye shall find...

Speaking of feeling the need to generate foolproof boundaries and rules for children, there is no such thing. Trying to think of every possible danger and situation that a young person might get themselves into is a recipe for a stressful home. What is very useful is to share experiences with other people who are in the lives of young people on a regular basis.

Think about it. In a work situation, if you are given a project to manage and bring to fruition, you will generally seek out other opinions, advice or guidance. The best leaders will always listen to the perspectives of others before taking decisive action.

I am an advocate for parents seeking out the perspectives of others on a regular basis in order to promote their own ability to reflect on their role as parent. This helps to maintain a perspective on how they are doing. Similarly, it is refreshing to hear a parent in a conversation with a group of teenagers saying that she is thinking about introducing a new rule into a given situation and asking what they think.

My point here is that we do not need to have all the answers. If we gave up this tiresome trait, we would have much more time to engage in meaningful conversation with teenagers. Such conversations can be used to generate rules and regulations that are reasonable, effective and representative of the wishes of all of those who are affected by them.

My experience is that culturally, Irish people were not taught explicitly how to stand back from their own thinking and behaviour and reflect on its strengths and weaknesses. Many of the current parents of teenagers whom I work with do not have a history of critical evaluation of their presence in the world and how they impact on those around them.

On top of this, these same parents were brought up with the rule that 'you did what you were told'. Whether that attitude is useful or not is irrelevant here – what is relevant is that it will not work with today's teenager who is growing up in a society that has taught him about rights and charters and the importance of 'I'.

- Parents need to take plenty of time to evaluate their own values and attitudes to rules that they were brought up with.

- They need to weigh the benefits and costs of introducing those rules into their homes.
- Then they need to decide how to create methods for evaluating how the rules impact on each family member.
- Finally, but most important, they must devise ways to ensure that flexibility can be built into the family system so that the rules can be amended if this is appropriate.

TOP TIPS

1. Ask teenagers for their insight into your most idiotic rules.
2. Know what you would like to hand on to your child about being in a row.
3. Don't make rules on your own – involve those who are affected by them.

Investments take time to mature

If all of this seems like hard work that continues for years, that is because it is.

Everybody in the family set-up is continually negotiating and renegotiating what happens on a daily basis and when this is working smoothly all is well and good. It's a big dance. In a smoothly functioning family everyone is in a perpetual dance with only occasional bumps as they engage in the constant movement of negotiation.

When things begin to malfunction and the rhythm of the dance becomes fragmented, it's time to analyse the entire rule system – how it was set up, what it looks like day to day, who is in charge of it, how differences of opinion can be introduced into it and how it can be changed.

If the teenager is not part of this analysis a cycle of breakdown in communication will be triggered, with inevitable distress for some if not all of the family. Why parents leave teenagers out of the process varies but might include forgetting to bring them into it, being frightened of bringing them into it, or being too lazy to bother bringing them into it.

Rules, regulations and laws work simply because people believe that in their absence normal day-to-day functioning and living would disintegrate. Society can provide countless examples that will support this belief, particularly in the histories of war-torn societies. It is the same within the family. Unless each member can see the value of having the rules and that there is a benefit to them, there is no logical reason to uphold them.

Bring the teenager into a mechanism about rules that will affect their lives and they will learn a host of lessons, including:

1. that you care and love them
2. that effort is required to maintain the 'law and order' of the family
3. that you can listen, argue and negotiate
4. how to use this mechanism when interacting in the world outside of home.

In this process teenagers may need to hear from you that it is normal for them to want to experiment with rules, test the limits and occasionally find that they either deliberately or inadvertently break them. This lets them off the hook of needing to fulfil any expectations you have of them being the perfect child.

However, they will also learn that deviations from rules in which they have an ownership will lead to consequences that can be uncomfortable. In my experience the most uncomfortable consequence for a teenager if they have stepped over a line is to actually sit calmly and discuss this in detail. The detail is necessary for an understanding to be arrived at. It gives the explanation as to why this happened and the impact on all those affected. To be most effective, this needs to be done with teenagers as soon as there is a rule break. Dealing in the here and now needs to become the pattern for how deviations will be addressed in the family.

Managing rule breaks

1. Bring all parties together.
2. Bring out all perspectives on the rule break for open discussion.
3. Allow yourself the opportunity to see where the teenager stands on the issue.
4. Allow the teenager the opportunity to learn that there is more to the world than simply their needs.
5. Teach them how to manage difference of opinion without abuse, violence or disrespect.

Psychologists call this method of maintaining order 'inductive discipline'. This is where a situation that traditionally might have called for punishment is actually turned into a learning opportunity.

In my experience it really does work better because it weakens the one thing that teenagers detest. They hate the use of power differences in a relationship in order to control them. The challenge for the parent or teacher is whether they can create a relationship with the teenager where they do not use the power difference as the main means of interacting with her or controlling her.

All of this is based on the notion that you have thought this through and are at ease in modelling this style of communication to your child. This will not be the case if you simply rehash what was done to you as a child. Neither will it be effective if what is done is simply about restoring authoritarian law and order irrespective of the views of those affected by it.

When there are rule breaks, teenagers will generally not respond well to parental ranting about how hard they have to work for the family, or that teenagers have it easy. This line of argument from parents is based on an attempt to get the teenager to understand emotionally where the parents are coming from.

This is a very tall order for all but the most mature and oldest teenagers (and, ironically, probably too big a task for most parents too). Teenagers operate much better with a *task-focused* approach than an *emotion-focused* approach to problem-solving.

So, very clear communication is needed about:

1. what exactly was the nature of the rule break
2. what exactly did it mean to the individual affected
3. what exactly did it mean to the family
4. what exactly can be done to acknowledge the hurt caused.

This will work better than trying to elicit emotions of guilt and shame by an oral outburst that has the potential to go around in circles for all involved.

Importance of meaning in rows

Making meaning clear is a very important task in managing any process by which rules and regulations are generated. How often does it happen that opposing parties are seen to have reached an agreement about a particular issue, only to find that after a few days' reflection, each comes up with a completely different opinion on the meaning of a key phrase?

Meaning-making is a highly complex psychological task that

involves emotional memory, behavioural memory, language functions, learning styles, language styles, communication styles and personality traits, to name but a few.

What is important is the understanding that two people experiencing the same event will derive meanings from it in completely different ways, sometimes to the point that you have to wonder if they are both actually referring to the same event. Therefore it is very important in any process that is explaining or generating new rules that there is a regular *check back* procedure to ensure that all parties involved are actually talking and agreeing (or disagreeing) about the same thing.

Most rows end up being about something that bears no relation to what started the row in the first place. This is normally because one or both parties have not acknowledged an earlier grievance and have stored it in their memory. When an opportunity comes along, their memory spots this and suddenly the disagreement over your daughter coming in late ends up being a slanging match about how you embarrassed her in front of her friends.

Row prevention

Recognising feelings and being able to respond to them is a key tool in preventing rows happening in the first place. If we acknowledged our emotional responses as they occurred, the fuel that feeds rows would simply not get the chance to build up. We would acknowledge that something is not quite right and work towards resolving issues in the here and now. This would prevent memory shedding its load into a situation that bears no relationship to the issue under disagreement.

It is also important to remember the developmental stage of the teenager in question. Those who are still in the first throes of adolescence still hold some of the belief that they are the centre of the universe. This is most likely to be seen when arguments occur: they feel the pain of the row more acutely, given that they are more inclined to believe that their entire world is under threat by the opponent.

A young person approaching the end of adolescence should be more capable of a more reasoned approach *if* their parents have modelled this type of rowing style to them.

TOP TIPS

1. Talk about your own experience of rules and the struggles you have had with them.
2. See rule breaks as opportunities for learning rather than opportunities for punishment.
3. Offer a 'way out' for the teenager when there is a rule break – don't insist on trying to shame them into apology or change.

Rows with friends

Rows involving friends and arguments about them often form a central part of teenagers' life experience. Teenagers are coming to terms with the new-found capacity to influence each other in a manner previously not experienced. For the most part it is better if parents let these run their own course and observe from a distance the struggles of teenagers as they try to establish rules for each other to abide by.

There are a number of key areas that parents need to be mindful of in order to be able to support the development of friendships for a teenager.

1. A typical teenager must be able to form friendships in the first instance. In order to do this she will have to have

developed an understanding of how and why friendships are formed and what types of people make good friends.

2. Once this has been established she will need to work out an understanding about the importance of closeness in friendships.

3. She will need to be able to distinguish between peers, acquaintances, friends and close friends.

4. She will need to be able to acquire different levels of intimacy in friendships in order to protect herself and promote her self-esteem.

5. Related to this, the concept of trust will become of paramount importance to teenagers as this is one area that is brutally subject to the idealism that is often the hallmark of adolescent thinking. It is often when trust is perceived to have been breached that the fragility of teenage thinking becomes apparent.

It is heart-wrenching to observe as their sense of the whole world is collapsing around them and how this seeps into all interactions. It often becomes the basis for many of the arguments that occur at home when the teenager decides to discharge their frustration at their friends on to the innocent scapegoats at home.

Hell hath no fury like a jealous teenager

Parents of most teenagers will readily describe the impact that jealousy in teenager friendships can have. This is an obvious issue as romantic relationships develop but is also likely to occur in more subtle ways as teenagers work to find their place in peer groups and social hierarchies. It becomes a particularly acute issue if teenagers are isolated from groups or become leaders of groups that work to isolate others in their immediate environs. In other words, if bullying becomes part of the teenager's experience.

Jealousy-based issues often serve to trigger a crisis within the group and one possible result of this is that certain friendships become strained or indeed reach the end of their natural life. Particularly in the first couple of years of adolescence, this can be quite a traumatic experience for the young person.

At this age the teenager will have the ability to understand that others will also form opinions about her role in how the ending of a friendship came about. So how do you manage this?

Managing jealousy rows

1. Try to understand the type of arguments and disagreements that teenagers engage in and then to make an offer of support. Is about trust, friendship, protection of honour, need for connection to the group or jealousy of material things?

2. Do not be surprised if your offer is rejected initially. Many teenagers will experience some level of embarrassment at being unable to sort out their own difficulties. This is when parents are likely to hear phrase, 'you wouldn't understand, anyway'.

3. Approach them with phrases like, 'I know you've had a row but I don't understand it', 'I'll listen if you want to explain the row to me' or 'It seems like you've all had a falling out, is there anything I can help with?'

4. If your teenager approaches you with a request for help, work with her to help her to define the particular problem from her perspective.

5. When she has her perspective clear, encourage her to look at alternative perspectives.

6. After this is the time to examine possible ways and means of resolving the problem.

While most young people are able to create a number of potential solutions, many of these are untried in the real world. Parents are in a good position to offer guidance on which of the potential solutions has the best probability of being successful. Being involved in this way allows the parent to keep informed about what is happening in the child's life while also teaching a conflict management and resolution skill that the young person will be able to transfer to many other situations that come their way.

And finally . . .

All in all there is an important role for rules, regulations and rows. Most family difficulties are the result of an over-emphasis on the importance of rules and regulations but with little thought given as to how rows can happen. Rows will happen and need to happen in families. They serve many useful functions but only if they are then used to generate learning. Learning then helps to influence how the important relationships between parents and teenage children develop over time. Above all, learning provides the platform for teenagers to go out into the world with some very useful strategies for negotiating the many new and exciting relationships that become the hallmark of their development.

CHAPTER 9

Exams: Who's Being Tested?

Why are we so hooked on education?

The Great Irish Famine took place between 1845 and 1849 and in its wake reduced the population from eight million to three million. Its consequences are etched in folk memories, songs and stories. It is a classic example of helplessness in the face of external, uncontrollable forces.

Consider the impact this situation had on the psychological make-up of the individual, the community and the country. Belief systems were based on external control with no sense of being able to master one's own destiny. Add to this having to contend with starvation on a daily basis and being helpless as family and friends died around you. The immediate consequence in the aftermath of this has to be one of trauma and subsequent humiliation.

We are closer to our history than we think

Parents of teenagers in Ireland today are on average no more than five generations removed from the famine and its humiliating devastation. Studies of attitudes across generations of families suggest that it takes between three and five generations to change belief systems that are part of the family culture. In other words, family attitudes live long in the memory.

This phenomenon of attitudes and beliefs being handed down through families is referred to as *intergenerational transmission.* It refers not just to the fact that certain information is handed on from one generation to the next but also to how that is actually done. Its purpose is to maintain traditions, distribute wisdom, consolidate family identity and teach following generations the skills and knowledge that will sustain and maintain the family system.

So one family prides itself on the value of sending children to school, another is more concerned with children having sound religious beliefs. One family believes in slapping a child while another is horrified at this. Parents who had healthy experiences of being a teenager delight at the prospect of their own teenage son growing into being an important contributor to the family.

All of this passing on of information is worthy and saves each generation from having to continually re-learn information that is already in the family. Such material has been experimented with and shaped into a valuable tool for the next generation so that it can better itself. Hence, families hand on knowledge about money, farming, work, religion and relationships.

Trauma stories

However, what happens when those attitudes and beliefs are subjected to a traumatic set of circumstances? In psychological terms, the trauma gets locked into the day-to-day experience of a person and he goes on to develop a new set of beliefs that are now based on the information that the trauma has generated.

Because trauma is based on fear, the new attitudes become based on fear. For example, prior to the famine the poor classes (most of the population) struggled, but that struggle did return a standard of living where at least access to food was regular, if meagre at times.

The famine changed all that. The attitudes and beliefs related to the ability to influence one's own destiny that sustained families through the generations was traumatically challenged.

With trauma, previously held beliefs get hidden beneath the raw memories of the trauma. It becomes difficult to access memories other than those related to the trauma. The new information becomes the norm, even when the trauma is long past and its obvious consequences have disappeared.

How to avoid the trauma happening again becomes paramount and in Irish family history the seeds of the idea that wealth and access to it is through *education* were sown. The seeds were further nurtured right through the twentieth century as Irish people travelled abroad seeking work to educate their children so that they would have a better life.

School – where history begins to shape his story and her story

Education plays a very powerful role in the history and psyche of the Irish nation. From pre-school to university the education principle permeates every aspect of life. Almost every child between the age of five and sixteen years attends school. There are schemes to support those who because of difficult social circumstances cannot attend school. There are liaison officers to ensure that children who do not attend regularly are monitored by state authorities to reverse the trend. For children with disabilities there is a support network of educational resources and an increasing choice for parents regarding attendance at mainstream school or special educational schools.

There is a set of very strong and principled reasons for such focused attention on the provision of educational services.

1. Education remains one of the single biggest defences against poverty.
2. Education opens doors to formal healthcare services.

3. Education acts as a barrier against a range of social and psychologically adverse conditions.
4. Education can be a launch pad to better employment opportunities.
5. Education leads to better social opportunities, due to the fact that people with similar social experiences tend to mix together.

Above all, education allows parents to derive satisfaction from the fact that they are facilitating an experience that they believe will enhance the lifestyle prospects of their children. Parents see education as a route to acquiring wealth, employment and family sustainability. Ultimately this can be turned into evidence for their success as parents.

The educated Irish

As a country, Ireland has grasped the task of education with vision and intensity. It is only forty years ago that secondary education was made freely available to children, thus creating the future generations that would take Ireland out of economic and social decline.

In the past fifteen years, the ensuing economic success has created pre-schools for those too young to attend formal education. In more recent times the notion of fourth-level education for lifelong learners has emerged as the new recruiting ground for third-level institutions.

Ireland is now a long way from the history of hedge schools and the handing down of stories of repression and pillage by foreign invaders. The value of education to parents, teachers and the state is evident in the often heated debates around the level of resources that are made available for the education of new teachers and the continuing call for better teacher–pupil ratios.

Third-level education providers are in the driving seat to promote and materialise the new knowledge-led economy of the twenty-first century. Education is at the heart and soul of the Irish parenting experience.

TOP TIPS

1. Identify your attitudes about education and see if they are fear-based.
2. Understand your own experience of school and see what influence it has on your attitude to education.
3. Ask your teenagers about their attitude to education and see what it is they value about it.

Education – could there be a dark side?

The protective effects of education against social, economic and health decline, along with the development of its provision almost from cradle to grave may have a downside. In my opinion the education system has also created an underlying anxiety for those responsible for ensuring that children receive education, i.e. parents, teachers and the education system itself.

This anxiety can be in part understood by the effect of our relatively recent history of starvation, repression and perceived helplessness in the face of trauma. Remember that it takes up to five generations to change belief systems and attitudes.

The parents of teenagers and their teachers are not that far removed from the history and stories of the legacy of the famine years, the loss of family to emigration in the mid-twentieth century and the cold economic realities of the 1980s. Current economic woes also stir the bad memories of these times.

The idea of lifelong education can also sow the seeds of doubt with regard to the possibility that we can never know enough. It will be interesting to monitor how this seed develops as we move to a knowledge- and research-led economy and away from a traditional manual and manufacturing economy. Could lifelong learning be the other side of the coin that reflects 'not good enough, not educated enough?'

The point of this is to highlight that education as we practise it has inbuilt anxiety that needs to be more carefully managed. We are living in a society where it is possible to be examined, assessed and evaluated from childhood to elderhood and we have given little thought to the impact of this on ourselves or on our children as we set this as a norm in society. This is bizarre, given that we know that one of the key blocks to effective learning is anxiety!

Education – the bright side

So what has all of this to do with examinations? Put simply, success at exams is *perceived* to protect against negative social conditions. Parents see education as a way of improving the lot of children and of society as a whole.

Parents hope that education will:

- enhance the quality of life for children
- enable them to make better-quality friends
- ultimately get them rewarding employment
- mean that that they will bring home better-quality boyfriends and girlfriends
- be able to afford to put a good-quality roof over their heads.

With such potential rewards it is no surprise that parents worry about exams, exam results and the consequences of these results. Teenagers will not worry about these in the same way and herein lies a source of misunderstanding and tension between parents and their adolescent children.

Teenagers may worry about exam performance, but the longer-term consequences are of little interest as they continue to see the world with (age-appropriate) idealistic values. The future is far away for them and 'everything will sort itself out'!

It is very difficult as a fifteen- or seventeen-year-old to fully comprehend the importance of the future in concrete terms when there is so much of that future ahead of you.

It is better to try and enjoy the here and now and let parents worry about job prospects.

Teenagers carry a sense that the world owes them something and therefore, in their thinking, poor exam outcome (as defined by teacher or parental values) can be compensated for at a later stage if it is that important. This compensation can take the form of repeating exams, taking a year out, doing another course, getting a job with opportunities for training built into it.

It is worth bearing in mind that there is some truth in this. Most parents of adolescents and the teachers of these children were brought up in an age where if you did not 'get the Leaving Cert', your chances in life were deemed to be highly restricted. Thankfully, that day is gone.

It is now possible to access university as a mature student with or without a Leaving Certificate. It is possible to study at third level in most subject areas without any formal second-level education. It is possible to engage in training and vocational courses that will lead to formal recognition in a range of work areas that were previously deemed as only for those who 'failed'.

It is possible to sit Leaving Certificate subjects at any age after the magical but mythical age of eighteen. It is even possible to sit different types of Leaving Certificate. In other words, today's teenagers have opportunities way beyond those available to their parents even two decades ago.

TOP TIPS

1. Education is important, but supporting the development of a content teenager is even more so. Education is only one part of their life experience.
2. Become aware of the amount of anxiety that surrounds learning and try not to add to it with unnecessary pressure or 'dodgy' future predictions.
3. Teenagers will not see the future as you predict it – they're probably better off!

Parents and exams – the fear of failure

So what happens to parents when their children enter the exam years? Probably, and most important in my view, their own experience and memory of being examined is resurrected along with the anxiety that they endured at that time.

From a psychological perspective this is a fairly standard but often forgotten reaction in stress situations, i.e. long after a stressful event, small reminders and triggers can set off a flood of memories that relate to the original incident.

Therefore, at exam time, parents' interaction with their children is influenced by the fear that their children will not do well enough. This fear reflects their own original fear when they were doing exams.

Some of this anxiety may be useful but most of it is not helpful in creating the type of supportive atmosphere required for learning. Too much of it leads to conversations that end up in the well-practised phrase, 'go to your room and study', which is more often used out of frustration and as a last-resort solution.

The anxiety of generations of family afraid that they will let their children down in some way that will ultimately lead to catastrophe is often caught up in such useless phrases as, 'I can't get him to study' or 'I've tried everything to make her study.'

Given that the teenager often does not experience the quality of worry that the parent experiences, the question must be asked as to whom is really being examined. In working with families, it often strikes me that there are a number of stakeholders other than the teenager who act as they if they are being examined.

Given that this is not actually the case, I have to assume that they are *feeling* as if they are being examined. It is this assumption that can undermine the creation of healthy study conditions for teenagers about to sit exams.

Parents under the spotlight

Parents fear that they will have failed their child if he does not do well. They are afraid that their failure will be catastrophic for the child. They also have to contend with long-held family attitudes regarding success, mastery and competence. They may even have to mourn the loss of their own educational dreams for their child as it becomes clear he will struggle with maths, languages or science.

Many parents speak of guilt in relation to the now common practice of parents working outside the home. Parents have described the guilt at not helping with their children's homework because they are uncomfortable about their own ability, particularly in the subject areas that are new in the curriculum since their schooldays.

Parents describe the struggle of managing their own feelings of incompetence when trying to grasp new subject areas. They are afraid that this incompetence might be seen by their children as a weakness. They were brought up with the lesson that 'parents know it all' and they struggle to say, 'I just don't know, but let's work out how to find out.'

Parents struggling to keep pace with financial demands report frustration at not being able to provide all the extra tuition, summer schools and intensive study courses that they are led to believe should be an integral part of the educational experience for children today.

Parents carry with them recent memories of hard times when economic and social outlooks were bleak. The experience of national achievement is not yet a generation old and will not remove so easily the clearly etched images of mass emigration and unemployment welfare queues. Particularly when those same images are becoming part of the daily news diet again.

The rapidity with which current debates about recession have replaced the consumer confidence of recent years shows how close to the surface the old fears live in the collective memory of the nation.

Equally, parents of teenagers can access the uncomfortable memories of their own school experience, which in all likelihood was based on a principle of fail or success, with little comfort in between. Not to mention the often horrible experience that many parents actually had in school at the hands of authoritarian individual teachers and regimes.

Interestingly, what parents very often fail to acknowledge is the fact that they were never instructed on how to support the learning needs of their children. So while it is useful to encourage young children to learn by repetition and using rote memory, using the same techniques with teenagers, who are equipped to manage more abstract and complex learning techniques, is a wasted opportunity.

We need to go beyond the idea of filling them with information. Parents need to redefine the role of their child as an active participant in his own learning. He is not a blank page waiting to be coloured in by someone else.

TOP TIPS

1. Your anxiety is yours – don't throw it in the direction of the teenager just because she is not that concerned about school.
2. Teach your teenagers how to manage their learning by asking how you can support them, not by telling them what to do.
3. Teenagers need to hear you say, 'I don't know.' You need to hear yourself say, 'I don't know.'

Teaching teens how to learn

People tend to have different learning styles, but this does not appear to have permeated into the daily practice of being a parent. So there is little information available to parents as to whether their child learns better by image or sound, whether she is a predominantly logical thinker or a more creative thinker, whether she learns more quickly in groups or as an individual.

If you take a step back from your child and remember the subjects that he is best at or enjoys the most, you will learn a lot about his learning style. A lot of time can be wasted trying to force a teenager into studying something in a way that really does not suit. For example, there is little point in forcing a quiet, reflective teenager into a learning group. He will often learn better on his own. But the active, practical thinker will flourish in the group.

Similarly, parents may be surprised to learn that little may be genuinely learned in a two-hour cramming session but that really useful material can be learned in short study bursts with breaks in between. Short study periods with specific study tasks followed by breaks will hold the attention of the teenager. They will also break up the monotony and distraction that goes with sessions that last for hours on end.

Supporting the learning needs of teenagers is still often reduced to how much time was spent in a room (often a bedroom) studying. Few parents are armed with the know-how to judge quality learning and fewer still are willing to chance that quality learning can often happen with friends, in fun ways that do not include pain and drudgery. Here are some ways to be more effective as a learning support to your teenager.

Supporting your teenager's learning

1. Learn about how your child learns.
2. Talk to him about this.
3. Ask teachers about how he learns best.
4. Offer yourself as a sounding board for his ideas.
5. Agree to have friends around for shared learning time on school projects.
6. You don't need to know all the detail – use your common sense to judge whether something seems logical or well presented.
7. Surprise him by highlighting what is good in his learning.
8. Balance the need for learning with the need for breaks.
9. Not everyone is Einstein – acknowledge his limitations and don't waste too much valuable time trying to secure insignificant changes to them.
10. Set up support networks with other parents to learn from how they support their teenager during the exam years.
11. Ensure that he gets physical exercise.
12. Make sure he gets good-quality nutrition.

Intelligent parenting doesn't worry about intelligence

Parents also make a decision about whether their child is 'intelligent' or not. This assumes that they actually know fully what it means and also that the examining system actually examines it. Both of these assumptions are most likely to be inaccurate.

Intelligence does not mean the material in or the grade for a language or science paper. Neither does it mean a particular score on an 'intelligence test', although this historical use of the term may help to explain parents' rather narrow view of intelligence. This is only part of the story.

Intelligence is much more sophisticated than that and nowadays it is actually taken to mean a number of important abilities. These include:

1. the ability to deal with abstract concepts such as morality
2. the ability to solve problems in ways other than simply using previous experience
3. the ability to learn and especially to be able to use symbols to enhance learning, i.e. short cuts to learning
4. and especially, the ability to use emotions in understanding and building relationships that can be used to enhance personal growth.

So in talking and thinking about intelligence, parents need to be able to see the broad spectrum that this entails in order not to miss out on the learning potential of their child. Even if a child struggles with general mental ability – ability to be an average performer across all the components that make up intelligence – she may well do very well in areas where she has what is called 'domain-specific knowledge'. This refers to being very good at particular things but not at everything.

This is often the basis of the biography of many a successful person when they tell the story of failing every exam at school but becoming very wealthy through business, music or playing football. Their *specific* knowledge and skill ensured success, not their *general* ability.

An example that comes to mind is the English footballer, David Beckham, a gifted footballer and very wealthy businessman. I can recall numerous occasions after a Beckham interview when he was castigated for being unable to put a sentence together correctly. As if this really mattered to him when he was so good at what he did.

Exams measure little and often!

This does lead to another assumption about exams: that they measure intelligence. They do not and they cannot. They measure some of the parts that make up some intelligence, and by and large only those that we can capture on paper. Exams as currently designed will not be able to give a result that tells you that your son is the next Beckham because 'bending it like Beckham' is not on the curriculum.

Neither, for that matter, is the art of being a Michelin-starred chef or how to be the head coach of the Irish rugby team, yet both of these professions require tremendous intelligence at a number of levels in order to be successful.

My point here is that the parents of today's generation of teenagers were brought up at a time when intelligence simply meant the scores that were achieved on one or two dates in their lives. What was tested was a narrow range of subjects that impact on life. It is important to avoid that narrow perspective when thinking about our own children's abilities and potential.

Essentially, what parents rely on when judging learning and trying to enhance its quality for their children is the message that they carry around about studying from their own schooldays. This message is often flawed because it is based on anxiety and fear of catastrophe (inherited from history and cultural influences).

It is this message that also triggers the intense anxiety parents have about exams. This is what makes it seem as if they are the ones who will sit at the exam desk and turn the pages of the exam script.

So it seems to me that parents, with all the best intentions, employ two of the worst techniques in an effort to ward off their own inherited anxiety about the importance of success at exams and the catastrophe of failure at exams.

1. They monitor that their children are getting and doing homework (as if by some miraculous process this equates to learning).
2. They believe that sending a teenager to his room for hours of study is the same thing as hours of learning being achieved.

Doing homework is only useful if your teenager is actually learning something. So ask questions that set out to check this. Or have them act as teacher to you to see if they can explain what they have learned. Have a friend come around and encourage the pair to examine each other to check what they have learned and what they have missed.

Good-quality learning can occur in short chunks of time. The hours of study can be broken down into ten- or twenty-minute segments and each of these segments can show learning. Have breaks after the segments to allow for information to settle in the memory.

We all need to manage the anxiety associated with learning and exams, simply because we know that anxiety blocks how and what we learn. It disturbs the pathways in our brains that allow memory to store material. It makes us tired, thus reducing the amount that we learn. But above all else it hampers the enjoyment that can come from learning.

TOP TIPS FOR MANAGING ANXIETY

1. Become aware of the physical reactions you have when you get anxious, e.g. a knot in the stomach, headache, feeling hot, etc.
2. Stay focused on the here and now and identify how you can ease the physical reactions you experience.
3. Stop trying to predict the future or crystal-ball an outcome. Work with what you can influence.

Teachers – their importance in the family loop

In this country there is a very strong relationship between the general population and its teachers. Many have positive experiences and memories of their teachers, but for others this is not the case. Either way, most nations use the teaching profession as the mechanism by which the intellectual capacity of the country is developed, maintained and passed on through the generations.

Analysis of the daily responsibilities of the teaching profession unveils a range of roles and duties that go well beyond the standard definition of what being a teacher is. Teachers are expected to:

*   act as the knowledgeable mentors of our children
*   carry responsibility for carefully developing future talent upon which continued economic and social success can be sustained

- assess for difficulties that might impede the talent of their students
- regulate moral development through modelling and instructing on social norms, values and achievement-oriented goals.

Teaching is one of very few professions that is regularly benchmarked against stark black and white standards of achievement, that being the success or otherwise of their students at state examination time. Such quantifiable and openly available information is currently the subject of possible further delineation in the form of school league tables, like those seen in the United Kingdom. To my mind parents currently have more than enough information to make decisions about teachers' competence.

Such annual results are often judged by parents and public alike as an indicator of the competence and capacity of the teacher. There is little reference made to the result being a product of the interaction between the teacher and the pupil or the teacher, school, student and family. In other words, exam results are often the end product of a set of relationships. Like all relationships, it takes two to tango. Focusing only on the role of the teacher misses the input of the student, the rest of the school and, in particular, parents.

Undoubtedly teachers have an enormous influence on the day-to-day experience of a young person in school. However, they have also become like an additional member of the family. They have contact with your teenager for seven hours a day. They watch his unfolding personality over a six-year period. They have access to thousands of pieces of information about him and can offer opinions on a whole host of important issues for him. Critically, they have a relationship with your teenager that needs to developed and nurtured in order for it to work.

Teachers are a key influence in how student motivation is first triggered and then turned into something useful for teenagers. Parents need to assist teachers in the practices outlined below, which have been shown to support student motivation. They can do this by maintaining regular contact with teachers, sitting on parents' councils, volunteering to assist with extra-curricular school activities, not always taking sides against teachers when teenagers are complaining and by asking teenagers how they support the teacher in the school.

In other words, parents, not just teachers, have responsibility for how the school community works. The following suggestions require parents to ask teachers how they are being carried out in class and if there is something that parents can do to ensure their success.

Supporting student motivation in the classroom

1. Teaching and grading practices that stress individual improvement rather than comparison to others.
2. Adopting practices that reflect high teacher expectations for all students' performance.
3. Adopting practices that ensure all students participate fully in learning activities in the classroom.
4. Using practices that involve hands-on activities.
5. Using practices that support student independence and decision-making.
6. Ensuring that teaching practices are compatible with the student's culture and home values insofar as is reasonable.
7. Generating teaching practices that help students understand the importance and the wider meaning of what they are being taught.

References

While the ideas, opinions and advice in this book are the author's, they are a culmination of evidence drawn from his clinical experience in conjunction with findings from psychological research. To that end, the following texts were used as reference material in the preparation of this book.

Adolescence (8th edn). John W. Santrock. McGraw-Hill: Boston; London, 2001.

Adolescent Coping: Theoretical and Research Perspectives. Erica Frydenberg. Routledge: London; New York, 1997.

Blackwell Handbook of Adolescence. Gerald Adams and Michael Berzonsky (eds). Oxford : Blackwell, 2005.

The Handbook of Child and Adolescent Clinical Psychology (2nd edn). Alan Carr. Routledge: London, 2006.

The Nature of Adolescence (3rd edn). John Coleman and Leo Hendry. Routledge: London, 2000.

8. Enhancing practices that create a positive and supportive teacher–student relationship.
9. Adopting practices that create a positive and supportive peer climate for all students.

All of the above seem to place strong responsibility on the teacher. However, if you look closely at them you will see that what is at the heart of these factors is the relationship between the teenager and the teacher. Parents, not teachers, ultimately determine how their child approaches this relationship.

Parents teach lessons about how to relate to authority and how to negotiate with this authority. Parents model respect and courtesy. Parents teach about assertiveness if the relationship is not fair and reasonable. Parents show the way on good manners and decency. In other words, parents provide the platform for how their teenager triggers the support role of the teacher.

Bridging the classroom and the outcome

In terms of the current pressure to link what actually happens in the classroom to academic outcomes there is a growing consensus in research to suggest that the following strategies are important. Parents therefore need to ask about these when they meet teachers and when they are looking at what school policies exist to support the teacher in bringing them about.

From learner to achiever

1. Students are asked to construct or produce knowledge rather than just reproducing facts and views expressed by teachers.
2. Disciplined inquiry in which teenagers are encouraged to engage in deep thinking that requires them to communicate their ideas in elaborate forms.
3. The work of students in school should be valued and recognised as being important beyond the school and classroom.
4. Regular feedback on progress so that students understand what they know and what they still need to learn and master.
5. Abundant opportunities to rethink one's work and clarify understanding.
6. Various teaching methods that recognise individual differences in levels of current knowledge, interests and learning styles and provide multiple ways of learning new material and demonstrating that learning.
7. Co-operative and highly interactive learning activities that allow students to work with each other and allow teachers to work with them in designing interesting learning activities.
8. Active instruction in the thinking skills that are needed to monitor one's own learning and progress.

We can dump all woes on the teacher!

Earlier in this chapter, I looked at intelligence and how parents might view intelligence. It is equally important for teachers to be aware of the tension between what they have to deliver in the classroom in order to be able to show that they have supported the 'state-defined' view of intelligence and what the psychological reality of intelligence is for the young person.

Teacher education programmes at universities strive to promote the idea that the student is much more than the sum of individual exam performances. Maintaining such thinking in the actual school system is much more difficult, given the pressure to produce all-round exam performers, even when this is not realistic. No matter what is said, exam results will still hold sway in parents' and students' eyes alike. Perhaps we need to examine differently or examine qualities other than ability to regurgitate facts. Our teenagers have so much more than that to offer.

My point here is that the profession of teaching is one that in many ways is strongly influenced by the normal anxiety associated with achievement. The difficulty in dealing with this is exacerbated because many of the factors are outside the immediate control of the teacher who is perceived as being responsible for them.

In that sense, the process of examining is as much about the teacher, and how he manages the associated stress related to the potential outcomes of his students, as it is about the student. Because the teacher is the one in front of the class, he is an easy target for the anxiety of parents and students. We must be careful and responsible that we only dump on teachers what they are responsible for. They have too much to offer to be carrying around our unwanted fears and worries.

School – the new member of the extended family

The school itself – its staff, students and infrastructure – is continuously being examined. Secondary school is where society has decided that its teenagers should spend seven hours a day (or more if involved in extra-curricular activity including study time, sports, etc.). There are dining halls, sports halls, school shops, school banks, homework clubs, exam study time, outdoor pursuits trips, foreign exchange schemes and a host of other educational and social domains related to the work of school. School is a tremendous hub of creativity and activity.

In other words, schools are communities with their own hierarchies, regulations, disciplinary mechanisms and reward schemes. Therefore, like any community, a school is under constant scrutiny with regard to how it performs in relation to its own goals. It is also being assessed in relation to the goals set by government at one end and parents at the other. No easy living here for members of this community.

School is also the place where the fantasy of the perfect education is expected to be made a reality. Parents send their children to school out of a moral sense of duty that is based on the notion that it is the best place for a child to receive an education. There is little questioning of this assumption in general conversation.

Parents assume that teaching will be of the highest quality but have little knowledge of how this quality can be measured. They have to assume that learning will be experienced in a manner uniquely tailored to their child without themselves knowing what this actually is. In other words, there is a lot of soft thinking associated with the education process. And like many fantasies, when we cannot make them a reality ourselves, we hand over the responsibility for them to another source – in this case, the school.

The difficulty with this is that we see it as our responsibility to hand over the responsibility. Handing over becomes the job. We think of this as the end in itself and create a set of beliefs to support this job. Beliefs such as:

- we have the right to set standards of achievement for the school

- the school will somehow set the needs of our own child on at least an equal par with those of others
- this will be done at all times
- we have an undeniable right to be annoyed if we deem the school to have failed the child.

Sometimes it sounds like we have become experts in school assessment simply because our child attends the school.

Some of these beliefs are valid, but the school and what it symbolises (our hopes and fantasies for our children) in many ways has to constantly scan the environment for the possible threat of accusation from parents and the state. Schools are essentially being examined both formally and informally and are subject to the normal anxiety that goes hand in hand with this.

Teachers do not perform in a vacuum: they are themselves influenced by the school atmosphere and culture within which the school operates. This refers to its own philosophy, ethos, policies and procedures, which form the foundation for how it delivers its key educational goals and objectives. Indeed, in keeping with the theme of relationships, a key relationship for any young person in many ways is the one that exists between him and the school. It's like another member of the family – one he spends seven hours a day with.

Very new research in this whole area examines what it is that makes school such a key relationship for young people. The understanding of school simply as a place where knowledge is imparted and exams are suffered is a major underestimation of the complexity of the type of relationship that exists between the young person and the school community.

School as surrogate parents

Some research goes so far as to suggest that the relating styles between the young person and the school mirror the relating styles between the young person and the family unit. Parents therefore need to build and sustain a relationship with the school. It is no longer a case of sending your child to school; it is about being actively involved with the community that is the school so that it works to its potential to enhance the development of your child.

It has been my experience that teenagers from secure, warm and supporting families tend to be able to trigger a similar environment in their school by virtue of how they get the various players in the school to interact with them. I have also worked with young people from psychologically disadvantaged families who have enough resilience themselves to be able to use the school environment as one of their only sources (but a hugely powerful one) of positive experience. This helps them to develop with a reasonable chance of experiencing healthy self-esteem, or at the least to counteract the unhealthy aspects of their home or neighbourhood.

If this is the case, schools need to be influenced by parents to exhibit certain characteristics that enable both the learning environment and the personal development environment for the young person to be enhanced. Such characteristics may include:

- a curriculum based on rigorous academic standards and current knowledge about how students learn best
- a curriculum that is relevant to the concerns of young people
- teaching methods that are designed to prepare all students to achieve the highest standards for them
- educators who are trained experts at teaching young people
- ongoing professional development opportunities for the staff involved with young people
- organisational structures that support the climate of intellectual development

- organisational structures that support a caring community climate with shared educational goals
- democratic governance that involves both the adults and the young people who attend the school
- extensive involvement of parents and the local community
- high levels of safety and practices that support good health.

Schools have direct responsibility for many of these characteristics, but my contention is that parents are also part of the school community. Therefore you have a responsibility for seeing whether the school is working to sustain your child.

Teenagers also have a responsibility for these characteristics. They will respond to this responsibility if they are central to how the school is managed. They will react less favourably if they are dictated to or treated as if their voice is less relevant.

What I want to highlight is that children and adolescents are processed through an educational system that has a strong undercurrent of anxiety. This has to be managed by a school system that is perceived as being the place where untested assumptions of parents will be delivered in a way which will set up the child for measurable success. This success will then lead to the ultimate delivery of parental dreams and wishes. No small order there!

Ultimately everyone involved is in some way being examined right through the educational experience. We don't like being examined so regularly. It is therefore no wonder that time for reflection on the process through which we channel and support the intellect of the future generations is sparse in parental conversations with their children. We prefer to think that it will be all right.

TOP TIPS

1. Stress the importance of improvement in learning rather than exam performance, in order to contain anxiety.
2. Create meaningful relationships with key school staff to enhance your sense of investment in your teenager's education.
3. With your teenager, promote the idea of his individual responsibility for improving the school experience for all involved. Every little helps.

Revolutionising the relationship with education

Is there, therefore, a need for a revolution in how we think about the journey for children and teenagers through the educational system? What do we do with research that suggests that neither classroom size nor the use of homework holds the magic key to successful academic outcomes for our young people? In a world of amazing technological advances, will the school as a building become redundant as children sit at home learning in virtual classrooms?

Key questions need to be addressed by parents so that the future development of young people is not hampered by the fear created by a pass/fail educational system. Such questions include the following.

1. Is there a need for an educational system for parents that teaches them about learning styles, multiple intelligences, peer learning groups, etc. so that they can be as up to date as possible with what works and does not work in learning?
2. Should parents and teachers be sent on courses together so that both understand the context in which teenagers learn?

3. How could we go about making teachers key relationship partners to the teenager and the family?
4. Above all, do we need to sit back and examine the impact of an educational system that primarily defines success as what happens in one set of results after spending fourteen years in school?

If all the stakeholders in the education journey are under constant examination, surely all should have access to the type of good-quality information that highlights how to manage successfully the examination process and the anxiety that it is built on. It is not fair or reasonable to leave teachers or young people to bear the responsibility for academic outcomes when in fact those outcomes should be more genuinely seen as the property of parental and family aspirations.

If we define success and achievement on the basis of one examination, we are also defining achievement as that which places each individual in some position in a hierarchy that is determined by individual talents, motivation and performance on a given day. This is not necessarily a bad thing in itself.

But there are alternatives. What if exams were not about individual performance but instead looked at the following?

1. The ability to produce a required set of outcomes based on group or team performance.
2. The ability to design a project that has a positive impact on the local community.
3. The more important tasks of reading, spelling and writing in ways that allow for clear expression of thinking.

If, as popular representations suggest, teenagers are grumpy, irritable, self-interested individuals, why reinforce this in education by continuing to have exams that reward individual performance? If we want to stop anti-social, loutish behaviour, is there not a parallel responsibility to educate about the principles and practices of more acceptable behaviour?

What rewards might we see in twenty years' time if education based on the principles of community spirit, individual responsibility and effective relating was resourced in order to undermine the self-interested, winner-takes-all philosophy that is all too prevalent in society today?

The education system in all developed countries is a massive societal undertaking and is no mean achievement to operate on a day-to-day basis. That is why it may hold much potential for how a society influences the evolution of its own development. The question that forms the title of this chapter was set to highlight the fact that the notion that it is only our young people who are subject to its influence is false.

Every member of society is in some way examined in terms of what we allow or do not allow to be taught in our schools and colleges. The philosophies that underlie the practices within schools are open to influence by parents and teenagers if they choose to take this responsibility on. Each parent of a school-going child has responsibility for ensuring that their child is helping to foster the community spirit found in the school and the wider community. The thousands of teenagers who receive important exam results at the end of each summer are, in many ways, symbols of what adults want in society.

And finally . . .

What the education system deems as being teenagers' success becomes our success and what it labels as failure represents our failure to get the best from our young people. More important, the things they are actually successful (or otherwise) at reflect the values that we identify with and cherish in the society that we live in.

If we continue to choose to eulogise 'A' grade academic achievement without a similar commitment to respect, worthiness, collective achievement, dignity and social responsibility, in twenty years, as the parents of today's generation of teenagers move into their senior years, locked gates and security pads will offer little resistance to the power of self-interest that we have further enhanced through the educational system.

CHAPTER 10

Boyfriends, Girlfriends, Neither or Both

Relationships are central to all human beings in terms of sustenance, support, pleasure, connection and fulfilment. For something so central, it is harder to imagine an area that fills parents with more anxiety than the sudden realisation that their teenager has the capacity and desire to enter into relationships in a way they have not previously experienced.

What is changing?

Of course, what was not previously experienced was the new capacity for romantic relationships and the potential for sexual activity. There is hardly another area of a young person's life that is so intense and meaningful to them and so filled with trepidation for their guardians. Tackling the issue really does feel like skating on very thin ice for parents. Teenagers curl up and cringe and the whole subject takes on a life of its own and sits like the elephant in the room that no one really wants to see.

We still cling to the rather rose-tinted notion that in the old days, teenagers had romantic desires but that in some way these were kept in check by an authoritarian society and strict parental discipline. It also helped that there was a lack of money for socialisation. The sheer power of being embarrassed into maintaining proper social standards by an ever-watching, religion-bound society also prevailed. Or did it?

A conversation with most thirty- and forty-somethings of today will quickly debunk this myth. Romantic desire, physical passion and broken hearts are not new to parents. In some way this explains parents' fear and occasional paranoia about the relationship lives of their teenagers – they know what they 'got up to' at that age and have to assume their children will do the same!

Is there an area that makes parents of teenagers more anxious than having to confront the reality of their sexual child? Their 'little one' is now capable of not only engaging in full sexual activity but in actually deriving pleasure from it. This then increases the likelihood that they might want it to become a normal part of their relationship lives. Shiver at the thought!

Teenage sex – maybe it's just another one of those myths

What do we know about current teenage sexual behaviour? To be blunt, it does not make for very comfortable reading if you are a parent hoping that your child will reach adulthood before fantasising about sex and all its associations. Research pertaining to western countries including Ireland has reported that fifteen per cent of men and eight per cent of women first engaged in sex when they were under sixteen years old.

A majority of the women in that group (sixty per cent) and more than a third of the men report that they subsequently regretted their early introduction to sexual activity. Wisdom with hindsight.

Most people now in their twenties will have had their first sexual experience before they were eighteen. How big a difference is this from forty years ago? Again, research tells us that the most common age at which men currently sixty years old had their first sexual experience was twenty, while for women it was twenty-three.

However, our focus here is the fact that currently, for people under the age of twenty-five, the age of their first sexual experience is, on average, seventeen years. What this fact also tells us is that if the average is seventeen, there are some children under that age who have began to explore their sexual identity through actual sexual behaviour.

Teenagers, our children, our 'little ones' are sexually active. Fact, not myth.

The implication of this is that we have to get our heads out of the proverbial sand, stop wondering and fretting about what and if teenagers do with their relationship and sexual lives and start talking to them directly about relationships, friendships, sexuality and sexual behaviour. Seems obvious when you read it. Reality hits a hard slap at the obvious when we start to examine what is still the experience for most teenagers today with regard to preparation for developing this crucial part of their identity.

TOP TIPS

1. The move into romantic relationships is a normal part of teenage development.
2. Begin conversations about relationships in the childhood years and let them evolve into sexual development slowly.
3. Work with the notion that your teenager is interested in sex and see what fears it raises for you. Decide whether you want to hand these fears on.

Are parents ready and able?

Often when I ask parents about how they have managed the process of talking to their children, and particularly their teenage children, about matters related to sex and sexuality, they will answer assuredly that they had no problem in telling their children about the 'facts of life'. This is indeed a positive step forward in our capacity to act in an adult way about something that is fundamental to the very existence of the human being.

It is also hopelessly inadequate, however. Few parents in my experience *talk with* their children about the facts of life. Most parents *tell* their children about *some* of the facts of life.

It will hardly be news to most thirteen-year-olds that if a sexually able and active teenage boy and girl have unprotected sexual intercourse there is a chance that the girl can become pregnant as a result of the dynamic interaction between a sperm and an ovum. Yet this is often what teenagers are left with after talking to parents.

Consider the following challenges to parents regarding how we handle education about sexual development.

1. How many parents and teenagers have had the discussion regarding sexuality and how it develops and changes over time, not because of any confusion but simply because that is how it works?
2. How many parents can comfortably explain to themselves what the significant influences on their own sexual development were, let alone use these to form the basis of a useful discussion for the teenager?
3. How many parents can explain to their children why being gay or lesbian still causes difficulties for some people in Ireland?
4. How many parents still use coded messages regarding underage sex and pregnancy as a means of controlling this aspect of the child's behaviour?
5. How as a parent would you support your child who insists on having full sexual intercourse?

Do we really have to?

Does my opinion that parents are not involved enough hold up with what we are informed by research? It seems so.

Research findings show that ninety-two per cent of people think that young people should get education on sexual intercourse, sexual feelings, contraception, safer sex, sexually transmitted infections and homosexuality. Eighty per cent think it should be provided in the home. This is good news – we draw satisfaction from acknowledging that this aspect of human lives is deserving of our time and attention in the place that has the potential to be the most influential – the home.

However, only twenty-one per cent of men and thirty-eight per cent of women under twenty-five have received sex education in the home.

Among those aged under twenty-five, nearly two-thirds of men and almost half of women did not find it easy to talk to their parents about sex. Something is wrong here.

If most of us think that education on sexual health, sexuality and sexual behaviour should be carried out within the home, and then most of us do not follow through on this, what type of conflicting message is being given to teenagers?

I believe it is a message that is perceived as confusing by teenagers. It goes something like, 'Your sexual development is important so long as someone else deals with it – until that time keep it away from this house.' I do not think that this is intended by parents but it is often the result felt by teenagers.

Remember that they now have the mental capacity to decipher subtle messages, contradictions and indeed hypocrisies. In other words, they spot the hidden embarrassment, shame and awkwardness that underlie the 'zone of discomfort' surrounding sex-related discussions. They then go on to make those feelings part of what their own sexuality means to them.

I am not arguing that we have to share all the information we have gathered on sex and sexuality with our young children. I am strongly advocating that by the age of eighteen years, adolescents should be armed with a fair and accurate representation of our understanding of this, if it is accepted that it is part of the responsibility of parents to mentor and guide development of young people.

And if parents struggle with doing this themselves, how will they support others who may be in a position to influence access to good-quality information regarding sexual information?

A case in point is parents who have struggled to accept that their teenage son or daughter is sexually active. Perhaps their final words on the matter are 'be safe, use protection'.

Here are my challenges to this.

1. Who teaches the teenager how to put on a condom?
2. How is their knowledge about contraception and how safe is it to assume that the method used is reasonable and practical?
3. Would you as a parent or teacher bring home a prosthetic penis or vagina and show the adolescent how exactly a condom (male or female) is worn?
4. If not, what are your reactions to making this type of education available through other channels?
5. How would you react if your child came home and reported that he had gone to the local GP to ask for the contraceptive pill for his girlfriend?
6. How would you react if you found a packet of contraceptive pills in your daughter's bedroom?

Now I'm really worried!

These are exactly the questions that need to be asked to try to move us on to a more mature approach to sexual education. You are responsible enough to work with your children on potty training, hand washing and teeth brushing. It must therefore become acceptable for you to ensure that practical sexual health education is a normal part of the developmental relationship between you and your children. It cannot be normal if as adults we skulk around it, terrorised by our own old stories regarding the deficiencies in this part of our lives.

If we struggle with this aspect of sex education, the consequences of unprotected sexual activity will prove even more difficult to manage. There is plenty of evidence that this is the case, with reported cases of sexually transmitted infections on a rapid upward curve. Such diseases can have extremely serious long-term health consequences for individuals and society.

As teenagers 'don't do' long-term, there is a particular onus on adults to be proactive in education that is informative, accurate and preventative. And parents need to do this in the here and now.

TOP TIPS

1. Education begins in the home – buy the books, get the manuals, talk to other parents. Get informed.
2. Learn about your own shame about the sexual side of your personality and try not to let this become part of how you relate to your teenager.
3. Don't talk to or tell teenagers about their development. Talk with them. You don't know what it is like for them, so ask and learn.

Do what and how?

1. First of all, arm yourself with accurate information from reliable sources.

2. Prepare to share with your teenager new things that you have learned.

3. Pre-empt some of the questions that might come your way from your teenager.

4. Do not commit the 'sit down, we need to have a talk' sin. There is no better way to sabotage your own efforts than to clumsily harass a teenager into a sex conversation. There is also no need to do this.

There are plenty of naturally occurring opportunities for conversations like this to be triggered by issues on TV soaps, magazine stories about teenage icons, relationship issues in the wider family, etc. Parents need to have their homework done so that they carry a confidence into the discussion that the teenager can react to. They also need the confidence to be able to say, 'I don't know' or 'Let's find out' should this be needed.

It is also worth considering how you will tell them about your own development. We tell children about lots of other aspects of our lives as we grew up. Why should sexual development be any different?

This does not mean going into every detail about every aspect of you sexual and relationship life. You can be open about to the joys and struggles of falling in love, having a crush on someone, how desire can almost take over your life, having your heart broken. You know, the normal stuff.

And it is that stuff that can naturally lead to specific conversations about sex, sexuality, healthy sex, unhealthy sex, pregnancy, contraception, etc.

Being tongue-tied about sex is no fun

I am constantly curious as to why it is that sex and all its related topics hold such a disabling influence on many parents. How is it that normally functioning, able and fluent people become completely tongue-tied when it comes to open conversation about sex with their children?

As with so much of our development, history is important. A sexually repressed state in recent times, a much more liberal state in current times – one possibly as damaging as the other as the generations in between get caught in the substantial swing from one extreme to the other.

One difficulty with sudden cultural shifts is that values and norms that held sway for such a long period of time are abandoned because their usefulness is seen as having been outlived. The abandonment process creates a vacuum until new values are explored, debated and finally embedded into everyday cultural practice.

Human behaviour generally does not function usefully when it exists in a vacuum as people struggle to find new ways of living while the hangover from the old ways still lingers. So today's parents of teenagers find that the values that they grew up with are longer valued. However, society has not yet matured enough to hand them new values that they can use in creating new boundaries and behaviours for their children. There is a knowledge gap.

A related point is the belief that 'anything is better than what we got' and this still has an influence. Many parents of teenagers emerged from the generation of parents who at best struggled and at worst utterly failed to educate, teach and guide on this important aspect of human development. So for today's parents anything they are able to do will be significantly better than what they received. While this is true there is room for much improvement.

TOP TIPS

1. Use normal everyday occurrences to begin conversations about relationships.
2. Identify your own values about sex and sexuality. In a world that is lacking in clear values these can be valuable to a teenager to work out their own.
3. Think back to your own development and identify what would have been useful. Offer this insight to your teenager to see what they think.

It's all normal – don't create a monster

There is a need to normalise our experiences about sex, sexual identity and sexual development. Sexual development (and all its associated concepts, such as gender, identity and orientation) is just another part of our journey through life. It begins in the womb when nature regulates various hormones to determine whether the embryo becomes a boy or girl. It moves through childhood as the environment naturally shapes in different ways the behaviour, thinking and emotional worlds of males and females in both subtle and obvious ways.

As adolescence approaches, nature moves to the forefront with the move to puberty. The capacity to be sexually active and the ability to procreate becomes as much a natural part of us as the depth of a boy's voice or development of breasts in a girl. Sexual development is normal, natural and fundamentally important to who we feel we are. That is not to say there is only one way to experience this. There is plenty of psychological research that shows that the actual experience of sexual development is as unique as each individual.

This is one reason why I am not overly interested in sexual identity as a central focus for this chapter. Sexual identity is simply a label that society creates to categorise what it perceives an aspect of a person's life as being. It narrows down sexuality into primarily whether a person is straight or gay. This is never going to capture the richness and complexity of people's sexual worlds.

When the identity label is applied to teenagers it also reduces their sexual development to a task that has to be achieved and once it is, that's it, done for life. Sometimes it feels like our response to the sexual world of the teenager is to 'keep 'em away from it and keep 'em straight!'

Believe in your responsibility to lead – don't hand over the power

But if sexual development happens to us all it must be what we do with it that creates the problems when we try to communicate and educate about it. Or rather what we do not do with it.

Parents can choose to ignore sex and displace responsibility for its mentoring onto others (schools, peer group, state agencies or government). They can simply hand over their power and responsibility to influence their children by thinking that they don't know how to have these conversations. It's easy to see how this attitude has crept into parenting styles.

After all, how many parents carry useful messages in their armoury which they can draw from when dealing with the topic? Many stall at the conversation, some choke on it, stutter out a few facts and see the job as being done. Others go into denial and hope the government does a good job of it and if it doesn't their energy can be directed at complaining about the state and its inadequate employees.

We can make ourselves helpless with this type of thinking. Handing more and more children's issues over to state agencies or expecting government to become that involved in the daily lives of our children only serves to undermine our power and responsibility to influence our children.

To balance against this, parents need to believe that sexual development is normal and that therefore engaging in conversation with a child about it can be seen as normal. Talking to your child about relationships is not going to produce a girlfriend or boyfriend. Neither is talking to your child going to create a sex-starved teenager.

Talking is much more likely to give your teenager information that is not available to him anywhere else: information that can help him think and make choices rather than just react to schoolyard myth and adolescent boasts. Parents can also deliver this information more usefully than anyone else as they have an understanding of how their child learns best.

When to start

Education about relationships and everything that goes with them needs to start well before puberty. Too many opportunities are missed by the time adolescence comes knocking and it is also likely that the anxiety produced by waiting will lead the parent into the classic trap of simply doing what was done to them.

It is the lead into the teenage years that will determine how a parent and the child can engage in meaningful and useful conversation about sex and the issues that go with it. The influence of avoidance, discomfort and embarrassment will be acutely felt at age thirteen if they have become the atmosphere within which previous relationship-related discussions have been experienced.

Daily life brings ample opportunities for guidance and education on sexual development:

• the arrival of new boyfriends in the extended family
• the marriage of neighbours

- births at home
- friends in school 'getting' new babies
- the content of television soaps.

There are multiple ordinary opportunities to talk freely about this aspect of development without recourse to the 'this is what sex is, don't do it' lesson.

Look, listen and learn from the child

Parents are rightly concerned that their child will not be able for this information. However, parents who are well attuned to their children will know how and what the child can manage. This is a skill that they have to use every day with regard to other aspects of development and in answering questions related to other aspects of living. It is a skill that parents have adopted from as soon as their child began that phase of development that is consumed by one question – 'why'.

Parents make hundreds of decisions based on what they judge the child can make sense of before launching into explanations and justifications – sex doesn't have to be any different. If you do get it wrong it's time for another gift to your child – the gift of saying that you got it wrong, how you got it wrong and what you have learned from the mistake.

It is important to remember that the vast bulk of our communication is not done through words alone and children from infancy onwards are genetically able to decipher and interpret non-verbal communication. If your style of carrying out your parenting duties is one of being passive or avoidant of uncomfortable topics, a child will have learned this well by the time adolescence has arrived.

They will adapt to you by developing a communication style that in some ways mirrors yours. So they will not be that keen on engaging in 'difficult' topics. Hence the need for some real homework on this before you launch in a blind panic into a hugely important area of development.

To do list

1. Know your own struggles with talking about relationships.
2. Work out what it is you are more comfortable with and talk about this first so that you can feel yourself getting comfortable with hearing yourself talk about it.
3. Read parenting blogs and learn from the experiences of others. Many of them will be really familiar to you.
4. Talk to other parents who have been there and done that. Learn that your fears are normal and manageable.

Time to grow up?

Ten years ago, I was in Berlin in a bookshop and I went to the school book section. There were shelves full of books for pre-schoolers and school-age children that showed cartoon pictures of children with all body parts and functions highlighted and named. This is the first step in normalising conversation about sexual development and it can begin early without drama or dread by simply using the natural curiosity-driven behaviour of young children.

Why is that, with young children, 'a hand is a hand, a finger is a finger but a penis is a willy?' How many parents of today's teenagers still struggle with using words like penis, vagina, ejaculation or orgasm when talking to their soon-to-be-adult children? If we expect teenagers to act in a grown-up manner we need to match that by treating their sexual development in a grown-up way.

TOP TIPS

1. Sexual development and how we relate to it is a lifelong experience – there is no need to make it an 'abnormal' event in the life of a teenager.
2. Start early and often with the conversations that children give a cue for with regard to relationships and sexual development.
3. Be attentive to what teenagers can manage at any one time. Little and often maintains learning. Too much conversation provokes anxiety.

Do I have to bare my soul?

Another possible reason why parents hesitate to have rich and detailed conversation with teenagers on issues related to sex, sexuality, sexual emotion and behaviour is the fear that somehow parents will be letting the child into the private world of the parent. This is a reasonable anxiety. Our sexual lives, fantasies and realities are exactly that – ours. They are often rich, exciting, edgy and fantasy-filled. They are used for creating intimacy with partners, self-stimulation and keeping sexual relationships alive and desirable. Sometimes they are embarrassing, painful and full of fear.

Maintaining reasonable boundaries around our private information is fair and proper and teenagers also need to learn that. This does not apply only to the sexual part of our identity – it can also be applied to the financial affairs of the family, the nature of friendships with others or the content of work practices.

With sexual development it is the hiding defensively behind walls of silence or bit-part conversations that, in my view, simply promotes the idea that our sexual worlds are shameful. This is not a message worth maintaining in society today, when we aspire to be free from an imposed sense of shame about ourselves.

Silent sexuality is a breeding ground for shame

I am constantly made aware of the power of shame when I work with adults and teenagers to create their life-story, particularly around the issue of sexual development. This phase of work still comes with a big warning sign that says 'don't go there, I dread talking about this'. Meaningful conversations about the sexual aspects of our lives still remain difficult to handle, despite all our so-called freedom.

I am saddened by the waste of time and energy that goes into maintaining a bedrock of shame as part of the personality. Staying shamed consumes energy because we will try to pretend that it is not really there. It is, however, prevalent in the make-up of so many people as they struggle with the lack of freedom within themselves when it comes to their own story about their sexual development from childhood right through to old age.

The first step in challenging the prevalent psychological distress associated with sexual shame is to make strong efforts not to pass this on to the next generation. Parents need to open up the communication lines to ensure this.

How will my teenager respond?

As with most subjects for conversations with teenagers, the topic of sex, sexuality and sexual development can be challenging, rewarding and informative. Most adolescents will converse openly and genuinely about a range of important sexual issues when the atmosphere of the environment that this occurs in is neutral and not overly judgmental. In other words, keep it ordinary. Don't wander into warnings or dire predictions. And if the conversation runs out, let it go. There will be plenty of other opportunities.

What I have learned from teenagers is that they have soaked up a message from their families along the lines that non-judgmental conversation is not often possible in the home environment. Sexual development is not a safe topic. And while broaching the various sex topics *in general* may be possible in many families, broaching the various sex topics *specifically* in relation to the individual teenager is more often than not a no-go area.

I have also learned from teenagers that a critical objective for them is not communication about sex itself. They will talk more with parents about their underlying beliefs about issues relating to sex and sexuality. If a teenager believes that you will be defensive, embarrassed or put off by such a conversation, he will not initiate it. My challenge to both the teenager and the parent is to try to find out where this attitude emerged from.

Information, misinformation, disinformation

Much of the information that teenagers hold comes from peers and it is inaccurate. This is also the case with beliefs about parents and their ability to remain steady and educative with regard to sex. In other words, teenagers believe that a parent is unable to have a conversation about sex because that is what they have heard from their peers.

As a parent, you need to undermine this potential myth by initiating conversations when opportune moments arise. Otherwise, your teenager will be left trying to work out your ability and motivation to talk about sex. And I hope that by now you have learned that trying to work out how others think is a fairly fruitless operation.

It's not just the kids who are growing up

Of course the realisation that your child has a boyfriend or girlfriend (or both) is a big sign of a developmental shift in growing up for both you and your child. It can be easy to see everything as being focused on what is happening for the teenager, but of course, like all relationships, a change on one side produces a change to the other side. This is why engaging with children can be simultaneously so rewarding and exhausting.

Every developmental shift for them produces one for you, so there is a need for constant response and adjustment to who you are as a person but also to who you are as a parent.

Parents often feel they are on thin ice when they suddenly realise that their daughter has found a boyfriend and they are unsure about her understanding of sexually transmitted diseases, morning after pills or emotional readiness for such a relationship. Picking up on the subtle hints that a son has a girlfriend can trigger thoughts of 'at least he can't get pregnant'.

Parents delve into memory to see what they were doing at the same age and realise that their son or daughter is relatively far ahead of them, and they flounder, not knowing the language that is in vogue regarding sexual activity. The awkward knowledge that young sons and daughters may be engaged in exactly the same activity as mothers and fathers is knowledge that neither side particularly wants to sit down with and share (interestingly, this seems to be the case right through life).

Again, I am not advocating that an objective of the parent–child relationship is to reach a stage where everything is up for sharing – common sense and privacy need to shape the boundary of any relationship. However, a lesson from my interaction with teenagers is that common sense on the part of the parents is often not that common.

TOP TIPS

1. Mind your privacy and maintain a healthy boundary between you and your teenager. The details are rarely important – it is more the learning that you acquired in your development that your teenager can use.
2. Stamp out shame – watch out for non-verbal messages that communicate that sexuality is a dark side of our personality.
3. Be aware that part of your anxiety may just be a sadness that your teenager is growing up and moving on. Allow that sadness to happen.

Ready for sex?

The emotional readiness argument that is often used in parent-directed conversations is an interesting one as its basis seems vague, to say the least. Yet somehow it holds some sort of truth for us. Exactly what is it that indicates readiness for sexual exploration? Is a mature fifteen-year-old more ready than an immature nineteen-year-old?

Readiness implies waiting for something – so exactly what is it that people are waiting for? Traditionally, people waited for the 'right' person, 'right' moment, 'right' occasion'. I think that these are red herrings in the struggle to come to terms with a teenager who is capable of and wanting to engage in something that has the adults in his life worried.

Anxiety based on their lack of a good model as to how to manage this part of the process of human development seems to cause parents to freeze and revert to the 'you should wait' response. There is nothing wrong with the response, but with teenagers the explanation that goes with the response is more important.

The bottom line is that the opportunities for sexual activity in younger teenagers exist in a way that is difficult for parents to accept without recourse to desperation. Hence the 'are they ready?' question. It can be used to pretend that you are doing something useful to stop sexual activity. Asking it is not enough. It requires a lot of teasing out before your teenager will see that she is the owner of choices in sexual exploration, sexual behaviour and sexual safety.

Readiness is an important concept to bring into conversations – not as another means of controlling the teenager but simply as another important angle to be addressed. Remember that most people who have engaged in sex early in their teenage years go on to regret it.

Readiness is difficult to address in the psychological world of the teenager who has fallen in love and when this love is felt fiercely. This is compounded by the absence of a 'patience for the future' philosophy. He wants to show physically right here, right now how much he loves her. Talking to him and being honest about what is going on for him will actually help to give him a sense of control over his feelings of love and lust.

Talking delays scoring!

Teenagers do bring idealism to their thinking that can be used to help them choose to delay onset of sexual activity and, in particular, full penetrative sex. The single most important factor in delaying first experience of sexual intercourse is the quality of sexual and relationship education *received from parents*. Talking about

- the different types of partner (respectful, dominant, using, fulfilling etc.)
- what teenagers 'ideally' would like in a relationship
- how sex can be confused with love

- serious relationships and fun relationships

can help to delay full sexual activity.

We also know that parents who engage in good-quality debate and interaction with their teenagers on all issues related to sexual development also have strong influences on the friends who make up their child's social network.

In other words, the conversations between teenagers and parents have the effect of directly influencing the sexual behaviour of the peer group, which of course has an effect on the behaviour of their child.

Parents produce positive peer pressure!

Be choosy when you're ready

One of the conversations that I hold with teenagers is based on the question of how they make the choice to have sex with a particular individual. I ask them to evaluate how this choice reflects the information that they have about that person. Presenting behaviour as strings of related choices brings home the message about guiding your own future.

I also pass on the 'old-fashioned' but reasonable rationale that intimacy in all its forms is actually a powerful and special connection between people. I ask if that is a value that the teenager would like to have. I explain this because it gives the teenager a reason for why people delay sexual gratification. Do not assume that teenagers will automatically 'know' this reason.

Most will answer 'yes' to wanting the special connection because it is right at the heart of their idealistic belief about people and the world. Once this emerges from them, I ask them to apply it back to the question of when to have sex and who with. This introduces an element of reflection on the natural sexual feelings that they are experiencing.

It is out of reflection that choice emerges. Once we feel we have choice we believe that we can strongly influence a situation. It is this influence that we must strive to generate in teenagers so that they can make fully informed decisions about their sexual lives.

This is successful communicating because, of course, focusing only on whether teenagers have sex or not is a complete waste of time. We cannot control that. We must work to influence the process by which that choice comes about for them. As parents we work to influence their thinking skills.

But I am ready!

Another struggle for parents engaged with teenagers is that the emotional maturity argument has in some ways been blown away by the upsurge in sexual activity among teenagers. Many teenagers have told me that they engage in sexual activity because it is enjoyable, it is expected of them or 'it's just what you do'. Not much evidence of the need for emotional readiness in any of this!

One conversation that I have had with teenagers does highlight clearly why open, direct conversations about sexual behaviour need to take place. There has been a substantial shift in the teenage definition of what comprises sexual behaviour at the introductory end of the scale, i.e. in the early stage of exploration.

What was known as 'petting' and 'heavy petting' twenty years ago is actually activity that most parents engaged in when they entered serious relationships. Full-on oral sex is now a norm for the early stages of a relationship and often comprises 'first date' activity. Now that is a shift in trends that parents will not want to read about.

From a health perspective, oral sex can produce diseases just as unwanted as penetrative sex. It's not all about preventing pregnancy. Sex education needs to be complete as well as comprehensive.

Sexual activity in teenagers has always been an issue, but never before have we been so familiar and informed about it in such an open way to the point that a myth of normality could easily be constructed around it.

Most younger teenage boys and girls are not regularly engaged in full sexual activity, but many of those who are often have sex regularly and frequently. This increases the likelihood of unplanned pregnancy and the current silent epidemic of sexually transmitted diseases which is showing a frightening rate of increase due to unsafe sex practices and an increase in numbers of sexual partners.

The lines of communication about sexual behaviour and health need to be open and honest. Irish and international research has shown that when there is *open* communication between parents and teenagers about relationships and sex, it increases the likelihood that the teenager will wait until they are seventeen or older to have sex for the first time.

The fact that such a young age is now seen as being 'old enough' is indeed a sign of the times, but that is the current reality that we have all helped to bring about. We therefore have a responsibility to educate young people in how to navigate it safely and responsibly.

TOP TIPS

1. Don't use the 'wait till you're ready' line unless you are clear about what you mean, and can express it clearly.
2. You are a key influence on the peer group – get the friends around, interact with them, make yourself real to them. They'll thank you later.

3. Emphasise the importance of making choices – sexual activity is not automatic pilot material. Teenagers make choices about it.

Don't let your past overtake the present

Parents with responsibility for teenagers will rightly ask about their rights to uphold their own beliefs and values. Parents have a right to their moral, religious and social values but they need to consider how they want these passed on to the next generation. Passing them on can only be done effectively if parents make them explicit in behaviour and conversation.

If parents do not reflect on their values in relation to sex and how they will communicate these values, it is my opinion that they will hear themselves fall into arguments and orders that they heard from their parents. These were messages that they probably promised never to use with their own children.

What is important is not to regurgitate the past simply as a way of avoiding or denying this particular phase of the teenager's development. It is also important not to avoid your own fears related to tackling the issue in a constructive way. What adolescents (and all children for that matter) will respect is clear and informed opinion, even if they actually disagree with it.

What drives them to distraction is when they cannot work out exactly what it is their parents expect or believe in. Or, more specifically, if there are contradictions between what adults want of them and what they see adults do on a daily basis. If there are contradictions in your beliefs about relationships, bring these out into the open. You don't have to have the answers for everything.

So what's the answer?

Is there an age when a parent can legitimately believe that it is permissible for their teenage child to engage in sexual intercourse? As with most important issues pertaining to human behaviour, the answer is both yes and no.

Most parents I meet would prefer their child to wait until they have left school (and maybe home, too), but this is often to do with an 'out of sight, out of mind' attitude to the fact that their child is becoming an adult. So these parents often answer 'no' to the question above.

The parents who answer 'yes' are often those who have found out that their teenagers are already well versed and practised in sexual activity and who then, with the benefit of hindsight, try to justify this with ideas about their child's maturity, wisdom and intelligence.

As alluded to earlier, the later in adolescence a teenager first engages in sexual activity, the less likely they are to regret it. There are more than enough opportunities in life to collect regret, so encouraging teenagers to delay onset of sexual activity is one opportunity to reduce the regret load.

Whatever answer is arrived at it is best negotiated with the teenager by holding their curiosity and desire as important as your anxieties and apprehensions. All of these need to be clearly put on the table. The conversation with all these dimensions out in the open will help the teenager to come to understand the normal nature of their desires as well as the benefits and pleasures that come with delayed gratification.

Research shows that most teenagers actually seek and respect the advice of family above and beyond that of friends, particularly on issues of personal importance to them. With regard to sexual behaviour and promoting healthy sexual development, what parents can do with their experience and wisdom is:

1. initiate the process of examining all the possibilities
2. show the teenager how to look at the possible consequences (moral, social, familial, peer)
3. share their opinion and experience of all of these in a non-defensive but energetic debate
4. highlight how to arrive at a decision that reflects all that was learned in the process.

Making use of a 'cost–benefit' conversation is a useful way of making sure that all aspects of the issue are put out for discussion. It's as important to acknowledge the benefits of a sexual relationship as it is to highlight the downside. Otherwise the teenager will perceive the exercise as being somewhat dishonest and will probably withdraw.

A parent reading this might well throw their eyes to heaven, but this process is exactly the one that school counsellors, psychologists, trusted friends and respected teachers use when talking to teenagers. Teenagers show that they have the capacity and competence to engage with this way of weighing up different possibilities. And remember, no process can prevent all mistakes all the time.

However, many families encounter difficulties as a result of the parents beginning this process late in the developmental process of the adolescent. It is of little use to begin these conversations when you think there is a boyfriend or girlfriend on the scene. Teenagers (and all children) will distrust the authoritarian parent who suddenly wants to become all-engaging and on-side. They will be particularly distrustful regarding issues related to sexual development.

Begin these conversations when your child gives you the cue or shows curiosity about relationships. It is never too late – it's probably never too early, either – to talk about relationships and how central they are to our lives.

Lesbian, gay, straight or bi – what's normal?

As for the subject of sexual identity, do parents automatically assume or hope for an adolescent who is heterosexual?

Probably – and with good reason. Unfortunately, it is still the experience of many gay people that their sexuality makes them a target for bullying, ridicule and, in extreme cases, isolation. Homosexuality is a topic for debate, labelling and stigmatising that does not apply to heterosexuality.

Playground humour, gay-bashing talk and intensely emotive public debate on issues such as gay marriage manage to produce an atmosphere where for the most part it can seem impossible to live a non-heterosexual life without fear of ridicule or worse.

Straight people do not have to identify themselves by their sexual orientation and until people of other sexual orientations do not have to either, there is threat to psychological esteem. Secrecy abounds for people with orientations that do not conform to traditional straight sexual practices and while this is changing in very large urban areas, little change has hit other places.

Recent research is challenging the very notion of the straight sex/gay sex split that is often assumed to be the norm. It shows that a significant number of people have engaged in sexual practices with both genders and that a significant minority have adopted this as a lifestyle. The challenge is how we can accommodate this into our thinking about the sexual development of a son or daughter whose sexual preferences are not in line with our expectations.

Confusion is not as confusing as it seems

Parents need to be aware that most teenagers are heterosexual, but a significant number have had homosexual experiences and an even bigger number have homosexual fantasies. It is inaccurate to assume that this represents confusion on the part of the teenager.

Some are confused by this but most are adept at accepting it as a normal part of development without ever bowing to confusion in the long term. It is important to note that they are not working out their identity like some mathematical formula. They are simply in the process of setting up the collection of experiences that will help them to ultimately decide or choose their sexual orientation, be it straight, gay or mixed.

I would argue that in most instances the notion of sexual identity confusion is just another handy way for parents and other moral guardians to avoid getting involved in the conversation that would help to support the teenager in her process through this phase of development. It is easier to think that confusion is the norm for teenagers and that therefore there is no need to talk about sexual development.

The only way to find out if such confusion exists is to create the environment in which it is safe to trigger these conversations. By conversations, I do not mean an interrogation of a teenager about their intimate sexual desires. I mean the type of general conversation that can be triggered by news stories in the papers, about which discussions can be generalised by the adult and teenager in a value-free way. This avoids the scenario of any confusion that might exist being compounded by having to deal with feelings of shame or guilt.

What if there is confusion?

Teenagers who are afraid of their confusion are a vulnerable group of young people. Their environment (home, school or community) has taught them fear and this can be isolating and depressing for them.

Isolation can close the communication avenues that would

normally be expected to help them manage and resolve the fear in the first instance and the issue of identity in the second instance.

Do not be afraid to seek professional help for yourself or your teenager if you believe that confusion about issues of sexual identity is causing distress for your teenager and yourself.

Sexual confusion does not need to be seen as a norm. It is better seen as scenario that needs support and encouragement so that the young person can learn more about who he is. I have worked with teenagers who have expressed some confusion about their sexual identity and I am struck by a theme that emerges, which highlights that often the confusion is not triggered from *within* them: it occurs when they try to fit in with what they think society says is normal about sexuality.

There is some evidence emerging that some older adolescents and young adults who die by suicide are dealing with sexual identity crises. The problem here is not sexual identity, no more than it is for those who die by suicide without similar issues. The problem is that a wall of fear, silence or terror has been generated, from which it is nearly impossible to resolve any issues related to sexual identity. This indicates a gap in society in terms of providing ways to understand the experience of those who do struggle with sexual development. Whether the wall of fear of rejection is real or perceived, it can trigger the isolation and black/white thinking that can lead to suicidal ideation and behaviour.

TOP TIPS

1. Be careful of mixed messages – shying away from conversations about relationships and sexual development contradicts your belief that both are important to the teenager.

2. It's not old-fashioned to advise delaying sexual activity – it's old-fashioned to order it.
3. Identity evolves over the lifespan – don't stress yourself with the need to get it sorted now.

No answers, no problem – stay open with your communication

The issue of openness to communication that may be uncomfortable is central to helping resolve this. With sexual identity, as with other issues, parents and guardians do not need to have answers. Indeed, falling into the well-meaning but mistaken trap of providing answers is faulty for a number of reasons.

1. You cannot experience the problem for the teenager in the way that they do, so any answer is likely to be patchy in its accuracy.
2. By simply providing answers you are denying the teenager the right to learn how to deal with uncertainty in a way that will be useful for future problem-solving.
3. You simply do not have the answer. There are likely to be a range of strands that make up an answer and these may not reveal themselves for many years.

That is to say, sexual identity as a part of personality development is an evolving process – an answer to today's question may simply be the question for tomorrow's dilemma.

If there is a questioning of sexual identity, the likelihood of being able to sort it immediately is thankfully slim. Just like the curiosity and ultimately exploration of the relationship for heterosexuals, teenagers who are questioning, curious or confused will need to access a range of life situations and relationships over time before arriving at any decision regarding identity.

This means striking up relationships with like-minded people, engaging in flirtation, moving from casual friendships into first romances, learning of the pleasure of physical stimulation and ultimately engaging in longer-term relationships. How much parents, teachers and friends want to be a part of this will play an important role in how the individual teenager will value himself and the society that he lives in.

Tasks that promote healthy sexual development

1. Increase the amount of your communication to children regarding sexual development prior to the teenage years. Work at changing teenagers' underlying beliefs about discussing sexuality with you.
2. Boys need to be addressed in a different manner from girls, given the fact that they are more likely to want to engage in sexual activity and more likely to do so.
3. Delaying sexual activity is best taught to teenagers by having conversations that highlight both the 'costs and benefits' of this.
4. Better control of access to and opportunity to consume alcohol is necessary given its role in decreasing inhibitions to sexual activity, while also increasing the probability of sexual violence experiences.
5. Parent training programmes that are based on sound principles of adult learning and education need to be available to parents as part of their own personal development.
6. State agencies need to monitor and address the trend in starting sexual activity at an earlier age as a way of informing all of the above.

Relationships and sexual development are central to the esteem of young people. They also impact strongly on the 'fear portfolio' of parents. Therefore I have outlined a series of tasks that need to happen in order to promote optimal sexual development against the backdrop of the significant societal shift that has taken place in intimate relationship activity.

And finally . . .

Just like any other aspect of teenage development, everything related to sexual maturity needs to become a central part of how the parent–child relationship evolves and matures. This can begin prior to the teenage years and if done early can pave the way for much easier conversations when the 'big' issues of sexual relationships and activity arise in reality.

Teenagers are capable of weighing up the issues if they are presented to them in a safe and supportive way. They do not respond favourably to orders, threats and dire predictions about their lives being wasted because they are sexually active.

Abstinence is good, but improbable for many. Delay is possible, but a struggle for many. It is parents who strongly influence the probabilities and possibilities. Handle this position with care and sensitivity and watch how your teenager responds with a maturity that can be surprising.

Above all else, understand that relationships are very important for the healthy development of teenagers. They are the mechanism by which they learn more about themselves. Curiosity, exploration, fantasy and wondering are normal. Being ashamed about these is not necessary and only serves to block what is a normal, natural part of the human condition. You are central to how this phase of development plays out for your children and it is a phase that can be full of play, fun, excitement, exploration and contentment.

CHAPTER 11

Boys and Girls – Different but Equal

Previous chapters have outlined ideas on a range of issues that impact on parents and teenagers as they negotiate their shared journey through a phase of development in the lifespan that has generated numerous fears, myths and unhelpful attitudes. My thinking is based on various theories that inform my clinical practice and access to quality research is important for how I review and reflect on my thinking.

Much of what I have written is applicable to a wide range of issues and audiences. I have written directly to parents in this book, but many of the ideas will be useful to others who come into regular contact with teenagers.

However, that there are great variations in human beings is a given and it is to the biggest one that I now turn my attention. Gender.

Nature says they're different, so let's work with that

This chapter outlines some of the differences between the development of boys and girls during the adolescent phase. Knowledge of these is useful to bear in mind when attempting to work out an understanding of the world of the teenager.

My opinion is that much time and energy has been wasted on trying to make boys and girls the same: which presumes that it can be done and also that it is healthy to do so. I am not convinced of either assumption. I am more comfortable with the notion of all being different. I propose that our task is to work with our general understandings of teenagers and see what fits with which individual.

So, if I am working with a teenage girl who is not interested in talking that much about feelings, I don't consider her abnormal. She doesn't like talking about feelings – it's that simple. The challenge is for me to work with her at how she does communicate. Similarly, if a teenage boy is not interested in every sport under the sun, that simply is the case. I don't need to change him just because his interests don't fit with the majority of his peers.

Are you ready to challenge yourself?

I have set out a range of differences between boys and girls in a different format from the rest of the book. This is not to encourage the reader just to glance through them as if collecting pieces of information for a table quiz. It is more to offer the opportunity to reflect and critically evaluate your beliefs, which may be affected by each of these research findings.

In other words, I would encourage you to question yourself using these pieces of information. Doing so promotes a clearer understanding of your own thinking. Having that clarity can be used to decide whether changes in your attitudes or behaviour are required in order to further enhance the relationships that will develop between you and the young people who share your life.

I also hope that seeing the differences will assist you in being responsible for the development of young people in a way that respects and reinforces the genuine differences between boys and girls. I believe it is a waste of valuable time trying to 'blandify' the entire human race. The fun in being alive comes from the fact that we are all different.

It is my practice not just to highlight the differences between the genders but to support these differences as one way of maintaining self-esteem.

It is damaging to adopt a one-way approach to all children regardless of age, but it has been my experience that sometimes parents automatically try to do this because they know no other way, or because they have not thought out the consequences of not doing so. Or because they have had success with one particular approach to parenting and will therefore try and repeat it. This rigidity in approach is completely understandable but will lead to difficulties in the relationship with the young person as she tries to express her own unique identity.

Equity not equality

Underlying this philosophy is a belief in the need for fair treatment of boys and girls. It is important that similar experiences are open to both. It is not important that they experience them in the same way.

Responsible parents and others have to work out a way of enjoying and supporting the differences between the male and female children who are in their charge while at the same time ensuring equity in treatment.

Note that I refer to equity, not equality, in the treatment of boys and girls. I do not believe that we are all equal or that an intelligent objective for any society is to try and make everybody equal. Equality in my mind means sameness – and we are not all the same. I am not as talented as the person who built my house (I am a DIY disaster and have little interest in changing that talent). Equally, I have heard people sing who cannot hold a note for love nor money, something which I can reasonably do for both or either!

Certain specific activities may require equality in how they are made available, for example equal opportunity for all interested in a particular post of employment. But to try to use this concept for most aspects of human development is a nonsense. Male and female, boys and girls, men and women, she and he, him and her – there is difference. Isn't it interesting, therefore, that when we talk about teenagers or adolescents or youth or youngsters, we do not have two separate words, one for male adolescents and one for female adolescents? We lump them all together as if they are the one thing.

Similarity and sameness are not the same

Of course, it would be ridiculous to argue that male teenagers and female teenagers do not share many of the same experiences. They do. Emotions, behaviours, physical reactions and thinking show many common threads for boys and girls. But it is important that while informing ourselves about teenagers' development *generally* we also hold the unique contributions that *specifically* being male or female brings to how boys and girls experience the world and to how they react and respond to it.

There is some very interesting research from the USA on what happens when young children are in crèche and where rough and tumble play is encouraged as a normal part of the daily routine. Physical play, the type traditionally associated with the play of boys, was found to enhance both the self-esteem of boys and girls and both used it in different ways to enhance the differences between them. Related to this is the finding that in schools where such rough and tumble play was discouraged or punished, the boys were actually more likely to act out in an aggressive manner and the girls were described as having poorer self-esteem.

So it seems as if we are biologically driven to be different and no amount of politically correct policies and procedures should try and become an obstacle to that, regardless of how well-intentioned the reason for such policies.

I similarly get worried when I hear of traumatic events that impact on schoolchildren where teams of counsellors are called in to offer support. Getting young people to talk about the loss of a friend or acquaintance through an illness, suicide or road accident is only useful if that is what the young person wants in the first place. Blanket counselling is dangerous if not driven by the expressed needs of those to whom it is offered. More specifically, the use of talk in trauma situations has to be carefully regulated as otherwise it can actually cause more harm than good by repeatedly exposing already vulnerable children to the very thing that is causing them hurt in the first place.

In a related point, boys and girls will use talk differently to manage this information in their heads. Girls will use more words more often to help process all the different elements of a story. Boys will not. Not because they are in denial, are repressed, don't feel, are quiet or incompetent, but because they operate differently. They are natural born males and do not need to be turned into females. We must simply work with what they offer us as we do with girls in the same situation, as this is a more equitable approach that will lead to healthier outcomes in the long term.

Equity – acting appropriately for the future

Equity is a far more influential and sophisticated concept than equality to work towards in our behaviours towards young people. For me, it is based on reasonable notions of fairness and even-handedness. These should reflect societal attitudes to all citizens, irrespective of the amount of maleness or femaleness that makes up their character.

Being equitable does not require policies and procedures – it needs an attitude of respect and openness, two attributes that happen to be cornerstones of what brings about successful parenting experiences.

Delighting in the differences – bring them on

So, to 102 things that highlight the differences between boys and girls and remind us of the rich rewards and frustrating failures that can symbolise our engagements with young people. First though, a caution to the reader.

The differences outlined here have been sourced from scientific research resources that I have used to develop my ideas as presented in this book. To the best of my ability, I have tried to ensure that they are not just 'one-off' findings but have been reported with consistency. However, as with all good science, they are open to new findings that may weaken, overshadow or completely debunk them with the passage of time.

In keeping with learning outlined in an earlier chapter, in this life there is nothing certain but death, and in the meantime we must work to make do with the uncertainty.

Puberty

1.   Significant numbers of girls experience first menstruation in the summer season. Season is not yet known to be a factor in onset of the development of boys.

2.   The average age at which breasts begin to develop for white girls is just under ten years of age and the process of developing mature breasts takes approximately 4.5 years.

3.   The average age for onset of menstruation is 12.8 years for white girls.

4.   Black girls begin puberty earlier than white girls and take longer to move from early to mid-adolescence.

5.   On average boys begin pubertal development one to two years later than girls.

6.   The average age for onset of puberty is eleven years for boys.

7.   Being an early developer has negative effects on girls' self-esteem.

8. Being an early developer has a positive effect on boys' self-esteem.

9. Acne may be one of the first visible signs of puberty in girls.

10. Female pubertal development is occurring earlier than in previous decades.

11. Development for boys is not happening earlier. We are not sure why this is.

12. If a father is absent in the childhood years of a girl she is more likely to begin physical maturation earlier than her peers.

13. In two-parent families where low levels of warmth are expressed, girls tend to mature earlier.

14. Breast development in girls produces emotional reactions for the girls themselves and social responses from others. Boys' initial pubertal changes are a much more private matter.

15. Very little is known about the meaning of puberty to boys themselves.

16. What little is known suggests that boy's responses to first ejaculation are more positive than female responses to first menstruation.

17. While the timing of onset of puberty is important for both boys and girls, the effects of either early or late onset are more serious for girls in terms of mental health problems.

18. Bodily change is more likely to elicit shame responses in girls than boys.

19. In early adolescence, girls are likely to spend more time in bed and wake up later due to their more advanced development.

20. Before puberty, girls manage stress better than boys; but after it, boys manage stress better.

KEY QUESTIONS

- What have I just learned that is a surprise to me?
- How can I apply this learning to my son or daughter?
- How can I change the way I engage with my son or daughter using this learning?

Social development

21. The process of transmitting values from parents to children is different in the way the mother–daughter pair and the father–son pair does this.
22. Mother and daughter discussion is more detailed and explicit.
23. Father and son discussion is more practical and implied.
24. In participation in sports, the impact of environmental influences over genetics is stronger for girls than boys.
25. Girls are more consistently concerned with fairness and equal access for others to groups than are boys.
26. As adolescent girls develop social relationships their emotional responses to these get stronger as they mature.
27. Boys' emotional responses to relationships do not become stronger as they mature.
28. Girls display more intimacy in their friendships than boys.
29. Girls are more likely to attribute higher quality to their friendships than boys.
30. Status hierarchy (where you stand in the pecking order) is more evident in adolescent female cliques than in male cliques.
31. Girls will display more indirect verbal aggression (e.g. spreading false rumours).
32. Boys will engage in more risk-taking behaviour.

33. Boys are more likely to get into physical fights as a result of using alcohol.

34. Boys are more likely to get into trouble with the police as a result of using alcohol.

35. Irish teenage girls report higher use of drugs than Irish boys.

36. Boys will have more significant conflict and behavioural difficulties when they live with a single mother.

37. Girls will have more significant behavioural difficulties when they live with a single father.

38. Boys have a tendency to be more seriously affected by divorce than girls.

39. Girls show greater reliance than boys on external forces such as approval by others.

40. 'Talk' is the mechanism that brings girls together and drives them apart.

41. 'Doing' is the elastic that influences the movement in boys' relationships.

KEY QUESTIONS

- What have I just learned that is a surprise to me?
- How can I apply this learning to my son or daughter?
- How can I change the way I engage with my son or daughter using this learning?

Sexual development

42. Girls who become sexually active before the age of seventeen are almost seventy per cent more likely to experience a crisis pregnancy in later life and three times more likely to seek an abortion in their lifetime than those who wait until they are older.

43. By the age of sixteen, fifteen per cent of teenage boys will have experienced sex.

44. By the age of sixteen, eight per cent of girls will have experienced sex.

45. Almost two-thirds of girls will later regret this.

46. One-third of boys will regret early experience of sex.

47. Depressed mood is more likely to be associated with sexual experience in girls than boys.

48. Sexual activity is still something to be proud of for boys.

49. Sexual activity is still something to be kept quiet by girls.

50. Boys are more comfortable with the idea of casual sex for themselves.

51. Male sexual minorities (e.g. homosexual, bisexual) are more stigmatised than female minorities.

52. Male sexual minorities have more violence perpetrated on them than female sexual minorities.

KEY QUESTIONS

- What have I just learned that is a surprise to me?
- How can I apply this learning to my son or daughter?
- How can I change the way I engage with my son or daughter using this learning?

Mental health

53. In experiences of depression, genetic influences are stronger for female adolescents than for their male counterparts.

54. Rates of depressed mood increase more significantly for girls than for boys in adolescence.

55. The gender difference for depression becomes more noticeable from the age of eleven years onwards.

56. Prior to age eleven, boys are more likely to be depressed.

57. Girls report more feelings of hopelessness, even when there are fewer risk factors for this, than boys.
58. Girls will report more awareness of feelings of shame, guilt, sadness and shyness than boys.
59. Adolescent boys are more likely to deny having feelings at all.
60. Attempted suicides are three times more common in girls.
61. Rates of deliberate self-harm are higher in female adolescents.
62. Younger teenage boys (up to fourteen years) are five times less likely to engage in deliberate self-harm than girls.
63. Older teenage boys (over fourteen years) are half as likely to engage in deliberate self-harm.
64. Increases in male completed suicides over the past two decades have not been matched in female completed suicides.
65. Girls tend to perceive events as being more stressful than boys.
66. In response to stress, boys are more likely to use practical, active coping skills than girls.
67. Boys are also more likely to deny a problem or withdraw from it.
68. Girls are more likely to expect the worst in a given situation.
69. Generally, girls will experience normal demands as being more threatening and complex than boys.
70. Girls are more likely to experience stress when someone in their social circle gets stressed: they also get stressed even though the other person's stress does not have a direct bearing on them.
71. Across the entire adolescent age range, older male teenagers have the highest prevalence of drug use.
72. There is some evidence for a hereditary influence in drug and alcohol abuse in boys.

73. For every one adolescent boy with an eating disorder there are nine girls with a similar disorder.

74. Girls are more likely to be sexually abused at the beginning of adolescence than at any other stage of it.

75. Boys are more commonly abused by someone from outside the family.

76. Girls are more commonly abused within the family.

77. Boys are more likely to adopt an 'ignore the problem' strategy.

78. Boys are more likely to try to use humour to sort a problem.

79. Girls are more likely to adopt a 'solve the problem' strategy.

KEY QUESTIONS

- What have I just learned that is a surprise to me?
- How can I apply this learning to my son or daughter?
- How can I change the way I engage with my son or daughter using this learning?

Career and vocational choice

80. Adolescent boys and girls hold different work values.

81. Boys prefer more tangible values, such as financial gain.

82. Girls prefer expressive and socially oriented values, such as friendships with work colleagues.

83. There is less support for boys wishing to pursue non-traditional careers than for girls who wish to choose non-traditional careers.

84. Girls are more likely to link personal achievement with helping others.

85. Boys place higher value on creativity, money and physical activity.

86. Fear of success is more often found in teenage girls than boys.

87. Fear of success is more likely to be found in girls who have high self-esteem (because of a belief that they 'should be able to do something').

88. High-achieving girls are less likely to use the usual coping strategies that girls use – they tend to engage in more problem-solving than emotionally focused strategies.

KEY QUESTIONS

- What have I just learned that is a surprise to me?
- How can I apply this learning to my son or daughter?
- How can I change the way I engage with my son or daughter using this learning?

Independence and autonomy

89. In general, girls expect to receive independence in terms of behaviour later than boys, but this difference is less pronounced than in the past.

90. An authoritarian parenting style in early childhood produces over-control of behaviour in adolescent girls.

91. An authoritarian parenting style in early childhood produces less control of behaviour in boys.

92. Girls will exhibit a stronger sense of connection to parents, teachers and unrelated adults.

93. Being independent is linked to more help-seeking behaviours in girls than in boys.

94. Boys will exhibit more excessive demands than girls for independence from parents and other adults.

95. Girls stop idealising parents at an earlier age than boys.

> **KEY QUESTIONS**
>
> - What have I just learned that is a surprise to me?
> - How can I apply this learning to my son or daughter?
> - How can I change the way I engage with my son or daughter using this learning?

Abilities

96. Adolescent boys can throw objects further and more accurately than girls.
97. Girls score higher on language skills.
98. Girls tend to be better at spelling.
99. Boys tend to be better at mechanical reasoning.
100. Girls will attribute their success at maths to hard work.
101. Boys will attribute their success at maths to their intellectual ability.
102. Adolescent girls report lower levels of perceived ability than boys.

> **KEY QUESTIONS**
>
> - What have I just learned that is a surprise to me?
> - How can I apply this learning to my son or daughter?
> - How can I change the way I engage with my son or daughter using this learning?

And finally...

Regardless of the all of the facts and figures, the similarities and differences and the scientific opinion, the bottom line is that teenagers are ordinary people. Therefore relating to them requires no more than the respect, sensitivity, courtesy and dignity that is required for any other person.

People of all ages have issues that have a particular meaning for them, times when they are more sensitive, less resourceful and more demanding of others. Likewise with teenagers.

It is our responses to teenagers and what they present that determine how we feel about interacting with them. We are responsible for handling our own responses be they positive or negative. Handling them does not mean throwing them back to someone else. It means understanding our response and then deciding what is the most useful thing to do with it. This applies to all ages.

Teenagers are our future. Parents are in the privileged position to guide their development in any number of ways. Choosing to see this as a partnership with them teaches them invaluable lessons as to how all sorts of relationships work. The reward travels both ways. Parents get free lessons in how the human condition unfolds with the passing of time!

Above all, parents can rest assured by the history of all the parents gone before, that despite feeling that you're not doing enough, 'more grows in the garden than the gardener knows he has sown'.